Kennedy's Recruit:
Tales from the Poverty Wars

by

Joseph T. Wilkins

Joseph T. Wilkins
P.O. Box 185
Oceanville, NJ 08231

Email: wilkinsjt001@comcast.net

Table of Contents

Foreword

"Before we help the poor," St. Francis of Assisi is said to have taught, "we must first beg their pardon." Good advice, and still good today. Nobody asks to be poor. In that same spirit, it may be a good idea when writing a book like this to apologize in advance to the reader for the inevitable tedium of telling him or her about one's background; a task which, however, mundane, provides the reader with necessary context – some sense, as we said in the Sixties, of where we're coming from.

A reader of an early draft of this book challenged me, with some exasperation, to declare whether it was a personal memoir or a history. "If it's a memoir, it's not personal enough," she said, "and if it's history it's too personal." "Too much politics," said another. "Too much of your wanting to get elected to Congress and not enough about the problems of the poor."

In truth, this book is both memoir and history, or at least tries to be. Meeting John F. Kennedy when I was a brand new college freshman and he was setting up his run for the White House was a compelling moment for me. He urged me and others like me to consider lives of public service. I came to think of myself as his recruit to that life. What I did not foresee is that politics, properly understood, is more about getting something worthwhile done than about getting elected, although that statement would provoke cynical laughter from today's millionaire campaign consultants. I never won a campaign for any elected public office. The more I tried to get "something done" the more those very efforts doomed my chances of winning election. The story of those efforts forms this book. It is a personal account, based on my notes and correspondence, old newspaper clips, my written reports long since filed away in the National Archives, and recollections of an active journey of personal development and inward discovery that took me from the earliest days of the great "War on Poverty" in 1964 to the day eight years later when I hung out my shingle as a lawyer in solo practice in Atlantic City.

It was a journey that once begun changed the course of my life.

Chapter 1: Beginnings

It is fifty years since the times I write about in this book. I was 25 then, a young man still reeling from the assassination of President John F. Kennedy; a stunned swimmer suddenly thrown into the turbulent rapids of the 1960's and swept along from one rock to the next trying desperately to regain control of the course of my life.

Until Kennedy was killed I knew where I wanted to go and how to get there. I used him as a personal inspiration, the way young men do with their heroes. His sudden death wrecked my plans and dreams.

I was born on New Year's Eve in 1938 in the security of a middle-class American family in a comfortable home in the Germantown section of Philadelphia, the son of a spirited Irish beauty and a small businessman then building a reputation as what he termed an "ecclesiastical decorator". He made his living providing the many Catholic churches of the city with drapes, altar furnishings, sanctuary rugs, candelabra and other items required for the great liturgical rituals. I had a sister two years older and another, Suzi, two years younger who, as with my young mother, was to die of tuberculosis before my fourth birthday.

By the time my mother died Pearl Harbor had launched World War II. When my widowed father received a draft notice for the Army he found room and board for my surviving sister and I in St Mary's Home, a semi-orphanage run by Polish nuns for the Archdiocese of Philadelphia on a great estate bequeathed to it in nearby Ambler, Pennsylvania. The estate had belonged to a wealthy doctor who built upon it a mansion in the style of Windsor Castle, complete with gray battlements and crenelated towers. For us children it was a grim existence in a splendid setting. The nuns, largely poor women from Poland who themselves had been raised in superstition and harsh treatment, knew no way to raise children save by regimentation and physical punishment. When we smaller children soiled ourselves, the nuns' remedy was to tie our soiled underwear around our necks for the rest of the day.

The estate, replete with sunken gardens, a great lake and many acres of woodland, was cash poor. We children were set to weed the yards, drives and wide cement walkways on our hands and knees under the stern watch of nuns speaking to each other in a strange language.

I survived the experience by stealing books from the estate library and hiding away in a secluded grotto where, a voracious reader even as a young child, I could escape to a different world of adventures and ideas.

Along with the Chippendale furniture and oriental rugs left behind by the doctor who bequeathed the castle to the church, he left an extensive, comprehensive and by the nuns totally unused library of books that ranged from mysteries to biographies to science to medicine and history. But we were forbidden from entering the library. Once when I was caught in it reaching for a book I had my knuckles whacked with a wooden ruler. The nuns taught us only from catechisms and textbooks bearing the formal approval of the Church. We were diligently shown how to look for the official Imprimatur – the official seal of permission for Catholics to read a book. Reading a book that was on the *Index Librorum Prohibitorum* was a sin punishable by God Himself for which you might ultimately burn in Hell. With a diligence bordering on medieval superstition the nuns distrusted all other books and the suspicious knowledge they contained.

If the nuns had taken an inventory of that small library at the castle they would have been shocked to find the room was a treasure trove of intellectual sin. There were English translations of books by Rabelais, Descartes, Voltaire, Pascal. There was *Les Miserables* by Victor Hugo, Gibbon's *Decline and Fall of the Roman Empire*, Machiavelli's The *Prince*, John Stuart Mill's *On Liberty* and Milton's *Paradise Lost*. Most of what those books contained was far beyond my comprehension, but they were all I had. There were no movies nor television, and we had no radios. For the four years I was there I smuggled out whichever book caught my eye on any given day and took it to my secret hiding place in the small grotto in the sunken garden where I could pore over it word by word. Here and there I could find and follow a thread of understanding. I had to take wild guesses at what the unfamiliar words meant in the context of their sentence. The library's dictionary was far too big to smuggle out and I dared not linger in the library to look something up. Proper pronunciation was out of the question. It was years before I learned that "chemistry" is pronounced "kem-is-tree" rather than the "shem-es-tree" I had supposed on the assumption that the soft "ch" in "church" was the right guide.

There were no children's books, of course, except for a few like Swift's *Gulliver's Travels*, Alexandre Dumas's *The Three Musketeers*, and Robert Louis Stevenson's *Robinson Crusoe*. Luckily, there was also Mark Twain's *Innocents Abroad* and his *Letters from Earth* and Chaucer's *Canterbury Tales*.

Best of all, there was Malory's *Le Morte d'Arthur* – the immortal and, to a small boy, glorious tales of King Arthur and the Knights of the Round Table. I read of Kings and Queens and questing knights who lived in castles just like mine, but where the evil dragons did not come and who went out and fought for chivalry and justice. My castle stayed a child's prison in the real world, but in my mind the fields were filled with tournaments and jousting knights and beautiful, kind ladies who looked very much like my mother. I'd read until daylight faded and be sent to bed without supper when I came back and refused to say where I'd been. I knew instinctively that once you give in to bullying you are lost. So long as I kept my secret grotto to myself I could keep reading books and dream of great adventures and quests for justice.

I'm sure it was that curious blend of distrust of inexplicable authority, harsh reality and the escapism of idealistic dreams that shaped my views of the world and of life. The lure and love of reading has never dimmed. Thomas Jefferson's declaration that he could not live without books made sense to me when first I heard it. I knew exactly what he meant. When in fifth grade a few years after we left the orphanage, we were asked to name the last book we had read, I answered with Eisenhower's 600 page

"Crusade in Europe." The nun at first refused to believe an 11 year old would read so adult a book, then warned me against getting "above yourself" in reading.

Except for summers in the homes of various relatives I was at St. Mary's until after the War. Then my father remarried and brought my sister and I home to live over the shop with his new wife and a succession of new brothers and sisters arriving almost annually until there were seven of us. In 1948 my father was doing well enough to buy a summer home in Brigantine, at the Jersey shore, which soon became our year-round home.

It was my father's early hope that I would become a priest. When I eventually discovered girls, his plans changed to my someday joining him in the church decorating business he had slowly built into a steady livelihood. I worked with him during summers, and for a year after high school, but the pull of books and some higher role in life than hanging draperies and carrying plaster saints to the side altars was too strong. Much to his disappointment I started college at LaSalle College in Philadelphia. There I developed a vague but emerging impulse toward law school and politics, an impulse arising out of my reading habits and growing love of history and biography, especially the post-war histories then pouring out including the books and biographies of figures like Winston Churchill, Franklin D. Roosevelt, and Dwight Eisenhower.

In my freshman year at LaSalle then-Senator John F. Kennedy, deeply into his ramp-up for the presidency, came to make a speech on his favorite subject for college events, "A Career in Politics". As a rookie columnist for the college paper, I was included in a small luncheon given him and came away after talking with him determined to someday be, like him, a member of the Senate Foreign Relations committee, moving at the center of world affairs.

It was a turning point in my life. All of my friends at home understood the dim prospects of employment in the Atlantic City area. To get a college education locally was impossible; the nearest college was almost forty miles away or twenty miles further on in Philadelphia. Many who left to get their education planned never to return. I did plan to return, but knew I'd have to find a way to make a living, and instinctively wanted to make that living independent of anybody else's payroll, and did not want to get trapped in my father's business. I took the college aptitude tests with no particular plan, but after a year of work with my father and living in Philadelphia went to nearby LaSalle College and applied. I had a vague notion of law school but, after meeting Kennedy, was convinced the path for me was to get a law degree, go home and practice law, go into politics, and so make my way in time to the U.S. Senate.

That dream never thereafter dimmed. When I graduated four years later, now married with two children and a third on the way, I headed directly for Washington in search of a day job to support the family while I attended night law school.

My stubborn pursuit of that goal was not only a trial to Maryanne, who faithfully stood up for me against family criticism, but an affront to common sense. As one unsympathetic priest coldly advised me, if I wanted to go to college and law school, I shouldn't have started a family. He may have been right, but such hypocritical advice came hard from my own church, which taught how great a sin it was to practice birth control.

So it was that on a blistering hot day in late June I trudged to the bridge leading out of Philadelphia with the grand total of 26 cents in my pocket, all in pennies. I hitched a ride to Washington and spent weeks living on small loans from friends, looking for work while Maryanne and the babies lived at her family's summer home in Brigantine.

The job I eventually landed was as a trainee budget analyst with the General Services Administration, as bureaucratic a career as can be imagined. Its saving grace was that the GSA provided supply and support services for the entire federal civil government, which taught me many things about the role and reach of the federal government. I developed the same appreciation of the federal bureaucracy Roman engineers had for good roads. My job also included helping prepare budget requests and justifications for the Congressional appropriations cycles, which offered the chance to spend a great deal of time on Capitol Hill attending budget hearings. I had the privilege of frequent visits to the Hill, a privilege I abused to sit in the Senate and House galleries and watch interesting debates and votes.

A few years on, having done well enough academically that I was elected to the Law Review I jumped at a chance to leave the GSA to work with the legal department of the trade association of the American soft drink bottlers. I thought the job would add dimension to my education about Washington. The move proved to be a mistake. My visits to the Hill stopped. I worked in a cramped back office grinding out weekly newsletters for politically conservative soft drink bottlers around the country who were interested in finding ways to avoid regulation of their products, their labor relations, and their marketing practices. My views on such issues were rooted in the traditional views of the Democratic Party, but were no more liberal at the time than those of Kennedy himself. He was for civil rights so, although I knew little about the subject, I was for civil rights, although not so much as to walk a few blocks down 16th street to hear Martin Luther King's famous speech at the Lincoln Memorial.

As time went on, I grew increasingly bored with the job at the bottler's lobby, and impatient at the daily lunches of the five man executive staff where every policy initiative of the Kennedy White House was criticized.

A vague discontent at working against my political leanings slowly grew. Cases I reviewed for the newsletter included many in which bottlers claimed their driver's helpers – the usually black helpers who actually toted the cases of soda into the store — were independent contractors, thus shielding the bottlers from liability for paying a minimum wage, paying into social security, or covering them under worker's compensation. Other legal cases involved how bottlers could defend against suits about consumer issues, such as "exploding bottles" which shattered if dropped, often cutting the legs of elderly women shoppers, and the "cockroach in a bottle" suits arising when bottles were allegedly left insufficiently cleaned before being re-filled and re-sold.

One example of working against my political leanings remains vivid to this day. The Kennedy Administration, at the urging of organized labor, proposed legislation mandating triple pay for overtime hours, in expectation such a penalty would force companies to hire new workers rather than squeeze the extra work time out of their existing workforce. The proposal drew heavy fire from the bottler's lobby, as from the entire business community. My lobby assigned me the job of writing a statement in opposition to the triple-pay bill, to be given by our association's president at the congressional hearing before the House Labor subcommittee handling the legislation. Although I had no strong convictions on the issue, I put together a reasonable statement in opposition. The statement was duly read, along with many others of similar protest. After the day's hearings, I met a friend who invited me to a Cherry Blossom party hosted by one of the Congressmen whose daughter hoped to be chosen as Cherry Blossom Princess – a prize openly determined largely on the basis of how much clout her father had in Congress.

Washington was then a town filled, especially in Springtime, with friendly drunks, pretty girls, and a tolerant attitude toward human foibles. The Cherry Blossom parties on Capitol Hill were legendary for all three. Caught up in the general merriment I helped myself to the refreshments and gravitated toward an elderly man in a wheelchair who was the center of a small but lively discussion. He was Elmer Holland, a very senior Democratic Congressman from Pittsburgh and chairman of the subcommittee handling the triple-pay bill. Three lobbyists had him cornered and were passionately trying to convince him the bill would destroy the economy. When at last they drifted off I struck up a compensation with him, in which he gave me persuasive reasons in support of the bill.

When he learned I had written a statement in opposition, he waved forgiveness for the offense and asked me to wheel him back to his office, where in short order I was drinking his Chivas Regal and listening to him talking about his life. The quotes are from memory of a long time ago, but are essentially accurate.

"The guys from the Manufacturers and the Chamber damn near got on their knees the other day begging me to go easy on 'em" Elmer said.

What they didn't know, or chose to ignore, was the Chairman's personal history. He had first run for Congress when he was working as a union organizer in the days when employers treated union organizers as blood enemies. I forget whether it was the Chamber or the NAM in particular who, he said, sent thugs out to kidnap him. He told me they drove him to a remote field and threatened to shoot him and hide his body if he kept up his union work. Then they left him in the field overnight and called his wife to tell her anonymously that he was dead.

Now, many years later, the NAM and the Chamber were begging him to go easy on them.

" 'Go easy on us, Elmer', they said. Know what I told 'em? I told them to go FUCK themselves!!!"

As could happen at such events in Washington, I had too much to drink, but that old man's anger came through with a vigor I remember to this moment. Next day I found in my pocket a tie pin with a ceramic center on which was inscribed "Elmer J. Holland for Congress". Ashamed to have accepted something of such obvious sentimental value from him, I took it back and gave it to his wife, who was also his Congressional Administrative Assistant and thanked me for returning it.

When that November the soft drink bottlers held their convention in Dallas, our five man executive staff left me behind in Washington to mind the store. They were excited to go because Vice President Lyndon Johnson, much admired among the bottlers because he counted among his business assets a stake in a Texas bottling company, was scheduled to make an appearance at the convention — a trivial appearance lost in the horror of that day's assassination.

Left behind in Washington on that Dallas trip, I spent the morning researching trademarks at the US Trademark Office, then at the corner of 21st and "K" Streets. I was working my way through the paper filings in those pre-computer days when somebody's radio interrupted its program with the report the President had been shot at in Dallas. Then came the awful news he'd been hit. Minutes later, standing by a car parked at the curb, I listened to the car radio announcing that President Kennedy was dead.

I spent that afternoon and evening in a daze, wandering around Capitol Hill and later the White House, where I saw the disrupted power of the nation dramatized by the arrival of helicopters and television lights and the comings and goings of black limousines.

On the night before the funeral, Maryanne and I went to pay our respects at the Capitol where he lay in state in his coffin. But when we saw the line, 40 abreast and almost a mile long, we knew it would be impossible for the end of that line to pass the coffin before the service was due to begin next morning. Instead we took the first places at the rope near the foot of the Capitol steps. There we stood, all night long, in a gathering crowd that swelled to the thousands as the hours wore on, all of us comforting each other. As daylight grew, so too did the pomp and ceremony as the great ones of the world came to pay their tribute. We stayed until the coffin was brought down the Capitol steps and placed on the horse-drawn caisson and marched off to the solemn beating of the drums.

A few days later, the bottler's executive staff returned from Dallas. At lunch we gathered around our usual round table. Our executive director Tom Baker expressed his regrets at the assassination but then remarked that "at least it's good to have somebody with gray hair in the White House again." He was not an unkind man, but his remark sickened me, as did the solemn nods of agreement around the table. Within a week I resigned, too angry and too foolish to line up another job first.

So began a year and a half of wandering in a personal wilderness. With a growing family to feed, the rent to pay and law school tuition a mounting debt, I grabbed the first available job, which was as a very junior labor law editor at the big commercial publisher the Bureau of National Affairs, reading the mimeographed decisions of the National Labor Relations Board and abstracting them for publication in the BNA's weekly *Labor Law Reporter*. Reading, analyzing and condensing those hair-splitting decisions handed down in quarrels over obscure and remarkably trivial matters was the dullest, driest and most unsatisfying work I have ever attempted.

To feed my need for some meaningful activity I squeezed in a few hours between the end of the work day and the beginning of evening law classes doing volunteer work at the Democratic National Committee. There President Johnson's men, many from Texas, were energetically at work replacing references to "the Kennedy Administration" on all the literature with "the Kennedy-Johnson Administration" and, wherever plausible, dropping the "Kennedy." Deeply resentful of all things Texan since the assassination I began to think of some form of active resistance to the Texas takeover. I soon learned it would be possible to get credentials to the 1964 Democratic Convention if I continued my volunteer work at the Democratic National Committee. Since the convention would take place in August in Atlantic City, next door to my home town of Brigantine where the family could easily find beds and enjoy the beach, I had a good chance to get insider passes. These, I secretly hoped, would position me to lend a backstage hand to the supporters of Robert F. Kennedy should a movement emerge to drop Johnson and draft RFK as nominee for President. In that hope I was not alone. Passions like mine were running deep among many Democrats and New Frontiersmen. Anything seemed possible. I stayed with the BNA until the convention loomed, then handed in my notice and headed back home.

That the majority of the rank and file at the Atlantic City convention would have bolted to Bobby Kennedy if given half a chance was shown when he stepped to the podium to introduce a memorial tribute to his brother. The huge crowd gave him a standing ovation that ran far longer than any seen in many years. But the convention was far too tightly controlled by the Johnson forces to allow any mutinies by those of us who longed for an RFK candidacy.

By the time the convention ended, I had landed a job working for a local Democratic political strongman and attorney who had brought in a recently converted Republican from Philadelphia as his new law partner and was running him for Congress. In the incredible Democratic landslide for Johnson that year, many long shots came in, including the erstwhile Republican who was now my Congressman-elect. Offered a job on his anticipated congressional staff by his partner, I naively replied that I would prefer his help getting a job working for Robert Kennedy on his Senate staff, RFK having been elected Senator from New York in that same landslide. To my surprise the strongman saw my request to work for somebody else as a sign of personal disloyalty. Still a political novice and idealist, his reaction was my first exposure to the morally obnoxious demand for unquestioning loyalty to the boss that is considered a virtue by political strongmen in America. In Hitler's Germany it was known as the *Führerprinzip*, where every soldier had to swear personal loyalty not to their country nor flag nor laws, but to Hitler himself, the *Führer*, who was above the law. I later saw the misfortunes that fell upon people like Nixon aides J.E.B. Stuart Magruder when he and other young men were disgraced and some went to prison for placing personal loyalty to the boss above their oaths of office.

The cost of my first lesson in how the *Führerprinzip* works was not as high as what Nixon's younger aides had to pay, but it was high. The strongman thought my request so treacherous he fired me.

From late that November through the Christmas season and all of January were the bleakest times in my life. We were living on the charity of our families as I trudged around Washington looking for a job that would let me return to my evening law classes.

There came at last the day early in February when I knew I had to give up my dream. There was no hope anywhere. I could no longer stretch the long-suffering patience of family and friends. Deep in gloom and self-pity, I spent the late afternoon walking the streets of Washington, saying good-bye to my hopes and bracing for the return home with my head down and my tail between my legs. I had neither appetite nor money for dinner, and was saving my last $5 for gas and tolls.

As I walked up Georgetown's Wisconsin Avenue from M Street heading for my car I was waiting at a curb for the light to change when Bill Green stopped next to me. At 26, he was one of the youngest Congressmen, having won a special election to the solidly Democratic seat vacated by the unexpected death of his father, the powerful long-term Democratic leader of Philadelphia. We were the same age, and knew each other. In fact Maryanne was a very distant cousin. We had shared a few drinks in Washington and at a congenial gathering during the Atlantic City Democratic Convention the previous August. His own staff, mostly inherited from his father, was full and he felt loyalty to them. But he had made a few phone calls to colleagues in a generous attempt to help me out. They didn't pan out, but I deeply appreciated his efforts. Being an astute politician, he knew my circumstance.

"Had dinner yet?" he asked. "I'm on my way to Billy Martin's for a burger and a beer. Come keep me company."

I knew I had enough to pay for a beer at Billy Martin's Tavern, and that I could nurse it for an hour or so. He was good company. When he realized I was heading home next day in defeat, he insisted on treating me to a burger and the beer to go with it. I did not have foolish expectations that suddenly a job would come of this chance meeting, but his graceful and cheerful company restored a great deal of my battered self-respect. As we left, he suggested I call his office in the morning and leave word where I could be reached if anything turned up.

By next morning my spirits had again sunk. Over coffee at a diner I scribbled a note on my napkin. Thanks to Maryanne, that coffee-stained napkin note written long ago survived decades in my various desk drawers. It was a bit melodramatic, but from the heart:

> *"2/3/65. A Farewell to Washington – the only town where you can eat dinner with a congressman, and quietly starve in a wintry blast the next day. Four years of hope and despair, boredom and challenge, beauty and filth. Finis!"*

I finished my coffee and stopped to call Bill Green's office on my way out to the car. His secretary asked me if I could make an appointment she had lined up for 11 a.m. at "that new poverty program".

"Just tell them the Congressman sent you," she instructed. "And ask them to call me for confirmation."

A few hours later, I was hired as a budget analyst by the brand new US Office of Economic Opportunity, effective immediately.

Chapter 2: The Inspector General

It must be conceded at the outset that I was an unlikely recruit in the War on Poverty. For one thing, I knew nothing about the enemy. My family was distinctly middle-class, from a father who owned a 4-worker business to a row home in Philadelphia and a summer place at the South Jersey Shore complete with a small boat for fishing and water-skiing. We weren't rich, but we certainly weren't poor, either. Nor did I care much who won this so-called "War," declared by President Johnson in hopes of establishing his own signature program in the aftermath of John F. Kennedy's assassination. My ambition, stirred by having met and talked with Kennedy while I was in college, was for a seat in the United States Senate, dealing with world affairs and the great issues of the day.

What took me to Bill Haddad's office that afternoon in February of 1965 was my hope for work that would let me finish my studies at night law school in Washington without boring me to death in the process. Thus far I had spent the nearly four years since graduating from college in Philadelphia struggling to get my law degree while feeding my rapidly growing family – the last year and a half lurching from the wrong job to the wrong job in the emotional aftermath of John F. Kennedy's assassination.

It had been less than a month since, on the rebound from working in Atlantic City on the campaign of a Republican-turned-Democrat running for Congress, I had landed a job as a budget analyst with the brand-new U.S. Office of Economic Opportunity — the OEO. I'd been trained for budget work in the government's General Services Administration when I'd first come to Washington. The problem was that at 25, however welcome the paycheck, I dreaded returning to the dullness of government budget work.

I had reported to work at the New Colonial Hotel, a building at the corner of 15th and M then serving as OEO's temporary headquarters while awaiting the wrecking ball. The budget office in which I landed was not a center of great activity. But on the upper floors social workers of all descriptions were designing the greatest government social initiative since FDR's first hundred days. Tantalizing snatches of elevator conversations hinted at the innovative kinds of grant applications that were being solicited and considered. Downstairs, I was assigned to figure out what government forms we'd need when the grants people upstairs started dishing out the money.

The "grants people" were an eclectic collection of liberal thinkers, social workers, college professors and civil rights activists ecstatic at their new mission: social reform across the board; eliminate poverty however they could. There was no roadmap. No civilization in the history of the world had ever eliminated poverty. "The poor ye shall always have with ye," the *Wall Street Journal* pontificated, quoting the Bible with smug assurance that the poor may be with ye but the rich would be with they.

After a few weeks OEO shifted headquarters four blocks west to a modern cube of a building at the corner of 19th and M, close by Washington's restaurant row. Assigned to draft a manual of procurement regulations for the new agency, I soon caught myself looking out the window wondering if the snow was falling fast enough for us to go home early. Although if it concerned my law studies or politics I could work around the clock with drive and focus, impatience with dull work was a character defect that made me my own worst enemy.

My sanity was preserved by two coworkers. Juanita and Francine were young black women with fast, often bawdy, wit and a cheerful tolerance of my all too obvious restlessness. They were good company and fun to swap jokes with. They specialized in reviewing travel vouchers for payment. If I was reading law books when the boss came down the hall they'd give me a heads-up with sly humor in time to avoid disaster. Juanita invited me to dinner at her home on a particularly desperate day when my eyes again drifted to the window looking for snow. I'm not sure how her husband Pete felt about her dragging home such a lost soul, but he was a good sport and the evening went well.

Next afternoon the director of OEO's budget office asked if I would be interested in an overtime assignment. "The Inspector General, " he said, "is having trouble paying his agents their travel expenses. Go see what they need."

I didn't know what an Inspector General did. According to the organization table his name was William F. Haddad. On paper the outfit seemed small; 11 people in all. The main thing was that he was upstairs and I was downstairs, and he was busy and I was bored. That was enough for me.

***

At four o'clock I went up the elevator and along the corridor to the Inspector General's office hoping to catch a glimpse of things before returning in the morning to start the assignment. To my surprise, four o'clock was not quitting time for them. It could have been midmorning for all the attention anybody paid to the clock. Nor was the staff as small as the 11 who appeared on the organization chart. At least 30 people were bustling about. Secretaries typed, phones rang, copying machines hummed, and people rushed this way and that clutching memos and ducking in and out of offices. A strange and welcome glow seemed to come from each office as I walked along the corridor. Clearly this was where the action was. I introduced myself to the secretary as "the guy from Budget here to help with the travel vouchers."

"Jesus, are you gonna be popular! We've got guys stranded all over the goddam country!" She pushed a pile of paper aside, punched a button on a telephone console whose every button was blinking, and passed the news. "Go on in," she nodded to a door through which a half-dozen guys and women passed in the few minutes I had been standing there.

It was a large corner office, which accommodated an L-shaped desk with a typewriter on the return, two multi–button telephone consoles with all buttons silently blinking, and a collection of memos, reports, letters and newspapers with stories circled in red. Elsewhere in the room were a conference table and six or eight chairs. On the wall behind the conference table was a huge map of the United States, showing every state, county and city, with names like "Gonzalez", "Williams," "Torres," and "Argrett" written on paper slips pinned to towns and cities, many in the South.

"Bill will be with you in a minute," a lean, elegant man rose and shook my hand. "I'm Bob Clampitt." He was in his 50s, an urbane man with an easy confidence and graceful moves. He was in his shirt sleeves, with the jacket of his pinstripe suit draped over a chair, Countess Mara tie loosened and collar unbuttoned. A pair of scarlet suspenders over a gray shirt with white collar and crisp white cuffs complete with black onyx cufflinks completed the outfit. All this was topped by a set of cool gray eyes and a head of black hair turning gray, carefully barbered but now tousled, giving him the look of a man who started the day fresh and fashionable and morphed by late afternoon into a world-weary city editor with hot leads to the latest government scandal and not enough reporters to nail them down by deadline. He was in fact a corporate lawyer from New York, drafted into the Poverty Wars by the man sitting behind the desk wrapping up a telephone conversation with obvious impatience at whoever he was talking to.

" Nelson," the man behind the desk said, "you can threaten all you want. We're not about to let the state decide who gets what. Sarge won't do it. If we let you do it in New York, we'll have every Southern governor demanding the whites get all the money. You know that as well as I do!" A moment's pause as he listened to the sputtering voice on the other end. "Go ahead, Nelson. Call Sarge. Hell, call the President! It won't change a damn thing." He hung up the phone with an amused look at Clampitt.

"Rockefeller wants his hands on the reins?" Clampitt asked. I realized with a sudden thrill I was at a much higher altitude of events than even I had dreamt of – at least for years to come.

"You know Nelson," came the reply. "George Wallace was on the phone this morning wanting the same thing — control over who gets the money. I had to tell the Governor of Alabama to go fuck himself this morning. If I have to, I'll tell the Governor of New York the same." He looked at me with quick speculation in his eyes. "Hi," he reached over the papers on his desk to shake hands. "I'm Bill Haddad. What can you do for us? I've got guys running out of money all over the country," he gestured toward the huge map and the colored push pins.

He and Clampitt explained that in order to get the inspections up and running as the money started to flow from the OEO, they hired a bunch of investigative reporters who were on strike from the *Baltimore Sun* and several other papers, and dispatched them to places where they expected trouble of one kind or another. Problems had already broken out in the deep South, where white politicians were vigorously opposing the inclusion of black-run programs in OEO's funding plans. The reporters, hired as consultants, were sent off before all the paperwork went through. They put their airfare, hotels and car rentals on their personal credit cards with naive expectations that money would be wired to them in the field. They had no idea how agonizingly slow and indifferent the bureaucracy was to their cash flow problems.

"Nobody here knows how to fill these forms out," Haddad pointed to the conference table, covered with half-completed travel vouchers and receipts loosely piled for everything from air fares to gas for the rental cars, "and the more time the secretaries spend on that stuff the less work we get done. Can you do anything?"

"We-e-ll," I stalled, painfully aware I had no idea of how one fills out travel vouchers, "I'll need help. I've got two good people downstairs. I need your okay to get them reassigned to work with me up here for a day or two." I could have shoveled all the paperwork into boxes and had them carted down to the budget office, but here was my chance. If I was going to plow through the mess, I wanted to do it in full view of Haddad and Clampitt, who might be grateful enough to give me a job in this exciting place.

“Sammie,” Haddad punched the intercom to his secretary, a tall Texas blonde named Sammie Baer, “Get hold of Bill Kelly in finance. Tell him Joe Wilkins is working on our problems, and we need him okayed to bring extra help.” By the time I arrived downstairs, the word had passed that I was to be given carte blanche.

“Take whoever you want,” my supervisor muttered as he put on his coat. “It’s authorized.” I caught Juanita and Francine as they were leaving and explained the situation.

“Let me get this straight,” Juanita laughed. “You got your sorry white ass in trouble saying you can do travel vouchers when you don’t know jack shit about travel vouchers? Now we’re supposed to bail you out?”

“If you don’t, my sorry white ass is done for.” I groveled shamelessly.

Juanita couldn’t keep a straight face. “Okay,” she laughed.

Next morning Juanita and Francine brought along two other travel clerks cut loose for the day from other assignments. I commandeered Bill Haddad’s conference table, and sat between Juanita and Francine. They’d whisper to me what to say next, I’d give the orders loud enough for Haddad to know I was running things, and the pile rapidly shrank. While the girls worked through it I called a friend from my General Services Administration days who understood the mechanics of how approved travel vouchers actually got paid. He suggested it was possible to get the Treasury to agree to a same-day advance of 80% of each voucher, with the rest to come after thorough review — a trick, he warned, for which I would need serious clout.

That gave me no concern. Listening to the background conversations at Haddad’s desk while we worked, I was becoming aware of how much clout Bill Haddad had. His title as Inspector General was misleading; it initially led me to assume he was some kind of super-auditor. In OEO, however, Haddad believed it was just as much the job of the Office of Inspections to make sure the brand-new Civil Rights Act of 1964 was enforced by those who received OEO grants as it was to audit the money spent for paperclips. He was a short, dark-haired guy with relentless energy and the ability to listen to people's stories with a sympathetic ear and a quick, incisive mind. He had come up the hard way as an investigative reporter with the *New York Herald Tribune*, and worked as a top aide to Jack Kennedy in the 1960 Presidential campaign. A Jacques Lowe photograph that ran in *Life* magazine tells how close Haddad became to JFK: The election was so close it was well into the morning after on the East Coast before news came that Kennedy carried Illinois and thus the White House. Lowe's photo showed JFK early on that morning, in a chair in the living room of Bobby Kennedy's home at the family compound in Hyannisport. The picture was taken from behind the TV he is watching. In the background is his inner circle; his brother Bobby and wife Ethel, Pierre Salinger, and his brother-in-law Steve Smith. Everyone is watching the television. The caption read "This is the moment when John Fitzgerald Kennedy learned he was elected President of the United States." The closest figure to the new President-elect at that historic moment was Bill Haddad, crouched beside Kennedy's chair.

JFK asked Sargent Shriver, his brother-in-law, to run a talent search for the best people to bring into his Administration. Haddad was a key man in that effort, which meant that grateful top government figures all over Washington, keenly aware that a Robert Kennedy administration might still come about someday, accepted his phone calls without hesitation. When Shriver established the Peace Corps, Kennedy's signature program, Haddad came aboard as his associate director.

When Lyndon Johnson sought the support of the bereaved liberals still reeling from the shock of JFK's death, he named Shriver as OEO's first Director. Bill Haddad became Shriver's right-hand man at the OEO under the title of Inspector General, which fell far short of indicating his true influence and power.

Shriver, keenly sensitive to the civil rights turmoil around the country and the potential for both corruption and controversy in launching a huge new federal program, asked Haddad to set up the Office of Inspections with a broad mission including the traditional monitoring for abuse and fraud, but especially monitoring for racial discrimination and for exclusion of the poor from decision-making. Given the kind of influence and energy Haddad brought to the job, the post became the Office of Inspections "and Special Projects" – a euphemism for wherever his energy took him.

***

When the travel vouchers were ready and I had made some phone calls to prepare the way, I told Haddad we could have the U.S. Treasury cut and deliver checks for 80% of our guys' travel expenses that afternoon if he would back my play. He looked at me with sharply appraising eyes.

"Sammie," he called to his secretary, "get me the White House."

The checks arrived that evening, which prompted Haddad to ask what it would take for me to go to work for him as his administrative officer. It was the question I'd been hoping for.

Almost every event in my life since John F. Kennedy's assassination had been reactive — emotionally confused and not very smart attempts to cope with the sudden collapse of my hopes and dreams. Kennedy was my personal hero and the reason I was interested in politics. When I met him at a college luncheon the year before he was elected, he was tan and graceful, intensely alive, fully engaged, and plainly enjoying life. I sat across the table from him for an hour and, fascinated with the emerging European Common Market, asked him a lot of questions about foreign affairs. He indulged me in this, foreign affairs being his favorite topic. I did not know the word *charisma* at the time, but he had it by the ton. I came away dreaming of becoming a member of the Senate Foreign Relations Committee.

A year and a half later he was President and I'd been accepted at the Catholic University's law school in Washington as a night student. At that happy moment I could make no claim to knowing much more about what was going on in America than what I read in the Kennedy-centric press of the time. Kennedy favored civil rights so I favored civil rights, and to about the same extent. When the press ran stories of how the hardscrabble life of people in West Virginia awakened Kennedy to the presence of poverty in America, I accepted that such poverty existed — although, as with racism, I had no more first-hand knowledge of it than he did.

In the short life of his Administration I had found my life's direction and purpose. His death left me shattered. In the year and a half since, I had stumbled through a series of dead-end jobs, trying to survive and get through law school. Now at last I had come to a place where the right choice could make the difference between mere survival and challenging growth. Here was my chance to break out of a bureaucratic rut. I glanced at those little pins on the map of the U.S., which had been intriguing me all day, and took the plunge.

"What I'd like are two things," I said. "First, a promotion. To get things done for you I need to move up a grade." That was true, and if he agreed it meant a $100 a month raise, which was a lot. My rent was $112 a month.

"And the second?" Haddad asked.

"I want to go out in the field like those guys," I nodded to the map. "I don't want to get stuck in an administrative job."

"But it's the mess here we need help with!" Haddad said. "My guys are reporters. They're used to landing in new places and figuring out what's going on. Have you ever done that?"

"No, but I never did travel vouchers either." I explained about Juanita and Francine. Clampitt, a lawyer, wasn't particularly happy with the stunt, but the news guy in Bill Haddad must have recognized a kindred spirit. And those same-day checks from the U.S. Treasury were a powerful argument on my behalf.

"Ok," he said. "Give me three months of administrative work and I'll send you out in the field with one of my seasoned guys and we'll see how you do. That good enough for you?"

"Yes, sir, General, sir," I gave him a mock salute.

"Get the hell out of here," he chuckled. "Your first job is get your transfer and promotion taken care of. I don't know how that's done, but I'll sign whatever you put in front of me."

***

Haddad wasn't kidding about needing quick administrative help. Working with his Office of Inspections was like joining an avalanche in progress. It was the nerve center of the OEO. The men he sent into the field were the eyes and ears of the national effort; the insights they came back with informed and shaped the central policies of the agency. In that respect the War on Poverty was like any other war; it could not be fought without real-time intelligence from the field. Thoughtful people of great accomplishment had studied the causes of poverty and evolved theories and concepts that might or might not work. Like barriers erected against an invading army, poverty was protected against reformers by a deep defensive structure of racism, ignorance, greed, political inertia and corruption, apathy and cynicism. Sending funds and grants blindly out would invite waste, scandal and savage criticism. Haddad's inspectors were the key to prevention of such abuse, and to correction of misdirected or counterproductive policies.

All that required attention to the humble details of administration, for which little provision had been made in the rush to kick-start the Office of Economic Opportunity in its formative months. Some problems were complex; others could be solved with a little creativity. For example, when the field guys came back from assignments, their final reports needed typing; for which the half-dozen secretaries were too few. We had no room for more. Since Shriver still had authority over the Peace Corps, we offered evening overtime at OEO to any Peace Corps secretary who wanted it. That doubled our secretarial force without requiring more space.

Bringing secretaries in on the night shift was easy enough. Holding on to them was another matter. I found a gem of a woman, smart and fast and calm in every storm. Haddad stole her. Three weeks later Shriver stole her from him. A month later the Chairman of the House Appropriations Committee offered her a hefty raise and off she went. These women, born 20 years later, would have made it into management without breathing hard. But they'd spent their formative years trapped by what became known as "the glass ceiling," working under men with such bureaucratic souls they couldn't order coffee without making the call personally. Haddad's style was to rush out his door telling a secretary things like: "Millie – call the White House. Get Bill Moyers on the phone. Tell him I need a decision on Chicago." Bill Moyers was Lyndon Johnson's top aide, which meant that a secretary whose previous boss couldn't delegate squat was now on her own dealing with the Special Assistant to the President of the United States. That was heady stuff, and those women blossomed like flowers after a spring shower.

I blossomed considerably myself. Being the only person understood by one and all to have administrative responsibilities I was much in demand, especially since we used an extraordinary number of consultants. We paid their travel expenses and, informally, provided them temporary desk space and secretarial services in our crowded quarters. Functionally there was no difference between the regular guys on the payroll and the consultants; both rotated between field trips and Washington conferences and reports.

Given Haddad's contacts, finding superb people to handle special assignments on a consulting basis was an easy shot. They came out of nowhere, spent a day or two in our office to get up to speed on whatever problem or program they were to check out, flew out to interview people and find out what was happening on the ground, returned to be debriefed, did their reports, filed their expense accounts and went home — or out on the next assignment. All this required personnel forms, authorization of travel orders and so on. I became the administrative coordinator of the Haddad racing stable of consultants.

My efforts to persuade Juanita and Francine to transfer from Budget failed. They preferred the peaceful routines of their home base. They did help by training a succession of our secretaries in the exotic art of travel vouchers.

Personnel matters were trickier. The flow of new consultants was heavy and unpredictable. One might be a reporter temporarily available because he was out on strike; the next might be an investment banker from the upper west side of New York. One day a plain-looking fellow stood meekly in front of my desk informing me Haddad sent him. I figured him for a guy having a run of bad luck who put the touch on Bill for a job. With recent memories of being in the same spot, I wanted to get him on board as soon as possible.

"To do what?" I asked.

"I'm supposed to do something in New Mexico," he said. I grabbed a form and asked him to fill it out, then looked it over before handing it off to be typed. The three references he listed were the President of the United States, the Majority Leader of the U.S. Senate, and the Speaker of the House. Assuming that in his desperation he was puffing things more than was reasonable, I was about to advise him to come up with lower-octane references. Then I saw his name and background. He was Milt Shapp, who became seriously rich by founding Jerrold Electronics, based on the idea of building community antennae in remote Pennsylvania towns to get better TV reception, then running cables to carry the signal from the main antenna to individual houses. This was the guy who invented cable TV.

I had him sign the form, then I signed Haddad's name. Haddad, swamped with demands on his time, would routinely shove forms requiring his signature back to me. "I don't have time for this crap," he said. "Sign them with my name." My forgery skills progressed to the point where Bill couldn't tell his own signature from my version of it. Of course, I made sure my own promotion and expenses were signed by Haddad in person.

While I wrestled the administrative mess into reasonable shape, the real world of the Sixties moved on. More by accident than my own inquisitiveness I absorbed the dimensions of the changes underway. Busy afternoons and evenings eventually ended in the elegant Embers lounge on the first floor. One left the glare of fluorescent-lighted offices and hallways, rode fluorescent-lighted elevators to the fluorescent-lighted lobby, then opened a shiny metal door and passed into the welcoming, softly lit and red-carpeted Embers, where flickering candles and little cups of salted peanuts graced each table. A long bar shone with the soft reflections of mahogany, brass and bottles. We pushed cocktail tables together so the circle of inspectors and reporters in from the field could expand to welcome the newest refugee to the sanctuary. Having read their reports upstairs, in the Embers I could hear the details fresh from men just back from the Deep South, from the Indian reservations, from the urban ghettoes and farm worker camps. I took it all in with the salted peanuts.

Eventually it penetrated even my naiveté that beyond the comforting ambience of the Embers searing events were taking place out in the cities and counties across the country. Martin Luther King, Jr. was arrested – again – while leading 700 marchers protesting voter discrimination in Selma, Alabama. On February 21, 1965, about the time I joined Inspections, Black Muslim leader Malcolm X was shot to death in a Manhattan hotel ballroom in front of 400 people, including his pregnant wife and 4 year old daughter. President Johnson began bombing North Vietnam in the operation known as "Rolling Thunder" as he ratcheted up the number of American troops in Vietnam and authorized their commanders to send them into combat. Another Selma civil rights march led by a young John Lewis was brutally broken up at the Pettus Bridge by a hundred Alabama State troopers and local police, with Lewis and others clubbed in the head and kicked while down. A week or two later Martin Luther King, Jr. led two or three thousand protesters on another Selma march. The rising tide of protestors multiplied to 25,000 in the week following the murder on a Selma road of white civil rights activist Viola Luizza from Detroit.

Such was my ignorance of the civil rights ferment I had little idea of who Malcolm X was, nor of his vast influence in the black community as I listened to those stories in the Embers. Fortunately little more was expected of "the guy from Budget."

I was learning faster than I realized. By sheer chance I was at the convergence point of great forces that were shaping America in the mid-Sixties; the explosion of black anger in the civil rights movement; the convulsive violence of the South's white supremacists as they confronted protest marchers with beatings and murders and massive resistance to all forms of integration; the tremendous power of the federal government's enforcement of the Civil Rights Act of 1964 and, at the very heart of the conflicts, the determination of Shriver, Haddad and their colleagues to make OEO the first federal program that, from its birth, aggressively guarded against racial discrimination. They poured money and energy into black-run programs, migrant programs, Indian programs, and others that, precisely because of that emphasis on civil rights, confronted the established authorities and the power structure everywhere. With unerring accuracy The Office of Economic Opportunity was pouring the gasoline of federal money on every smouldering hot spot in American society. Even as that was happening in the land, President Johnson escalated the war in Vietnam, ignoring protestors who saw the war as an unwarranted and out of control military adventure.

***

A surge of new consultants came in to produce the OEO's first "Report to Congress." Photographers like Mort Engleberg fanned out across the country to capture scenes of American poverty as it existed in 1965. Writers from major publications in New York and Los Angeles dropped their bags in our office, got their assignments from Haddad and Clampitt, and were dispatched to the sites where our programs were beginning to take shape, in search of anecdotes and personal stories of the people we were helping.

The overall editor for the Report was Ira Mothner, a senior editor of

LOOK magazine borrowed for the occasion. The layout man was Bob Engle, senior cover editor for *Newsweek* magazine. Among many other writers were Dave Seaton from King Features Syndicate, Tom Kelly, a reporter from the *Washington Daily News*, syndicated columnist Don McLean, George Clifford, a sports and feature reporter for the *Daily News*, and Gershon Jacobson, a writer for *Der Tag Morgen Journal*, the *Yiddish Day Jewish Journal*, and *Yediot Acharonot*, Israel's largest daily.

Central to the Report's preparation was Gary Lefkowitz, a Brooklyn native who learned printing as a trade and was making good money as a printing cost estimator for Rand-McNally when he joined the Peace Corps. After two years in India he came home still wanting to do something for the country. He applied at The Office of Economic Opportunity and was walking out the door when he encountered Bill Haddad, whose name and reputation he knew from the Peace Corps. He became one of Haddad's most trusted lieutenants.

The Report to Congress was an around-the-clock, high pressure operation, carried on in the midst of other around-the-clock, high pressure operations. I first met Lefkowitz at 2 o'clock one morning when Haddad asked me to relieve him so Gary could get some sleep. He was running the physical side of assembling the congressional presentation, coordinating a workforce of writers, editors, typists, printers and assistants. He showed me the next steps that could be done in his absence, and went home to sleep. When he came back he hardly got home for three more days.

A few days later, around 1 A.M., I told Haddad no more galley proofs would be available for his approval for about 45 minutes. He cleared the top of a conference table, folded his coat under his head for a pillow, and took a nap until the new proofs arrived.

With the constantly accelerating cycle of comings and goings, I was fast becoming one of the few besides Haddad who knew everybody, or at least whom everybody knew. Gary and I hit it off . The approval of the printer's bill being part of my job, he kept me by his side as he reviewed proofs at the printer's, negotiated changes, wheedled writers, photographers and artists into necessary changes of length or cropping, and turned his informed professional eye on such esoteric printer's details as page bleeding, dithering, tones and other microscopic adjustments far beyond my untrained eye.

There came a night when the final draft was at the printers, and we had nothing to do until the proofs came back. A dozen or so reporters, writers and photographers had to hang around so they could okay the final before the production run. Some of them were veterans, as either staffers or reporters, of John F. Kennedy's presidential campaign. Several at Haddad's conference table that night were regulars on the "Caroline," Kennedy's family-owned campaign plane. A case of cold beer was brought in, and the evening turned into an Irish wake. He was dead less than 18 months. Many around that table had not seen each other since the campaign of 1960. Story after story was told, a treasury of Kennedy lore that held me mesmerized, including tales of how, when barnstorming California, a beautiful starlet would board at one stop, disappear into Kennedy's private cabin, and emerge to get off at the next stop slightly disheveled and smiling sheepishly. None of those stories ever saw print in those respectful days. Having met Kennedy, I had no trouble believing them.

The impetus Kennedy introduced to the government sprang in large part from the energies and leadership of guys like Shriver and Haddad and the kind of people they in turn could bring into play. For my part, I was happy to have entered this new world of drive and commitment.

Inside OEO, however, the difference between the high energy of Haddad's operation and bureaucratic foot-dragging in other parts of the agency provoked friction early on.

The conflict first became evident in trivial things. The evening secretarial shift we set up outnumbered the desks and typewriters available to them. The typists had to compete with the writers themselves, all news guys for whom pounding out rough drafts of their reports on typewriters was faster than dictating them. Most offices weren't locked, so we told people to take their typing to the nearest empty office to work. Since every other office except Inspections was empty by 5 or 6 o'clock, that solution worked fine; except that not everybody left their borrowed desks in clean condition, causing complaints from their regular occupants next day. OEO's director of management, a man with a deep love of bureaucratic niceties and a corresponding dislike of Haddad's constant pushing to get things done, fired off a memo asking the practice be stopped. We ignored it. In another display of chickenshit bureaucracy, a secretary confronted with a word on which the spelling was uncertain went out one evening and with her own money bought a dictionary so the memo could go off to the White House immediately. The bureaucrats refused to reimburse her the $7.50 she paid for the dictionary, on the grounds she hadn't gotten the right authorization signed before making the purchase.

Such incidents, while trivial, were symptoms of more serious problems developing under the surface. While needed OEO grants were being authorized for programs in which civil rights compliance was vital, especially in the still segregationist South, OEO's management was taking months to actually get the money to them. Nor was it helpful to have to untangle miles of red-tape to get our inspectors on board and into the field as safeguards against the wilful racial discrimination that persisted in the South. At first it seemed only a problem of slow management. In fact the foot-dragging reflected a division between those eager to forge a new approach to social justice, including justice for blacks, Hispanics and Native Americans, and those who wanted to fund and nourish the old-line and largely white labor, social workers and government agencies left over from FDR's New Deal of thirty years earlier.

Chapter 3: "It's What's Happening, Baby!"

It lay beyond my personal horizon at the time, but one of OEO's earliest problems was that nobody trusted us. The OEO was a government program at a time when liberals and conservatives alike were voicing distrust of the federal government. Traditional avenues to recruit young people to enroll in a government program were unlikely to work. It was especially unlikely that young black men from urban ghettoes would show up at the local employment office and fill out forms. In search of ways to reach and motivate the poorest teenagers in the great urban slums and persuade them to join OEO's Job Corps – no easy project when distrust of all things government was ingrained — somebody suggested using television to carry the OEO message. Not the old television of public service announcements nor the middle-class and middle-age television of Ed Sullivan and Walter Cronkite: this was to be a new, no-holds-barred show using the most popular musical groups and teen-hit celebrities to make our pitch with the music kids listened to and in the street language they spoke. Bill Haddad, related by marriage and friendship to CBS founder and longtime chairman William S. Paley, persuaded CBS to donate free air time. To produce the show, Haddad recruited the flamboyant New York disc jockey Murray Kaufman, known as "Murray the K" and "the Fifth Beatle" for his influence in bringing the Beatles to America. The show was to be called "It's What's Happening, Baby!" It was a revolutionary idea. Television had not progressed much beyond showing only the upper half of Elvis Presley's gyrating body. Even the wildly popular Beatles were considered almost too hot to handle on TV. CBS donated 90 valuable minutes of national air time.

The performers donated their services. On our side, the Office of Economic Opportunity agreed to pick up the performer's expenses – a commitment made with little understanding of how different was the view of each side as to what constituted reimbursable expenses.

With a promise like that, it wasn't long before the producers and performers began screaming for reimbursement of their rapidly mounting and self-defined "expenses". The bewildered budget officers in my old office were swamped. As Haddad's newly-minted resident expert on getting expenses paid to his troops, he asked me to see what could be done to break the slow-payment logjam that was threatening the show's production.

Other than understanding it would be a kind of public service TV appeal, I was slow to pick up what the show was all about. Haddad assured me we were getting the best groups going. I recognized none of their names. Juggling jobs, babies, college and law school had kept me out of step with the changes in the world of popular music that came in with the Beatles.

By late May the show's production reached the crisis stage. Angry telephone calls demanding money came in from New York, from Los Angeles, from Nashville and elsewhere. Murray the K called to say people were crowding his office wanting their money. Haddad sent me to New York. I left feeling important just to be on a plane at government expense. In New York I showed up at Murray the K's office, complete with a briefcase full of blank travel and expense vouchers.

I didn't intend it, but it was a dramatic entrance. "Here he is," Murray beckoned me in through a crowd of show business people gathered round his desk, perched on his sofa and sitting on the floor, "this is the guy from Washington with the money!" All eyes fastened hungrily on my briefcase, as if it were stuffed with cash. It took Murray the K long minutes to calm everybody down when they realized they'd have to fill out forms and wait for checks.

"Okay, okay," he got them relatively quiet, "let the guy do his job. Whaddya need, kid?"

"First thing," I said, "is receipts."

"What kinda receipts?" a guy in a lavender suit asked. "We don't do receipts for a lotta stuff."

"Well," I said, "I'll need receipts for stuff like taxicabs and — " I was hooted down with vociferous disbelief. It dawned on me there was a considerable culture gap between show business folks and governmental budget types.

"Taxi's?" a long-haired guy in the corner laughed. "Are you outta your fuckin' mind? You ever ask a New York cabbie for a fuckin' receipt?"

"I got $300 in taxi expenses!" another yelled across the din. "Jesus Christ, how you think you get around in New York? On Tinkerbell's back?"

I got back to Washington in one piece, and spent the next week sorting out the mess. Not everything went smoothly. Murray the K called in shock when word reached him the *per diem* – the government's allowable daily rate for incidental travel expenses other than transportation and lodging, was $16. "That's crazy! I spend 16 bucks by the time I get a shine and a cup of coffee!" To show business types, taxi receipts and *per diem* were minor bureaucratic irritants. Some thought on a larger scale: one big name group's manager wanted to charter a flight to the West Coast and take with him four beautiful special assistants from a modeling agency of dubious reputation "to recruit talent for the show." He expected the Government to pay for the flight and the girls, and was mad as hell when we wouldn't back him up.

As the day approached for the broadcast, we had no idea what kind of response to expect from the show. To find out if the language was likely to reach the kids, Haddad suggested that the script be proof-read by OEO's Xerox machine operators. These were black kids from the DC slums hired for the sole purpose of making copies. The Xerox company trained them in how to clean, maintain and run the machines, which were complicated and expensive monsters prone to breakdowns if not babied and tended. OEO paid them the minimum hourly wage and assigned each kid to his own machine, which gave them an introduction to the working world and a job that was more useful than anticipated. The Xerox machine kids were exactly the kind of kids the TV show was intended to reach. They liked the proposed scripts.

Since the show would make the point that the government would provide high school dropouts a new chance in life, Murray the K would tell the kids to write to "New Chance" and let us know they were interested. We arranged with the post office for delivery of all "New Chance" mail to the Office of Economic Opportunity.

No one knew wether we'd get a hundred letters or a hundred thousand; but whatever letters we got would have to be answered. We planned to set up conference tables in a room to which the mail was to be delivered. Haddad, with his usual zest and eagerness, insisted the tables be set up in his large corner office so he could see the results for himself.

The show aired on CBS late in June of 1965. Its performers included over twenty of the leading groups in popular music, including Sonny and Cher singing "I've got you, babe," Tom Jones performing "It's not unusual," Dionne Warwick, Martha and the Vandellas, Marvin Gaye, The Supremes, The Righteous Brothers, The Temptations, Johnny Mathis, Ray Charles, The Ronettes, The Four Tops, and Little Anthony. Murray the K popped up throughout the acts, pitching the Job Corps in street language. It was a high-energy, all-out blast aimed right at the young. There was an assumption that the program would have its strongest effect on black kids in the urban slums. It was aimed at America's slums, but it hit America's heartland.

Next morning all hell broke loose in Haddad's office. Senators and Congressmen and the movers and shakers of America had all the phones lit up spouting outrage that a U.S. Government agency had sponsored shocking and depraved music and gutter language hardly decipherable to their educated ears. One Senator claimed he almost vomited when he saw the show. Others were aghast at the prospect that federal money was used to promote demoralized dancing and degenerate music. Telegrams bearing angry messages arrived from influential people and piled up on Haddad's conference table. Next morning the telegrams slowed, but were replaced by a flow of more articulate outrage, this time flawlessly typed on expensive creamy paper with engraved letterheads from corporate executives and wealthy people eager to blow off steam. As the mail mounted through the day we marshaled extra secretaries to type up replies.

Not until the third day did the stationery, and the tone, begin to change. Letters from ordinary people poured in; many still against what we did, and more than a few outraged at the sight of blacks and whites dancing in the same musical numbers. Still, the weight was shifting to those who applauded the effort, however "misguided" as they described it, to reach the kids in the slums. Ministers and rabbis, local union leaders and civil rights figures, main street businessmen and college professors wrote in. The pile on the conference table, by now an exhibit for interested sightseers from throughout the OEO, grew impressively. Hope spread in the office that opinion was shifting our way.

Then the real storm hit. Letters started coming in scrawled in pencil on lined paper torn from cheap copybooks and mailed in crumpled envelopes from all over the East Coast, filled with bad grammar and worse spelling. They came in by the thousands, mail in large and uncertain handwriting; mail on postcards; mail on every variety of paper that could be found in the houses of the poor, all with gut-wrenching messages. One of the early such letters brought tears to everyone's eyes with a message something like – I wish I had saved it — "Deer Job Corp. Pleas help me. I am 15 years old and pregnant with second babie. Can I be a sekratary." Another: "Dear Mr. President. I made a mistake and I need a new chance." Still another: "I got pregnant and dropped out. I'm going to have a baby and they won't let me back in but how can I teach the baby things I don't know myself." That one had a P.S. "Please don't tell anyone about me because nobody knows but me and the baby's father and you." These were dropouts who were bound by chains they couldn't see to a life they didn't want.

Reading that mail was a stunning personal experience that had a lifelong effect on me. Until then, the problems of the poor had always seemed statistics to me, or book-learned literary shadows from Steinbeck novels. Yet from that pile of letters came the voice of a young and poor America I didn't know really existed. It was the first time I understood the real power of government in a democracy to give hope to the poor and spur the dreams of the young. I have never forgotten that lesson.

The tide of letters rolled in from further west next day, and the next, as mail arrived from Appalachia, from the Deep South, from hardscrabble farmhouses and Indian reservations and picker's camps up and down the West Coast. There were coffee-stained letters from mothers desperate for their children's future; from young men in their twenties who had never held a job; from girls whose bright hopes shone from the paper sometimes torn from brown grocery bags on which they wrote. By the time it slowed, the outraged letters on creamy expensive stationery of the first day were buried under bags and bags of mail from the young who heard the message. The Office of Economic Opportunity thought it was reaching out to the urban slums, but its message reached far beyond, to every part of the country.

The letters touched all who saw them. OEO's man for congressional relations was Gillis Long, a Democratic ex-congressman from Louisiana and a member of Louisiana's most famous political family. He had left Congress to run for governor of Louisiana, lost, and was sitting out the year at OEO waiting to run for Congress next election. Gillis came to Haddad's office worried about the tremendous heat he was feeling from his former colleagues on Capitol Hill. I took him in to see the letters piled up on the conference tables, around which half a dozen people were now working. Taking a handful of letters from the pile I invited him to read them. He stayed well over an hour. Tears came to his eyes as he realized what was happening.

The letters revealed a great gulf between those on top and those down and out. One of the strongest protests came from Republican Senator Peter Dominick of Colorado. Yet from his home state came a letter from a young man with 3 small children who was a plumber until he injured his back and was thrown out of work. His wife was a high school dropout and couldn't get a job, and two of his children were ill. He wanted to be a police radio dispatcher; it had become his hope for getting out of the hole he was in. He didn't have the high school degree he needed to qualify and wrote us.

His letter did not plead; he stated his case with a simple dignity that made me wonder at the gap between their world and the world of the U.S. Senate to which I aspired. I wondered how any Senator could so vigorously damn the same show from which one of his constituents at the bottom of the ladder could draw such hope.

The mail overflowed the tables we set up, until we had to move the whole thing to another, larger room. Volunteers from throughout the agency came to help sort it out, organized by a fellow named Bill Campbell, and by Bill Nichols, one of Haddad's consultants who along the way had worked on the famous "Dragnet" TV series and other shows. They put together teams of volunteers who sorted the letters, categorized them as best they could in terms of age, geography, and the most likely applicable program for them, and prepared individual answers to the bulk of them. They forwarded the letters to the Job Corps, to the Neighborhood Youth Corps or other offices whose staff could follow-up with those who wrote for help.

Even in the face of such a resounding success, the bureaucrats still balked. OEO's Director of Management, panicked at the Congressional protests against the program, froze the reimbursement of all expenses, reneging on the promises OEO had made. In one instance I received a memo from his finance office, advising me that I might be personally responsible for a $92.50 bill for the rental of typewriters in New York in connection with the TV show. It cited a procurement regulation holding people personally liable for items charged without prior authorization. He forgot or did not know that my first days at OEO were spent drafting those procurement regulations. I was glad to be able to point out an appropriate loophole that let me off the hook.

Whatever excesses show business people indulged in by government standards, the facts were that CBS gave us enormously valuable air time for free; Murray the K and the greatest groups in entertainment donated their services, and the show reached tens of thousands of needy kids and adults with information that could lead them to jobs and a better life.

Chapter 4: Head Start

One day as I was hurrying down the corridor, Jack Gonzales grabbed my arm and pulled me into his office, saying "Joe, I need help on Head Start!"

Jack Gonzalez was in charge of Haddad's Inspections operations for the Southern region. He was a loose-tie, rolled-up shirt sleeves kind of guy. He worked in the Food and Drug Administration when Senator Estes Kefauver of Tennessee launched a congressional investigation into the high prices of prescription medicines. Gonzalez withstood pressure from his agency to water down testimony about how the drug companies artificially boosted the cost of drugs by inflating research costs and discouraging physicians from issuing prescriptions for generic drugs. Bill Haddad, impressed with his tough integrity, brought him into the OEO.

"What's Head Start?" I asked. In those early days OEO was coming up with one new program after another, with catchy names like "Upward Bound", "Job Corps", "Vista" and so on. I knew practically nothing about Head Start except it involved little kids.

As Gonzales explained, the concept had been part of the earliest discussions of the anti-poverty program. Studies showed that children of the poorest families were behind before they even started school. By the third or fourth grade many were already failing. Much of the problem arose because schools were local affairs, paid for by local property taxes based on local real estate values. Rich neighborhoods of more expensive homes could afford good schools and good teachers. Poor neighborhoods and towns had no equivalent tax base to pay decent salaries or keep class sizes low. The result was marginal teachers facing oversized classes. Another key element was the failure of the parents to get involved. Poor parents often did badly in school themselves and had neither the know-how nor the confidence to hold up their end of the parent-teacher relationship. The design for Head Start included involving the parents in an influential way. Bringing the entire family into contact with the school system might give them confidence and a sense of identity with traditional middle-class educational values.

It was, Gonzales said, "the hottest program we've got. The President's behind it, his wife's behind it, the public loves the idea, and Shriver is nuts about it. It's a crash program. They funded some programs last summer, but this year they want it rolling big time, and they want it done right. We only have a few weeks to get up to speed. A lotta pressure — lotta pressure."

According to Gonzales, Shriver had ordered a special task force set up to review the Head Start applications that were pouring in from all over the country from school districts, churches, and the newly-formed local Community Action Agencies. Recognizing the South's fierce resistance to integration of schools, Shriver was determined that Head Start would be free of the racial discrimination that had poisoned the schools of the South since Reconstruction. While the task force was to handle all other aspects of Head Start applications, Shriver wanted Haddad to monitor their civil rights compliance and the programs that resulted. It would be a huge and controversial job.

"Bill said you could handle the administrative stuff for me," Jack said.

"What do you need?" I asked.

"I have to hire a bunch of guys in a hurry, and get them into the field. Plus we'll need secretaries and travel money and all that stuff."

"Jesus, Jack! Haddad's already hiring guys so fast the finance guys are shitting themselves! How many you need?"

"At least ten right away; maybe 15 or 20 altogether."

"Where will you put them?" I asked in disbelief. Every desk was filled day and night. We already had moonlighters in half the other offices on the floor.

"I'm going to set up shop back at the New Colonial," Jack answered. "That reminds me; we'll need telephones. Oh, and copy machines. Thanks, Joe. Gotta go."

That was a lot to drop in my lap, but minor stuff compared to the challenges Gonzales faced. Under the new Civil Rights Law, outfits seeking federal grants were required to send in official certifications of compliance with the Act. In the view of the average government bureaucrat, what happened on the ground didn't matter. If they sent in the right piece of paper, they did not have a civil rights problem and could get federal money. There were already indications of Southern fights to come, and the internal stresses that would bedevil the OEO's own headquarters. On March 12, 1965 Bob Clampitt advised Haddad:

> Last week Jack Gonzales told me that the Director of the Central Savannah River Project has reneged on a commitment to hire a Negro staff member .... It seems that a 'housing man' told Central Savannah that they did not have to hire Negroes and that they could insist on a letter from OEO stating the requirements for Negro staff – so they hired two white staffers. I ... confirmed the story. I then ... asked that a hold be put on the letters of credit which were about to go out.

Haddad passed the memo on to Shriver that same day, with his own covering note:

> There is no doubt that we now face a crisis and a test in Georgia. .... These Georgians knew what the hell was going on. They're trying to renege following the usual patter of the South, putting us to the test, watching our reaction, and then going on from there. ... Unless we show the steel, we'll have real trouble.

An internal Community Action Programs memo further showed what Haddad was up against in OEO headquarters:

> Theodore M. Berry to Frederick O.R. Hayes, March 31, 1965:

> I would recommend that funds be released.... Haddad will probably have objections ... the second is the more serious one. It is that we should not continue to fund all-white commissions even though their CAP programs were run under acceptable bi-racial policy commissions. This, I find almost totally objectionable. It would mean the voiding, in effect, of an obligation to which the full faith and credit of the United States has been pledged, without action by the grantee that is violative of either the spirit or letter of the conditions under which he accepted the grant.

The home truth was that no one, either in the South or at OEO, gave any credence to signed statements of civil rights compliance. Southerners considered them updated versions of the loyalty oaths demanded by the victorious North after the Civil War – oaths extracted under threat of force and therefore weightless. Southern program officials signed the assurances of civil rights compliance never expecting anybody to actually implement racial equality. What Gonzales was about to do was ignore their signatures and check the facts on the ground.

To do that, he put together a force made up of two different kinds of agents. The first level were news reporters, who came in for a day or two, read the applications to see if there were any obvious trouble spots, and then called the local board members, staff, and local reporters to determine what the racial picture might be. If they suspected substantial non-compliance, they'd talk it over with Gonzales, who would usually schedule a field trip to follow up. If the reporters found real problems on the ground, Gonzales would send guys who had experience investigating federal programs for fraud and abuse. For this he borrowed guys from the Inspections office of other agencies like the Department of Agriculture or Labor; usually ex-FBI guys trained to gather evidence and give testimony in court. Some guys came from the Air Force to work on a volunteer basis. Meanwhile, Haddad and Clampitt contacted leading law firms around the country and got them to volunteer the services of their ablest young lawyers over the summer.

Those who came in for that work included people like Don Petit, an investigative reporter for the *Miami Herald.* Frank Grimsley was an ex-FBI agent and attorney who worked on the special squad set up by Attorney General Robert F. Kennedy to investigate, and ultimately convict, Teamster's Union President Jimmy Hoffa for jury tampering. Grimsley was Kennedy's man in the South. He could put his fingers on more information about what was going on in Southern states than anybody else. Jim Brenner (Clifford J. Brenner) and Jim Duggan were Republican lawyers in New York who worked on a special rackets commission set up by Governor Rockefeller and staffed by lawyers, C.P.A.'s and state troopers – until the trail of corruption led them into the ranks of the Republican-dominated New York state legislature, whereupon they came to work one morning to learn the commission was out of business. They and a third lawyer, a quiet, unassuming and razor-sharp guy named Peter Spruance, joined Gonzales's team.

Jim Brenner had the deceptively innocent appearance of a chubby Harry Truman. In fact he was a Major in the U.S. Marine Corps Reserve trained in guerrilla warfare and did intelligence work when on active duty.

Bob Martin, a Wall Street lawyer, was recruited on a temporary basis and never went back to private lawyering. Others included Al Krumlauf of Florida, John J. Casey of New Orleans, and John Daum, a tall, lanky *summa cum laude* graduate of Harvard who joined for a stint between college and Yale Law School.

Al From came aboard, fresh out of college. He was a young southerner trained in journalism and close to ex-Louisiana Congressman Gillis Long, OEO's congressional liaison. In later life, Al From founded the Democratic Leadership Council, and was eventually credited by Bill Clinton as the man who set him up for his successful run for President in 1992, bringing the Democrats back to the White House after years of disastrous defeats.

Bill Seward came to us from conservative Senator and former Republican Presidential candidate Barry Goldwater's office, jumping from one of the most conservative jobs imaginable to OEO, which was already perceived as a hotbed of liberalism. Seward, a top aide in Goldwater's office, grew disenchanted when what he saw as right-wing extremists claimed Goldwater as their own and moved in on the relatively easy-going Senate atmosphere.

***

Still working off my commitment to clear Haddad's administrative decks, I had not yet had the promised chance to go into the field. What I knew of the Head Start controversies I learned largely in the Embers lounge from reporters and agents just back from the battles. Their accounts were vivid. The fiercest fight was taking place in Mississippi, where a black-organized group called the Child Development Group of Mississippi, or CDGM, was approved for Head Start money to the outrage of the white establishment. The most powerful leader of that white establishment was Mississippi's Democratic U.S. Senator John Stennis, a power in the Senate and a fierce and crafty opponent of civil rights. For long years he had blocked the appointment of any federal judges in the state who were not demonstrably racist. He had filibustered civil rights legislation time and again, and made no bones about his belief that black people were incapable of self-government.

CDGM attracted angry young black activists determined to organize Mississippi's impoverished black families into a political force by registering voters under the new Civil Rights Act and the eagerly anticipated Voting Rights Act of 1965. Registering voters could not in any way be considered a legitimate use of Head Start funds, as Stennis vigorously protested to Shriver. He demanded that CDGM's funds be cut off. Shriver's efforts to get the paid Head Start staffers to quit registering voters on Head Start's time and concentrate on the little kids failed. The CDGM controversy became as much a symbol of the racial fights of the South as the beating of civil rights workers. Those of its leaders who may have started out moderates were radicalized by the clash between the white racists and black extremists. Shriver was assailed by both sides, by the black leaders for selling out the cause of civil rights; and by the whites as a Northern radical hell-bent on destroying society.

Throughout the South the Head Start battles were being fought against the background of the Supreme Court's 1954 decision in *Brown v. Board of Education* that racial segregation in the schools must be ended "with all deliberate speed." Meyer S. "Sandy" Frucher, a brilliant young liberal from New York who eventually had a distinguished financial career and became CEO of the Philadelphia Stock Exchange and more recently vice-chairman of the NASDAQ OMX group, wrote in a memo to Haddad; "Many Negro teachers are being squeezed out of their jobs in the South as Negro schools (and school systems) are closed and white schools integrated .... there is an apparent effort on the part of some white-directed Southern school systems to retaliate against individual Negro teachers due to court-ordered ... integration of schools."

I was learning how the boldest policies depend for their effect on the dedication and energy of the people entrusted to implement them. Haddad's commitment to civil rights for the kids and teachers in Head Start was personal and energetic, and for the most part shared by the Inspections staff, as it was by OEO Director, Sargent Shriver and sporadically elsewhere in the agency. There was no home in OEO for people opposed to civil rights. But there was a great difference between those who, as I did at the time, thought something ought to be done about civil rights, and those who insisted on doing that something immediately, whatever the consequences. Slowly I was coming to understand that, thirty years after FDR's New Deal, the impetus of his social reforms had slowed considerably — especially when it came to extending the reach of such reforms to blacks and Hispanics. In that sense, many government officials, union leaders and progressive politicians were still fighting the last war. Their roots were liberal; their politics staunchly in favor of the little guy and the working man. But they saw their role as winning more protection and better working conditions for union workers. They balked at taking blacks and Hispanics into the unions against the prejudices of their rank and file members. They found it acceptable to make grants to old-style labor unions and employment bureaus to train new workers, but resisted making grants for the same purposes to black or Hispanic organizations newly established by minority workers who were effectively barred from white unions or locals. There was also a generation gap; a bit of the old guard savoring its aging triumphs, reluctant to give way to the young turks impatient for action. In OEO overt racial prejudice had no champions. But the political power of largely white and largely Democratic-leaning unions protected their interests within the OEO. Unions had long ago learned to fight for a seat at any table where issues of labor were decided, and that clearly included OEO. Shriver's Deputy Director of OEO, for example, was a prominent old-line labor leader named Jack Conway from the AFL-CIO.

To that was added a measure of bureaucratic inertia in OEO's management – a tendency, to use an analogy between the War on Poverty and traditional wars, of the rear echelons to see haste as disruptive even as the troops in the front lines wanted faster logistics. The combination of management's slowness and labor's different priorities led to friction within the agency – friction that was reinforced by events in the field. Grants made to black-run organizations for Head Start or for job training provoked protest from white educators and white union locals; protests that were communicated quickly to their congressmen and national associations, and from there to the White House and to OEO.

The result was that even as Jack Gonzales was scheduling field trips and Haddad and Clampitt were recruiting consultants, management approvals for those consultants were held up for obscure reasons, and usually without notice to us. Requested approvals would sit ignored on someone's desk until we in Inspections could personally track them down and get grudging action. Then they'd move to a higher desk and sit there for another week or two. It was a deliberate "slow walk" approach that effectively threatened the whole project. Without consultants on board Gonzales didn't have the manpower to do the necessary field inspections; without field inspections, meaningful civil rights enforcement in Head Start programs in the Deep South would be impossible. Weeks and days mattered: with summer coming and the programs due to start, we were approaching a crisis. On May 27th Clampitt dashed off an angry memo to Haddad:

> ....We proceeded to line up the best people we could find – several of them are top reporters and editorial writers for the Baltimore Sun – to do field checks. We assembled about 10 people ... all their papers were prepared and sent to Personnel ... and that has been the end of it. No one has been processed; no one has been sworn in ....
> ...we were facing an overwhelmingly difficult time schedule which has now, because of delays ... become virtually impossible....

That afternoon Haddad fired off his own memo to Shriver:

> ... We have already lost 2 weeks while personnel papers have sat on somebody's desk.
> ....There are 375 instances which could be explosive ....
> We have the people ready ... and have all the bureaucratic details squared away, including prepared itineraries in each State....

Shriver passed the memo on to Jack Conway with his handwritten note in the margin:

> May I assume that these checks were cleared today under a system satisfactory to Julius Richmond [Head Start official], you, and Haddad? Sarge. 5/28/65

Conway caved, returning Shriver's memo with his own handwritten surrender note in the margin:

> Sarge – Yes – procedures were worked out as we agreed they would be. J.

With the bureaucratic logjam at last broken, Gonzales moved vigorously. By August 16, 1965 he was able to report that his inspectors had completed 537 field trips and conducted 2,153 telephone checks — finding 79 instances of racial discrimination severe enough to warrant "red-flagging" them for legal action against the local racists.

Back in Washington I heard many of their stories at the Embers – stories that hinted at a kind of poverty I was slow to understand; tales of black kids in homes that sounded straight out of the days of slavery; instances of racial inequality startling to hear. Frank Grimsley told me of a white teacher who had funds to hire an aide to help out in the classroom. The aide was to be paid $1.25 an hour. The teacher hired three aides for the money; one white at 65 cents an hour, and two black at 30 cents an hour each. The paycheck was made out to the white aide, thus depriving the black aides the minimum wage required by federal law, as well as credit toward their Social Security, workman's compensation, or other worker benefits. Al Krumlauf told of two centers, one white and one black, which he suggested be consolidated. "Can't do it," said the director. "They're too far apart." Krumlauf, who grew up in the South, drove the route for himself. In fact they were three blocks apart, and the kids were on school buses to begin with.

One investigative reporter checking out a Head Start program in the South made a telephone check and told Gonzales his gut instinct was that the program was suspect, however compliant it was on paper. Jack sent him down to look closer. The white program director insisted black kids had the same opportunity to attend Head Start as white kids. He claimed to be puzzled as to why black parents didn't send their kids. To drive home his point he produced a map showing how the school buses were sent on routes through the black communities just as they were through the white. Only when the reporter went out to interview parents in the black community did he learn the buses went through the black community at 6 AM, and through the white community two hours later, which was when the Head Start program actually began.

Some early changes could be seen. Once it became known through the South that OEO was taking a "show me" attitude about civil rights compliance and would check out the facts on the ground, Southerners who actually wanted to end segregation were able to assert themselves with their local colleagues. The high drama of governors standing at the school house door denying black children entrance began, although only here and there, to give way to common sense.

Don Grooms put together an informal collection of the stories brought back by our guys in the field. Of one Southern program the report was that:

> "a local official insisted to OEO inspector Macon Foster they were doing their best to integrate the program; even told the reporter that some of the white kids out in the country even rode 'the Negro bus.' Macon was intrigued. 'What do you mean, the 'Negro' bus?' 'Well,' replied the official, 'it has a Negro bus driver.' "

Of another instance Grooms wrote:

> "John Casey from New Orleans was checking out a Head Start program in rural Georgia. 'Oh, yes,' a school superintendent said. 'We believe in equal opportunity and we've had the best relations in this community for the past 75 years. We are going to have a bi-racial staff and all those little children are free to go to any center they want. We're color blind down here.' Casey turned away to get a drink from a nearby water fountain. The superintendent quickly warned him: 'Don't drink from that fountain. It's the colored one.'"

Not every story was pessimistic, Grooms noted. Bob Anthony, a quiet, bald and mustached career agent borrowed from the Department of Agriculture

> "... investigated a segregated program in Elizabeth City, North Carolina and suggested they might consolidate the Negro and white center several blocks apart. Bob went on to another town and came back to find they had put all the Negro and white children into the white center along with their teachers. The Director was so happy to see him again and thanked him profusely for his help, after telling him 'I didn't sleep for two days.' "

Al Krumlauf, a tanned, smooth-dressing investigator from Atlanta,

> "reported on the Head Start program in Tampa, Florida. The Director, who was restricted in his attempt to run a bi-racial program by the school board, pulled a fast one on everybody – the school board, and the parents.
>
> "Two dual centers were operating in one mixed community. The Director decided to give them the treatment for the first 3 weeks of the program – hamburgers and french fries for lunch, field trips to Marineland to see the whales, and parties for the parents. Then at the end of 3 weeks he announced the consolidation of the two centers to run a more economical operation.
>
> "As the Director put it, 'What is a parent to do when his child wants to know why he can't go back to Head Start to eat hamburgers and french fries and go look at the whale?'

That sort of anecdote, and the far more detailed field reports making sure Head Start lived up to its promise of racial equality between the children of poor whites and the children of poor blacks, provided Shriver with powerful support when angry critics charged that programs could not possibly be integrated in Southern states, or that his refusal to fund segregated programs was unwarranted because they had filed certificates of compliance with the civil rights act.

"Sarge would rather rely on a single fact than a dozen arguments," Gonzales told his inspectors. They provided him with just that.

***

Applications for OEO grants were moving toward us in a rising stream, including hastily thrown-together grabs for federal money designed more to secure patronage jobs for local politicians than to fight poverty. All it took was the quick formation of a non-profit organization. In many instances the heart of the application was inflated salaries for the inner circle who put the proposal together. The grants managers in the Community Action office had not yet developed channels of communication by which they could see beyond the paper application.

Haddad's choices to run the Inspections for the various regions were interesting men. While Gonzales was tied up full time with the Head Start project, Bob Martin filled in for him running the Inspections agents for all other OEO programs in the South. The Northeast was handled by Jack Williams. Williams, an investigative reporter for the Buffalo Evening News and for Rochester papers, had served for a while as assistant city manager of Rochester. He ran unsuccessfully on the Democratic ticket for Congress in Republican Ken Keating's home district in New York in 1964.

The Southwest and far West were handled by Vicente Ximines, who organized the Viva – Kennedy clubs for the 1960 campaign. Raised poor, he found his way through FDR's Civilian Conservation Corps, which was run in Texas by a very young Lyndon B. Johnson. Ximines had gone on to become a bombardier in WW II, and saw action in North Africa.

Some Southwestern boards claiming to have a majority of Mexican-American members in fact had none who spoke English well enough to have any say in the programs at all. In others, poor people without telephones or means to travel to meetings in rural areas were helpless to keep the power structure from completely dominating programs designed to help the poor.

To prevent this, Haddad set up an "early warning" operation. News reporters came in to the Inspections office during the evenings, read news clips gathered from all over the country by a commercial newsclipping service, and if they sensed a problem, made calls to check it out. A small newspaper in Wisconsin or Kansas, for example, might run a story about the local poverty program's new high-salaried executive director being the husband of the chairman of its board of directors. One of our guys, spotting that story, would start making calls. More often than not, the mere knowledge that someone was watching set things up on a better basis. We had no technical authority to limit such salaries, but we could threaten to revoke funding for the entire program or to refuse renewal of the grant when its term ended unless changes were made,.

The system's effectiveness was enhanced by the evening hours we worked, usually to at least 11 PM Washington, D.C. time. Calls made by our moonlighting reporters would catch board members and program directors at home in the evening, where they were often willing to discuss their progress and problems with greater privacy and candor than was possible in their offices. As the hours grew later in our Washington office, we were able to reach contacts in the Mountain and Pacific time zones, either at their office or at home. All this created a sense that the OEO was an active, involved partner in their efforts.

A spin-off of that approach was what came to be called the "Swit-Brown Operation". Dave Swit, a veteran AP correspondent out of Atlanta, teamed up with an old-line New Deal economist named E. Wayles Brown. They secured the names and phone numbers of the Chairmen and Executive Directors of every funded program, whether it was the subject of complaints or not, and spent several hours each evening calling just to ask them how things were going. Problems came to light that could be made known to the right OEO operating staff in Washington and taken care of. Many of the local people were overjoyed to be talking with somebody back in Washington who was knowledgeable about the programs.

Not every problem originated in the field, as Dave Swit and Wayles Browne learned. A frequent complaint was that OEO, having announced a grant, would not get around to sending the money for weeks and quite often months. Programs that had taken the grant award to the bank and borrowed money to get started had no way to recover the interest they had to pay on the loans and, at the very time their activities were getting into full swing, were finding the banks sticky about advancing more money until they saw proof of incoming cash.

Where there were more severe problems — outright scandal, exorbitant expenses, or very public screw-ups that sooner or later were bound to result in angry inquiries from congressmen and senators, we often had notice of the problem and could alert the right people in Washington to correct it before the incoming fire landed. Few things were more pleasing to OEO's Congressional Liasion man Gillis Long than to reply to a congressional complaint with assurances that we had already discovered the problem and fixed it.

Of course, OEO's Community Action analysts and grantmakers and certainly our management people were not happy to have their mistakes found out. Theoretically, OEO was in the position of achieving some of its goals by calibrating the use of the carrot of federal funding with the stick of civil rights enforcement. Haddad, through Jack Gonzales's inspections, proved the stick was available and effective. The problem was that when Southern compliance should have been encouraged with reasonably prompt funding, the CAP and the Management divisions proved obstructive.

Late in June, for example, Dave Swit noted a complaint from Chattahoochie, Georgia:

> This grant, for about $10,000 was submitted in December or January, and approved by OEO in February. He's since been sent, and has returned, the usual mess of forms. But still NO

MONEY.

Haddad forwarded it to Management Director Bill Kelly, sending a memo copy to Shriver:

Re: CAP – Delay in Funds

We're getting a series of similar complaints about failure to receive our money after approved funding. Could you please give me a report on this one.

Shriver, angry, sent his copy of the memo to Bill Kelly, adding his handwritten note:

If true, this is rotten.
Sarge

Kelly pinned the blame on the Community Action Programs office, by memo dated July 1, 1965.

Re: Chattahoochee grant
As of June 30, the approved file on subject grant had not been received in Management. When a complete file is received from CAP, the processing time is usually one day. There are several factors that delay a transfer of funds, but the delay is in CAP, not Management.

Such infighting grew serious. In the early days of the agency, Shriver personally signed his approval on every grant in a Friday "sign-off conference." Initially, the conferees consisted of Shriver, his deputy Jack Conway, Ted Berry or Tom Karter from the Community Action Program, Bill Kelly from Management, Bill Haddad, and several other top officials. Karter or Berry would introduce an application that the CAP reviewers deemed acceptable, such as a grant for an after school program in Denver or St. Louis that might be $600,000 or so and ask if anyone had objections.

If not, Shriver signed the grant on the spot and it would be sent out.

As the increasing volume of applications to be processed led to more cursory reviews, some grants were made where the local board had no representation at all from the poor, or where the grantee organization was fiscally unsound, overtly political or racially biased. Haddad grew uncomfortable sitting at the conferences and watching Shriver sign off on applications with too little knowledge of their makeup. He knew from his days as an investigative reporter that grants made to political machines or racially discriminating organizations would eventually erupt in public controversy. Yet without prior warnings of what applications would be presented on a given Friday, he had no way of insuring adequate review. He asked for two day's notice on any applications scheduled for the next sign-off conference, to which the CAP director grudgingly agreed. However, in the internal agency politics that often prevailed, the two- day notice would be forgotten. This was important, because Shriver's deputy, Jack Conway, was an old-line Labor man who favored steering grant money into old-line agencies, such as vo-tech schools where union influences were strong. They were all too often unions that kept high barriers against the admission of blacks, Mexicans, and Puerto Ricans. Since Conway's views often dovetailed with those of the CAP director and with those of Bill Kelly in Management, the Inspections staff suspected the failures to provide the two-day advance notice was deliberate.

Haddad, sharing the suspicion, decided to try to convince Shriver that the applications were so often full of loopholes and contradictions that the two- day notice should be made mandatory — in effect, giving Haddad the power to hold up any application that did not bear his signature.

Happily, lower-level CAP analysts were on our side. They were discontent with the indifference of Conway and their superiors to the need to give the poor a say in things. Word leaked about several key programs Conway intended to put through without advance notice to us.

One Thursday evening Bob Clampitt, Bob Martin, John Daum and

I and several others were having dinner at the Boar's Head, a steak and chop house on M Street a half-block from OEO. Daum was called to the phone. He returned to the table with news that Fred Hayes of CAP was going to try to railroad the Los Angeles application through at the sign-off conference next day without the promised two-day notice. Daum and Martin returned to OEO and secured the full Los Angeles application. It was for a basketful of programs, asking for $11 or $12 million, and it consisted of several volumes each about the size of the Manhattan telephone directory. That night Daum and Martin thoroughly scrutinized the application, finding within it dozens of inconsistencies, unfeasible projects, and persuasive evidence that the application and the programs it would fund would do little more than create a cornucopia of political jobs to be divided between California's most powerful Democratic figures, including Mayor Sam Yorty, local Congressman Gus Hawkins, and Governor Pat Brown. Based on the research done that night Daum and Martin produced a critique of the application which was given to Haddad before Friday's 3 PM sign-off conference. When the Los Angeles application was introduced by CAP official Fred Hayes with the statement that it was being introduced as an emergency measure because they had gotten it ready at the last possible moment and couldn't provide the two-day notice to Inspections, Haddad exposed the application for the fraud that it was. Shriver, chagrined at what CAP had tried to pull, announced he would not sign off on that nor any future applications unless and until Bill Haddad signed them first.

Armed with that new power, we were able to spot applications time and again that had false data in them — many having been submitted by groups with whose leaders no OEO official had ever discussed the program, its meaning nor their obligations to insure the involvement of the poor and the observance of civil rights. We developed a "sign-off checklist" to record approval or disapproval on specific areas such as involvement of the poor, absence of conflicts of interest, overly burdensome political influence, and so on.

As the administrative tangles within Inspections came under control and the review of the programs increased our workload, I was gradually given responsibilities more focused on the programs than solely on administrative detail. Vince Ximines, hard-pressed to cover the applications from the West, asked me to do telephone checks on individual programs in California, Arizona, Nevada, and New Mexico.

Reading the reports and listening to the Embers stories told by inspectors in from the field served as a beginner's course in how to look for signs of a troubled program, and the right questions to ask in telephone interviews. For the first time in my life, I was in contact with the real stuff of public policy. I was thrilled with this role.

An application from New Mexico illustrated the kind of thing I was expected to catch. The Governor's office wanted funds to run a statewide program to alert the poor to the opportunities available to them if they applied for programs. By itself it made sense, except that the guy who would run it was the Governor's protégée, he was studying for his master's in speech, and he wanted to use anti-poverty funds to buy a twin-engine Apache airplane to fly around the state giving speeches. I called and asked how many pueblos had airfields equipped to handle his flights, within walking distance of the homes of the poor. He was not happy. I passed my objections up the line with the marginal comment that "What the hell, maybe I'm just jealous!" The program was funded without the airplane.

***

Even as Head Start reached high gear in the summer of 1965, the Watts riot broke out in Los Angeles. On August 11th, with the temperature a blazing 93 degrees at a time when air conditioners in slum housing were almost non-existent, the police arrested a black man on a charge of drunken driving and took him to the station house. Rumors flew that they had killed him. Behind them began a riot that was to last for six days of fire and rage in the black community. By the time it ended, 34 people were dead and over 1,000 injured. Some 600 buildings were damaged or destroyed by fire. All of this was watched, thanks to television's relentless coverage and reach, throughout the country and around the world. From then on incidents of racial confrontations, whether provoked by police brutality or created by black protest marches, were front-page and prime-time news everywhere. The use of cattle-prods and water hoses on blacks were no longer unreported local events; they produced images that reached into homes almost every day. Across the country white cops in black neighborhoods were walking among human powder-kegs. The anger which erupted in Watts was boiling over throughout America's big cities.

Within OEO, Haddad's fight against the Los Angeles CAP application as a travesty of keeping the poor out of the decision-making process seemed of a piece with the riots of a few days later– if not in the sense of proximate cause, then certainly in the overall understanding that people who destroy their own community in rage have no sense of ownership in that community. After years of denying blacks a chance to work together with their neighbors to improve their lot, it was no surprise that they felt no identity with their own neighborhoods.

***

-Chapter 5: The Job Corps

Our workload was heavy and the pace was fast. Grant applications poured in to OEO from all over the country. With less than a year under his belt since the agency was created by Congress, Sargent Shriver was pushing hard to get the programs up and running according to his own vision. Some were in-house programs like Head Start, Vista and the Community Action Program; others, like the Job Corps, were run by the Department of Labor under authority delegated by Shriver.

To keep a close watch on such programs, Haddad followed the pattern that proved successful with Head Start – early and constant telephone contacts; close monitoring of all news stories; and field inspections wherever needed. For the Job Corps, the early inspection teams included Dave Seaton, Gary Lefkowitz, Ira Mothner, Jim Brenner and several others. It took them about a month of constant travel to Job Corps centers to build a picture of how the program was doing.

Many of the early Job Corps centers were unprepared to cope with the flood of angry, anti-social, anti-authority, and troubled kids that arrived at their gates. Aside from the enormous reach of the TV show "It's What's Happening, Baby", the Job Corps suffered from poor screening procedures and internal assignment. Young men with long arrest records, often for violent behavior, narcotics addiction and in-school violence were sent to rural centers far from their neighborhoods where it was difficult to lay down the right line between necessary discipline and overdoing it. In one Texas Job Corps camp the recreation area was surrounded by barbed wire. Teenage enrollees from the slums could not enter without a pass, often controlled by white ex-military guys, making the whole experience more like prison than a job-preparation program. In others, contracts given to universities or private corporations to run the centers yielded dismal results when basic discipline was ignored in favor of academic theories of social improvement. The early days were rough, as one of the Job Corps' greatest success stories,

Olympic boxing champion and world heavyweight champion George Foreman, eloquently described in his autobiography *By George*.

Some things were clearly out of control. A women's Job Corps center was the source of various complaints. It was, as one inspector dryly commented, headed by a woman who wore a mannish haircut, a man's business suit, smoked cigars, and conversationally offered her opinion that spanking was the best remedy for "these delinquent girls." (A few years later, the same thing was evidently still going on several months into the Nixon Administration. Republican Senator Margaret Chase Smith wrote an angry letter to George Schultz, then Secretary of Labor:

> "I have been told by a source I consider to be reliable that one of the reasons why the decision was made to close the Women's Job Corps Center at Poland Spring, Maine, was because it had been discovered and determined that organized lesbianism was being conducted there and that involved in the organized lesbianism were members of the staff as well as the girls assigned to the center. This is a very serious charge. I would appreciate having the full facts in this matter."

In another women's center key officials were running a ring of prostitutes — a profession too well known and too often practiced among the rough diamonds who gravitated to the Job Corps. Comments about locating federally subsidized whorehouses in nice neighborhoods gained ground as such news found its way into circulation.

Changing the self-image of tough kids was part of the challenge. George Morrison, a black kid from the slums hired to run Xerox machines at OEO and eventually enrolled as a $25 a day consultant by Bill Haddad came up with the idea of awarding prep-school blazers to young men in the urban Job Corps centers. Doing a telephone check on the women's centers in mid-August I encountered a severe problem with a Job Corps center in St.

Petersburg, Florida. Girls accustomed to dressing as hookers were being visited by tough-looking boyfriends cruising through nearby residential streets and scaring hell out of the neighbors. These girls, often from the streets of Harlem, Watts or Detroit, had their own ideas about grooming. To survive in the urban jungle they had to attract men, either as prostitutes or, where gangs ruled the streets, for protection. This meant heavy make-up, short skirts, tight clothing, a provocative walk, bold stares, and virtually every mannerism and characteristic that would make a young woman repugnant to an employer seeking a receptionist or secretary. The girls thought looking for a job was the same as trolling for a John, and used the same approach. It didn't help when a newspaper reported that a significant portion of the girls had illegitimate babies.

Borrowing George Morrison's idea I sent Haddad a memo suggesting blazers for the girls would be a great way to improve their self-image, and might cool the hostility of the neighbors. Haddad passed the memo on to the Director of the Job Corps with his endorsement. The idea was picked up. I was told it worked. The affair was of little weight, but I was learning the possibilities of creative thinking in public programs — and the need to support it when it came along.

Chapter 6: Into the Field — Boston

By July of 1965 I had cleared up the worst of the administrative problems in the Office of Inspections. The consultants were getting paid, their travel expenses were up to date, and enough secretaries were available and equipped with typewriters to get their reports done. Now I wanted to get out into the field and see things for myself. Bill Haddad kept his promise to give me the chance. He did not do the thing by halves. Knowing my hope to run someday for office, he told me to write up a press release for his signature announcing my appointment as "Special Assistant to the Inspector General." When he read my draft he decided I was too modest. He added three sentences that did much to boost my confidence:

> "Joe brings to this office not only an extraordinary drive which enables him to work around the clock, but a sensitive knowledge of the problems we face all over the country," Haddad wrote. "He has a rare administrative ability and a maturity of judgment rarely found in someone his age. He will make an excellent contribution to the team Mr. Shriver is assembling for his war on Poverty."

The release, complete with my picture (taken as a personal favor by Mort Engleberg, who years later produced the iconic 1977 Burt Reynolds film "Smokey and the Bandit"), went out to the *Philadelphia Inquirer*, my hometown *Atlantic City Press*, and dozens of weeklies throughout Southern New Jersey's 2nd Congressional District on which my distant political hopes were fixed. With its publication I had become a minor – a very minor – public figure at home. I thought it a huge step toward my political dreams.

In preparation for my first assignment as one of Haddad's field agents, I was issued a set of impressive credentials. White politicians and bureaucrats in the South had developed the tactic of challenging our guys when asked to open the books, answer questions, and permit access to their staffs, all of whom were either paid with or fighting for control over the federal funds OEO was handing out for anti-poverty programs. To combat such obstructionism, Haddad and Clampitt designed a set of credentials that left no room for argument. About the size and appearance of a U.S. passport with its deep blue cover, mine bore the Great Seal of the United States embossed in gold on the cover. Above that, in bold-and-gold lettering were the words **"EXECUTIVE OFFICE OF THE PRESIDENT"**. Inside, in Old English bolded script against a white background was:

Office of Economic Opportunity
United States of America

This is to certify that

JOSEPH T. WILKINS

whose signature and photograph appear below
is duly appointed

INSPECTOR

and, as such, is authorized to conduct investigations, audits and inspections in connection with the administration of all contracts and programs in which the Office of Economic Opportunity is, or may be a party of interest and is to have access to all information and material to which the director, O.E.O. would have access.

It was signed "Sargent Shriver," and was pretty impressive looking. My signature appeared next to my photograph. We were at the height of the early James Bond craze. Competition around the office for the prized number "007" was intense. I had to settle for "16".

Next came a blanket travel authorization good for 12 months for travel "From Washington, D.C. to points within the continental U.S. as necessary to conduct OEO business" by air, rail, or bus, and authorizing me to charge rental cars and hotel rooms, and hire stenographic services in the field, all for the catch-all purpose described as: "to inspect OEO field programs and to consult with the Inspector General." With the blanket authorization came a book of computer punched-cards similar to U.S. Government checks, which, presented at the ticket counter, would get you plane tickets to wherever you wanted.

All this was heady stuff. The downside was that I had already missed a year of night law school and taking on the traveling assignments I so greatly desired probably meant deferring my studies for another year. With only two semesters still to complete, it was not clear when I might ever finish. On the other hand, turning down the travel meant a return to administrative duties, where few challenges beckoned. I chose the travel.

***

For my rookie field trip, Haddad put me under the wing of Jack Williams, a veteran investigative reporter then in charge of field inspections in the Northeast region. Jack, whose casual air masked a mind honed by years of investigating corruption in big-city politics, took me with him to Roxbury-North Dorchester, where OEO's community action funds were arriving in the volatile center of Boston's racial battles over the integration of neighborhood schools.

"Ever serve as an election observer?" Jack asked as we landed at Boston's Logan Airport on a hot afternoon in late July.

"Sure," I said, explaining how challenging suspect voters at the polls was part of the congressional campaign I'd worked on in Atlantic City the previous November.

Williams listened with amusement. The election in Boston, he said, had nothing to do with such sophisticated concepts as accredited challengers, election laws and other niceties. It arose because Congress embedded in the law creating the Office of Economic Opportunity a mandate dear to liberal ideology – that the poor should have a say in deciding how to spend the money appropriated on their behalf. They were to have, as the OEO legislation put it, "maximum feasible participation" in the design and running of their own programs. This idea made no sense to me. I had been trained as a budget analyst; was putting myself through law school. I believed in government by elected political leaders, with policies carried out by trained government officials, operating within the context of appropriation laws and administrative regulations. There was a whiff of anarchy about letting tax money escape the control of people trained to account for it. I had learned, even without going into the field, that racial discrimination had to be actively fought. No one hearing of little kids denied access to Head Start because of their color could have remained ignorant of the extent and virulence of white racism. But not everybody who was black was poor, and certainly not all the poor were black. Leaving clear racial discrimination aside, what exactly did "maximum feasible participation" of the poor mean? Nobody had yet figured it out. Were the poor to serve as advisors? Or deciders? Were they to be paid? Could you separate out racism from poverty in the first place? If so, how?

In any event, who was to decide which of the poor should call the shots on behalf of the rest? Letting the poor elect their own representatives was a good theory on paper. Whether it would work in practice was what we had come to Boston to observe. There were no carefully drawn election districts, nor procedure to register voters and get them to the polls in this decidedly non-political election, nor, for that matter, people or procedures to count such votes as might be cast. Even with those handicaps, the theory might have had a chance if, say, everybody were white, or everybody were black, so the choices could be worked out without racial tensions.

What existed on the ground in Boston however was active hostility between the working class Irish Catholic whites of North Dorchester and the impoverished black populations of Roxbury, lumped together for anti-poverty purposes into the same district. The Irish Catholics raised in old neighborhoods anchored by church and settlement houses for three and four generations were to wrestle for control of anti-poverty funds with blacks who, as one settlement-house director sneered, "have no jobs, no property, no responsibility and have only been here, what, ten years or so?"

That same ten years measured almost precisely the time for which the mandate of the U.S. Supreme Court in *Brown vs Topeka Board of Education* to integrate America's schools "with all deliberate speed" had been fought by white parents all over the country. The immediate question of who would control OEO money in Roxbury/North Dorchester had nothing directly to do with the public schools. Yet the same underlying racial conflict was at its heart. In Boston the fight was so intense it was almost impossible for any public issue to be decided except in terms of how that decision would advance or retard school integration.

It would have taken a Solomon to reconcile the Irish and the blacks in Roxbury-North Dorchester. There was no Solomon. There was only an Irish Catholic lady named Louise Day Hicks, who rose to the powerful position of President of the Boston Schools Committee with jurisdiction over all the public schools in Boston and a deep conviction that court-ordered integration of the schools in her charge should be vigorously fought. In Roxbury the blacks hated her as a bigot pandering to white racist voters. In North Dorchester the Irish saw her as their only champion in an elitist world of federal judges and high-minded state government officials whose own kids were safely tucked away in white suburban schools.

Thus far ABCD, the city-wide non-profit Action for Boston Community Development corporation set up by the Ford Foundation as a prototype for the OEO's Community Action Agencies, had received $2.5 million in OEO funds. More, much more, was envisioned — if and when the roles of the poor, black and white alike, were sorted out.

We headed from the airport to the neighborhoods only to learn that the elections we were to observe next day had been held the previous day. Or had been cancelled. Or forbidden by a court injunction. Or were due to go on as scheduled.

The confusion was deliberate, brought about on one side by the leadership of the Denison House, a settlement house recognized as the bulwark of the Irish community in North Dorchester based on its 85 year history of serving the neighborhood; and on the other side by the all-black "Ad Hoc Committee," a loosely organized federation of civil rights groups in Roxbury.

The Denison House leaders scheduled elections for June 28th. The Ad Hoc Committee, funded by a small grant from the Ford Foundation seeking to promote community participation, sent a sound truck through the streets announcing there was no such election scheduled. That confusion sank the first try at an election and set the stage for the next, which was scheduled by the Ad Hoc Committee for July 29th. This the Denison House fought in court, getting a temporary restraining order on July 28th barring the election until a hearing could be held next morning.

The restraining order triggered an emergency meeting of the Ad Hoc Committee in its Roxbury storefront headquarters. Jack Williams and I attended as observers. The question argued by the black Roxburians was what to do if the injunction was not lifted. Should they stop the election, thereby losing any practical prospect of choosing their own representatives, or should they hold the election and risk being sent to jail for contempt of court?

All hated the idea of complying with the injunction, which they considered nothing more than oppression from power-structure people who had ruled their lives too long. The power structure in Boston, as Williams murmured in an aside to me, "is both powered and structured." I had never seen civil disobedience in action and listened to the discussion with fascination. No one bothered making the comparison, yet here, I thought, was a debate among the poor blacks of Boston that traced its heritage back nearly two hundred years to the days of the Boston Tea Party.

The vote favored holding the election and risking jail. When the result was announced, one member asked to switch his vote. He was a blind black man who had run his own used-car reconditioning business for nearly three years. He said that, while he was willing to vote himself into jail, he did not feel it right to vote absent members into jail with him. The Committee agreed to meet again in the morning after the status of the injunction was decided by the Court.

Next morning, the court lifted the injunction. The election, considerably hobbled by its on-again, off-again status and confusion over polling hours, locations and ballots, went ahead.

Part of our mission was to make sure the election districts roughly encompassed the areas in which the poor were concentrated. The boundaries were taken from old maps prepared for urban renewal work, which had in turn been based on census tract reports. I assumed they fairly represented where the poor lived. Williams, who took nothing for granted, asked me to double check.

"How can I tell without having the census data in front of me?" I asked.

"You can tell the difference between a shiny new bicycle and a rusty old one, can't you?" he asked. "Get out there and use your eyes!"

I cruised the streets for half a day, noting area by area what I saw. Jack was right. Here would be houses with sagging doors, broken down fences, broken toys strewn about the yards. A few blocks away was better siding, bicycles which, if not brand new, at least still had some shine to them. Cars and trucks in both areas might be in side yards needing repairs, but the models in one neighborhood would be a good 10 years older than those in another. The contrast between the neighborhoods had little to do with what the urban renewal maps showed. It had much to do with where the jobs were — or weren't. In truth, however, the difference between the neighborhoods was between hard-up and dirt-poor. Neither included signs of comfortable incomes or home improvements.

By day's end, the tactics of Denison House backfired. Their supporters boycotted the election. Only the poor remained, and most of the 586 votes came from them. Denison House's director vowed to fight on in court. I asked him why he was so opposed to having the blacks participate in making decisions about their fate.

"They're not responsible people, d'ye see," he said. "We want someone with a job; some property – you know – a taxpayer; somebody who'd have a proper interest in making the neighborhood better." His logic appealed to my still-bureaucratic soul, but his words clashed sharply with the blind black speaker of the night before, who seemed to me as responsible a voice as you could ask for.

Back in Washington, Jack let me write the first draft of the report that would ultimately go on to Shriver. I organized the facts and the interviews meticulously over 11 single-spaced pages of eye-glazing reporting. Then I learned an important difference between news reporters and the rest of the world. Williams sat at a typewriter and hammered out a new lead, which summarized in a sentence what it had taken me 11 pages to say:

> "Boston's CAP board is moving toward its highly-touted involvement of the poor with about the pace, and degree of commitment, of a handful of cold Jello moving across a blotter."

***

Chapter 7: Bosses and Boll Weevils

Haddad had given me the promised big break just in time. Shortly after I returned from Boston he wrapped up the one-year commitment he made to Shriver when the OEO was born, and moved back to New York, his first love. The effect of his departure was like the end of the first stage of a space shot; the powerful launching thrust ended, but the trajectories of its programs — and particularly Head Start, had been set with energy and determination.

Haddad's deputy, Bob Clampitt, made it clear it wouldn't be long before he, too, moved on. Shriver asked Edgar May, his Special Assistant, to take on the job of Inspector General. May, a veteran investigative reporter, had won the Pulitzer Prize in 1961 for "Our Costly Dilemma," a series on New York State's public welfare services he wrote for the *Buffalo Evening News* that involved serving three months as a welfare caseworker. A Vermont native with a strong commitment to social justice, Ed May had to follow a tough act.

Anxious to avoid backsliding into administrative work, I lobbied Ed May, Jack Williams and Jack Gonzales for more field assignments. To my relief, they were agreeable. A pattern evolved in which I spent several days on telephone checks of programs, then went out on field trips of a week or so, came back to write my reports and do more telephone checks, and then headed into the field again.

A telephone check of a program took most of a day, including a few hours to write it up. There were well over a thousand local Community Action Agencies then running throughout the country. Many had simmering controversies in need of resolution. For example, on Portland, Oregon I worked the telephones for several days. Portland had, as elsewhere, a struggle for control of OEO funds between the white power structure and the black community. This one had a special twist. The black representatives of the poor were fighting a two-front war; against the white power structure on the one hand, and against a black lawyer on the make for a reputation as a civil rights fighter on the other. In many places, the poor were not involved because they neither knew they were supposed to be, nor had a way to organize themselves. In Portland, and particularly its blighted Albena neighborhood, the very opposite was true. The poor in Albena sent for OEO's booklets and literature and followed them faithfully — too faithfully for their own good. They set up the "Albena Citizens War on Poverty Committee." When they learned that such boards were supposed to be broadly representative of the community, they widened their committee to include the non-poor — the whites and residents of greater Portland. They learned too late of their mistake, when a black attorney who lived elsewhere but maintained his practice in Albena came on the scene. The enlarged Albena Committee took over a small OEO grant the group had secured before deciding to enlarge itself, and elected the lawyer President, over the objections of the original group. The lawyer appointed a personnel committee to review applications for the job of director of the proposed community center, resigned as President, applied for the job, was approved by the committee he had appointed, and set himself up as a full-time civil rights advocate paid for by funds designed to fight poverty.

Meanwhile, the Mayor of Portland had set up a rival committee made up of public officials and his political allies, which applied for OEO funds in competition with the Albena Committee. The Mayor's Committee got the bulk of the money.

After more than a dozen telephone interviews confirmed the Mayor's Committee would not recruit poor members, I recommended that OEO reject renewal funding for the Mayor's Committee and fund the Albena Committee instead. That recommendation was accepted, but triggered unexpected and adverse national consequences. Democratic Congresswoman Edith Green, a former school teacher representing Portland in Congress, was so angry at the affront to the power structure she represented that she set out to amend the Economic Opportunity Act to bar OEO from funding a community action agency unless it won official approval by the chief political body of the community. Her amendment became known as "the bosses and boll weevil amendment" designed to wrest control of local programs from community groups and hand them over to the big city political bosses in the North and the county courthouse bosses – called "boll weevils" after the insects that infest cotton – in the South.

In Portland as around the country, the strongest resistance we encountered to involvement of the poor came not from the ineffective and powerless Republican minority in Congress, but from the long-entrenched Democratic politicians protective of the infrastructure that kept them in office. This was a conclusion I subconsciously resisted, having grown up with a vague understanding that all Democrats were on the side of the little guy. The idea that any Democrat would put preservation in office above social justice smacked to me of heresy. This was, after all, the party of FDR, of Harry Truman, and of JFK. In retrospect, my own naiveté astounds me.

***

Chapter 8: The Sioux Reservations of South Dakota

Faced with a short staff and a heavy list of field trips, Ed May concluded the time had come for me to fly solo. He sent me to see how the VISTA volunteers on the Rosebud Sioux Reservation in South Dakota were making out.

VISTA is the acronym for " Volunteers In Service To America," – the domestic version of the Peace Corps. Young men and women (most only a few years younger than myself, at 25) volunteered to work among America's poor for a year. After their initial training at programs set up by universities under contract to the OEO, they were dispatched to sponsoring organizations around the country, receiving a small stipend for personal expenses. Sponsors varied from small town centers to migrant camps to urban slums – and Indian reservations like Rosebud.

I was thrilled to be on my own. It was my first chance to see the West except for the time when, years earlier as a Marine Corps reservist I'd flown cross-country to summer training in California. But on that trip the flights ran through the night going and coming, leaving no chance even for aerial sightseeing.

This time my flight took me via Chicago to Pierre, South Dakota. The final leg was on a plane with steer-horns mounted over the cockpit door. Stetson hats, cowboy boots and string neckties with silver and turquoise clasps were much in evidence. My seat mate, a cattle rancher from North Dakota, chuckled when I told him I was bound for the Rosebud Reservation. "Don't expect much," he said. "We weren't about to give 'em good land. And when they found gold in the Black Hills we kicked them off that part anyway."

The Sioux reservations of South Dakota are vast expanses of rolling hills and prairie. The land is poor, and grows grass suitable for grazing perhaps one year in three. Distances between towns are great, and their populations minuscule by Eastern standards. It is a primitive country, with little electricity and less running water.

As I drove the hundred miles from Pierre to Rosebud I could see prairie grass and nothing else stretching to the horizon in every direction. Lost in bemusement at the emptiness of the landscape, I glanced at the speedometer and was shocked to see I was doing over 100 miles an hour. I dropped it to 80, thinking that if I blew a tire nobody would find me for a week. Until then I had had no concept of how the isolation of the land would limit what the VISTA volunteers could do.

There was no available motel room in Rosebud. I headed east a few miles to Mission, whose motel consisted of eight rooms and an office. There were no cafes or restaurants open, which was a jolt: I grew up in the Atlantic City area, where bars stayed open all night offering sandwiches, steaks and seafood for conventioneers, cabbies and cops. Here, the only food available was the candy-and-pretzel vending machine outside the office. My room did have a television – a black and white set, with only one channel on which the game show that Sunday night was "What's My Line?" Even that could barely be seen through the snowy static. It was the earliest I'd gone to bed since I was ten years old.

On the Rosebud Sioux Reservation a dozen Vista volunteers worked under the sponsorship of the Rosebud Sioux tribal council. My first stop was Spring Creek, a community of about 200 persons spread throughout the surrounding low hills. Many families of 14 or 15 lived in dilapidated old trailers, shacks, and "chicken brooders" — miniature Quonset Huts used in the war to breed chickens and later given to the Indians. In the East, they might have been used as large playhouses for little children. For the Sioux, they were primitive shelter from snow and rain. Few of the living quarters of the Indians had any electricity. Virtually none had running water, and heat was usually provided by wood stove or gas heater. Transportation for the Indians was usually on foot, sometimes by horse, and occasionally by old, hard-used cars.

Father Pate, a local priest helpful to thc volunteers, pointed out what he described as a typical Indian car to me. It was a station wagon, about 12 or more years old, with the left rear tire going soft and the left front wheel out of line. I followed the car for 10 miles until it turned into the yard of a shack just outside of Spring Creek and the passengers got out. It was driven by an Indian man wearing an ancient and battered slouch hat. His passengers included several small children, two dogs, and an Indian woman.

The first VISTA volunteers I met were Sandra Lindsay, 24, and Betty Wornecke, 21. They lived in a moderate sized trailer at Spring Creek. Its bottom was surrounded with bales of hay to insulate the floor from winter winds. The interior of the trailer was replete with dozens of children's books, crayoned drawings, and games for tots. Directly opposite the door I saw an old magazine photo, crumpled somewhat, but smoothed out and taped to the wall. The photo showed John F. Kennedy, smiling and sunburnt as he left the back yard of his Georgetown home clad in white trousers and a light brown sports coat.

Two puppies were curled up inside the trailer. One was named Sam. The girls introduced the other simply as "a friend of Sam's." The trailer had an oil heater and a gas stove for cooking which used bottled gas. Electricity was available through a line run from a nearby church. There was no running water. For showers, the girls told me, they used the nearby schoolhouse. At night, they said, they often had as many as 20 kids sitting around talking and listening to the radio. For many kids, coming to the trailer was their only entertainment aside from drinking.

Sandy said a few male VISTA's would be a big help, because Indian boys were reluctant to put much weight on what the female VISTA's had to say.

To set up a study center for the kids, the girls were cleaning and painting a meeting hall formerly used by the church — a one-room building with electricity, oil heat, and eight windows. The wood floor and walls were bare. With the help of the local teenagers, the girls had sanded and refinished the floor and were about to paint the hall. Although the toilet was an outhouse 20 feet away, the hall was the only place available for miles around that had heat and light in winter.

Both girls said their training program could have been more practical. "I know it sounds silly for a girl to say," Sandy told me, "but I wish someone had taught me how to cook. I never did at home and now I have to start from scratch. And we should learn some carpentry and auto mechanics. At least enough to build a shelf or change spark plugs. It's not very feminine, but I wish we had been taught something about hygiene, like how to build a latrine .... and we should learn how to drive stick-shifts and pickup trucks. I only know how to drive an automatic. That's not much help when you want to use somebody's pickup or some of these old cars."

Neither girl felt she was in personal danger because of remoteness. "When they're sober, the Indians are wonderful," one of them told me, "and when they're drunk, they stay away and won't come near the trailer. They do a lot of fighting, but it's all kept to themselves. And of course, now they know us and there are usually some Indian kids around keeping us company."

My next stop was at St. Francis, about 15 miles from Rosebud. This was the seat of the Catholic mission on the reservation, and included a large church boarding school, a gas station, a general store, and about 15 or 20 homes. A trailer housed the two volunteers working there: Yvonne Thibodeaux, 20, from Lake Charles, Louisiana and Deborah Piggins, 21, from Newark, New Jersey.

Such church-run boarding schools were normal on the reservations. The long distances between tiny settlements and the overwhelming poverty made going from home to school on a daily basis impossible. The ones I saw were run by the Catholics. According to Yvonne and Debbie, St. Francis held little attraction for the youths from the nearby area because of its stress on boarding school activities and its religious atmosphere. As one said: "Kids don't want to go to church after school; they want a place where they can have a Coke and listen to some music while they're studying."

While I was there, two little Girl Scouts visited the trailer. I was captivated by their beauty. Little Laughing Thunder, age 9 and Miss Fire Cloud, 11, were bright, merry-eyed, and extremely shy, but had formed an affection for the girls and, with many of their friends, came to the trailer for tutoring and talk. At first they were quiet at church mice, but soon accepted my presence. Little Laughing Thunder turned out to be an energetic and inquisitive chatterbox filled with questions about life elsewhere.

Mission, where I had found a motel room, was a medium-sized town about 12 miles from Rosebud which boasted three gas stations, a hotel, the Mission boarding school, and a large Quonset hut that served as a movie theater (50 cents), a café, and a community theater. Anna Sulanowski, a 19 year old from Detroit, was the sole volunteer in Mission. She lived with an elderly Irish widow named Mrs. Halligan and worked with a 4H group run by the county extension agent. She also worked on a housing survey until, as she explained to me, she concluded that asking the Indians personal questions about their outhouses and debts caused offense and hampered her work.

After the long day, I dreaded returning to my motel room and its one-channel television. The Quonset hut movie theater, according to the motel clerk, offered sandwiches and near-beer. A sandwich and movie sounded pretty good to me compared to the vending machine pretzels. The first half of the hut was given over to a bar running down one side, and bare wooden tables opposite. At the back of the hut six rows of wooden folding chairs faced a pull-down home movie screen on which a John Wayne movie was playing. I took a seat at the near end, which let me see the length of the bar, the tables, the wood chairs, and John Wayne killing Indians. Hoping to avoid paying for the sins of the 7th Cavalry I bought a drink for the man sitting next to me – an Indian with an incredibly weathered face and gray hair. He accepted the drink as we watched the movie. For a while it looked like the Indians were winning. Just as the young Indian chief jumped his horse over the wagon-hitch and got shot by the Duke, my neighbor turned to me with a look of enormous sadness. I spent the rest of the night trying to convince myself he was just a drunk working through his personal problems, and wondering if either John Wayne or the U.S. Government were as innocent as I had been raised to believe.

Next morning I headed to Parmalee — one of the poorest communities on the reservation. It was largely a ghost town. A gas station, a store, and several deserted buildings at a crossroad made up the town proper. The roads leading to the junction were dotted with shacks, chicken brooders, and trailers. I met three volunteers at Parmalee: Liz Thomas, from Little Rock, Arkansas; Kathy O'Toole, from San Clemente, California, and Ray Abbott, 23, from Newburyport, Massachusetts. The girls, in their teens, lived in a trailer near the general store. It had electricity and oil heat, but no running water. The girls' morale was high. They neither had nor wanted transportation. In their view hitchhiking was a good way to get to know the people.

Ray Abbott was young, dynamic, and wholly his own man. He lived in one room of a deserted store with no running water. Originally stationed in Mission, he found it too civilized, and moved to Parmalee in search of more challenge. He was working on the housing survey and preparing to set up carpentry and home repair projects with local boys. He told me he had an airplane pilot's license, although he was content to be afoot in Parmalee, convinced that a vehicle would alienate the people he and the other volunteers were trying to reach.

Soldiers Creek, about 22 miles from Rosebud, was not so much a community as the only place in the district where two dwellings were in sight of each other. Two young men were stationed there; Bob Fuller, 19 and Ken Burnett, 20. There were interesting stories about Fuller. I learned from Father Pate, the mission priest, that the sponsor expected volunteers of more experience and age than the ones it got. Faced with the group of young volunteers, the Tribal Council held a meeting to parcel out work assignments. After setting the girls up in various communities with the hope they would start preschool projects, the Council came to Fuller, a rangy young man with an unruly shock of brown hair. They asked what experience he had. The interview, as related by Father Pate, went something like this:

"I graduated from high school two months ago. I don't have any experience."

"Well, what can you do? Do you know any carpentry? Electricity? Construction?"

According to Father Pate, Fuller stood and informed the Council that he had "a back, a brain, two good eyes and two good hands," and demanded "can you use me?" When the Council stopped laughing, it assigned Fuller to Soldiers Creek to work on 4H with the young men. After a while, Fuller felt he was getting nowhere in the community, partly because of his youth, partly because of his white skin, and partly because he was an Easterner. At a local rodeo, somebody dared him to ride a bronc bareback. As Fuller told me the story: "I got on the damn thing and it started bucking like hell. They said using both hands was cheating, so I grabbed the horse's mane with one hand and kept the other in the air. I was scared as hell, but for all I knew, if you fell off they'd leave you there for the bronc to jump on. So I held on." Pretty soon the bucking stopped, and Fuller was still on horseback. The crowd loved it, and gave Fuller a big hand.

By coincidence I saw a survey form in Father Pate's office which Fuller had filled out, making a marginal note to: "Look at this one twice, they're really down and out," then reported on a family of 10 living in a two-room frame house "with rats, mice, no water, two dogs, and a $200 grocery bill a year-old."

That night, determined to avoid both the motel room and the John Wayne re-run at the Quonset Hut, I invited the three VISTAs from Parmalee to dinner. To get a good steak, we had to make an 80 mile round-trip to Valentine, Nebraska. I heard a good deal about life on the reservation from them, and next day from Father Pate. They told me there was a great deal of drunkenness, which started about the age of 13 or 14 for the Indians, both girls and boys. Marriage, he said, was a rarity anymore among the Indians, because the family structure had been wiped out by the BIA relocation program over the previous two decades. Prostitution and venereal disease were high, as were incest and illegitimacy. A prostitute's price on the reservation was about the price of a bottle of beer, which Father Pate seemed to consider as much an indictment of reservation economics as of morals. There was some money in the area, he admitted, but it belonged to the white off-reservation ranchers who leased the Indian lands cheaply for grazing cattle.

The BIA (U.S. Bureau of Indian Affairs) relocation program Father Pate referred to was one of the most unfortunate government programs ever conceived. For more than a century opinion was divided between two theories among the white men who then decided such things; whether it would be better to shoot the Indians or let them starve on the theory that the only good Indian was a dead Indian; or whether the Christian thing to do would be to teach them the ways of "civilized man." One way or another, both attempts were tried. The first led to massacres and the infamous "trails of tears" that forced decimated Indian tribes to march at gunpoint from their home grounds across half a continent and into reservations too barren to support them. The second, created by the B.I.A. — the agency charged with controlling the Indians under the pretext of looking after their needs — operated on the theory that the problem with the Indians was cultural and that if Indian babies were taken as infants from their tribe and family and raised in government or religious boarding schools they would learn and live by the ways of white civilization, from Bible reading to wearing neckties.

It didn't work. When they grew up the Indian children drifted back to the reservation, rejecting the grafting of white civilization attempted on them.

It was hard to tell where the apathy of the Indians left off and their total dependency on others began. I knew from books that somewhere, sometime, they had been a strong and independent people — nomadic tribes of fierce warriors and proud spirits. Now all that remained seemed to be the crushed spirits of a thoroughly defeated race. Father Pate told me of when he first arrived on the reservation years before. After helping a burned-out family find other shelter he bought a supply of groceries to get them through for a few days. "Next Sunday morning," he told me, "the old man showed up with a shopping list. It seemed perfectly natural to him to assume that I would keep providing whatever food they needed."

I flew back to Washington with new understanding of the American Indians. Having yearned to see for myself what Indian reservations were all about, after seeing it I could not resist summing up my report with personal observations:

> "The people of this land are not farmers or cattlemen;" I wrote. "They are Indians who live in country not good enough for cattle. They are not down on their luck or bypassed by society; they were beaten and placed on poor land and made wards of an alien government which promptly lost interest in them as people. Their poverty is not an accident of history. It is the intended and predictable result of conscious actions. Their apathy is not the smoldering resentment of the chafing ghetto dwellers; it is the timeless resignation of an emasculated race. No one says "The clock is ticking" for the Indians.

More recently I ran across an anti-government slogan: "If you think the Government is there to take care of you, ask the Indians how they made out." I thought immediately of Rosebud.

***

After I handed in my report on the Rosebud Reservation and took care of other Washington chores, I was sent back to South Dakota, this time to evaluate the VISTA program on the Oglala Sioux reservation at Pine Ridge, the great reservation that sprawls across the Dakota hills west of Rosebud.

When I landed in Pierre this time, the annual bull sale was underway. This international event drew cattle buyers from all over North and South America and from as far away as Australia and Europe. Getting a rental car was no easy feat. I was told I'd have to wait overnight. That changed when the girl at the rental agency saw my impressive credentials with the "Executive Office of the President" on the cover. She must have assumed I was the President's right hand man. Within the hour I was in a car heading two hundred miles southwest to Pine Ridge.

I drove for a long time through the Badlands of South Dakota, through prairies, hills and dramatic canyons. On the drive, a low cloud formation left a blue sky partially veiled by mist. After a while I pulled to the side to stretch my legs. I had seen no other car for an hour, nor house nor tree nor crossroad nor telephone pole. To a guy who grew up a block from the tides and surf of the Atlantic Ocean the silence was impressive. I saw an airplane high overhead, the intervening mist making it a ghostly-seeming reminder of modern times. Perhaps it was an omen: I did not realize the history of ghost dancers and massacres that awaited me at Wounded Knee.

The Pine Ridge Sioux reservation was, according to their application, the second largest Indian Reservation in the nation, extending over an area of 2 million acres of moderate to poor land. It seemed a trifle more affluent than its neighbor Rosebud to the east. There were eight VISTA volunteers assigned there under the nominal sponsorship of the tribal council president.

The community of Pine Ridge was the tribal headquarters of the Oglala Sioux. It contained the Indian Hospital, the Old Folks Home, a boarding school, the tribal council, the BIA, and the new Pine Ridge community action program. There were several blocks of relatively nice-looking homes, a restaurant and several gas stations. A loosely aligned series of cabins served as a motel.

When the first, and older, volunteers arrived, they were put to work running the Old Folks Home. There had been staff problems at the Home. The cook and his wife were alleged to be unreliable because they drank heavily; so the VISTAs were assigned to cook and wash dishes for the old folks. I interviewed one volunteer who placidly spent part of her day cooking at the home and the other part working in the tribal office on such tasks as securing caskets for the funerals of impoverished Indians. When I asked her to accompany me to the office next door to gain privacy for our interview, she asked one of the senior men working in the office if she could "be excused for a few minutes, to talk to the man from Washington." Permission to leave was granted. The whole incident was obviously routine, but I was disconcerted to see such subservience by a volunteer.

Shortly after the arrival of the first group, five younger VISTAs evidently made of sterner stuff appeared on the scene. From their first day they objected to doing housework at the Old Folks Home. Eventually they got themselves reassigned further out into the reservation; some to Porcupine Creek, about 18 miles from Pine Ridge. It boasted a water tower, school, and community center. There were several such community centers on the Pine Ridge Reservation. They were good-sized structures of natural wood and stone, something like a small ski lodge, complete with large wall and huge fireplace inside, and had electricity, running water, and central heating.

At Porcupine Creek I met Jim Shepard, a 23 year old volunteer from San Antonio, Texas. Several hours before I met him Shepard had been blasted out of a trailer by a gas explosion. He was still shaken by the experience. He had been asked by an Indian family living in the trailer next to his to help light their gas stove. Upon entering the trailer, Shepard placed his glasses on a nearby table and bent over to look at the stove. A coal oil heater standing across the trailer threw a spark. The trailer was demolished in the resulting gas explosion. The Indian family escaped through a rear door. Shepard was knocked unconscious and hurled about 20 feet by the force of the blast. His hair was singed, and his clothing burnt. I took him to the hospital, but he did not want to hang around two or three hours to see a doctor. Because of his condition, I asked him to spend the night with me at my motel. He slept little and vomited several times through the night. By morning he was feeling better. I left him on his promise to see a doctor for x-rays the following day. Since his glasses were lost in the explosion, he promised to limit his driving only to what was absolutely essential and during daylight until his parents could mail him replacements.

Originally stationed at Pine Ridge, Shepard didn't think he had joined VISTA to wash dishes or cook for an old folks home. He insisted on reassignment out into the field, making himself unpopular among the original, more docile, volunteers who said they thought his training should have taught him "the right attitude" to accept routine assignments.

In Porcupine, Shepard organized 4H projects and helped the preschool project by distributing supplies of toys and educational materials to the locations to be used for classes. His transportation was a GSA pickup truck, which did not suit him because it had unwanted government markings. "The best thing would be to get an old, beat-up truck," he insisted. "The Indians don't go for you when you're a government man, and that truck makes you a government man."

Shepard's major problem initially was acceptance in the community. He told me a local citizen and would-be community leader named George Iron Cloud opposed the VISTAs as a tribal project and was out to scuttle VISTA on the grounds that it was "a political arm of the tribal administration". Shepard's major support in the community was John Running Bear, who was in the hospital recovering from knife wounds.

I spoke with Charles Scout, the head of the family whose trailer blew up around Shepard. The Scout family was using the community center for shelter, and expected to move into another old trailer as soon as one could be found. Scout appreciated Shepard's efforts to light his stove, and muttered that he (Scout) had connected the gas line wrong, causing the explosion. Scout thought Jim Shepard was "okay", although he told me he did not know what the other volunteers did.

***

Like many American boys, I grew up reading with sympathy the story of George Armstrong Custer and the Battle of the Little Bighorn in which he and hundreds of troops under his command in the 7th Cavalry were wiped out by the Sioux under Chief Sitting Bull. Between the history books and the movies it was impossible not to have heard that story. It was however, entirely possible to grow up never having heard of Wounded Knee. I never heard of it until somebody at Pine Ridge, hearing I was going to visit Porcupine Creek, suggested I go see the battlefield at Wounded Knee. "The last big fight between the Indians and the cavalry," I was told. "Don't miss it."

I drove out expecting to see a classic battlefield with historical plaques marking skirmishes and gallant charges between warriors on horseback and the immortal 7th Cavalry – a western version of Bunker Hill, or the Battle of New Orleans, or Gettysburg. It was, however, quite different.

The place was as empty as the gray sky above, an expanse of prairie, gullies and low hills over which the November wind blew quietly. Here and there stone markers stood, alone for hundreds of feet before you encountered the next. There was a pair of weathered stone gate posts near a few stone monuments that bore plaques briefly describing the massacre on December 29, 1890 of hundreds of Indians, including women and children, who were shot dead and buried in a mass grave. By November of 1965 that tragedy was only 75 years back in history — well within the memory of old Indians still living on the Pine Ridge reservation.

The Lakota Sioux tribe, led in their resistance to white domination by chief Bigfoot, had been driven almost to extinction. A conviction grew among the Indian holy men that the Great Spirit would save their people. The conviction found strong expression in the "Ghost Dance" performed by holy men wearing "Ghost Dancer Shirts" of buckskin adorned with symbols and beads. It was believed the shirts would magically change the white man's bullets to dust. Word spread that Chief Sitting Bull himself was to join them; a hope that had died when he was shot and killed a few days earlier at Standing Rock. Still, when the 7th Cavalry surrounded the band at Wounded Knee, herded them into a small gully, and ordered them to disarm, most of the tribe obeyed.

Stories differ as to whether the shooting started when an old Indian wrestled to hold onto his gun and it went off accidentally, or whether young warriors pulled out rifles hidden under blankets, or whether a cavalry trooper mistook a sudden movement as hostile and opened fire. Whatever the spark, the cavalry opened fire on the Indian prisoners huddled in the gully below their feet. They used four Hotchkiss guns — light field artillery capable of rapid fire. When the shooting ended, between 150 and 350 Indians, including women and children, lay dead – many shot while trying to get out of the gully and run away across the open prairie. Of the 500 or so cavalry troopers 25 were killed, either by the Indian warriors or by uncontrolled sweeping fire from their own Hotchkiss guns.

I could not tell, walking about that place and trying to figure out what happened, who was right or wrong. Nor am I given to superstition or mysticism. Yet with no more knowledge than what I read on the plaques and saw in the terrain, I stood on the lip of that gully and understood that something more than individual people had died there. The apathy I saw everywhere among the Indians was no longer so puzzling.

***

I drove to Wanblee, about 80 miles from Pine Ridge. Two volunteers were stationed there; Sue Beebe and Anna Strickland. I had first met Sue Beebe at the Pine Ridge Indian Hospital while taking Jim Shepard there for a checkup. She had with her a 14 year old Indian girl from Wanblee, who was scheduled for an x-ray. She was extremely shy, although she had obviously formed a strong admiration for Sue. I was told that since she had started coming around to see Sue and Anne she had done less drinking and was beginning to bring her girlfriends with her to the trailer.

In Sue and Anna's trailer at Wanblee I saw children's drawings taped to every wall in the trailer, a large stack of children's records on the floor, and lots of children's books scattered around. Sue admitted that of the 200 pounds of baggage allowed her as a VISTA volunteer, she used up 196 pounds for children's books from home. Her parents later sent her clothes, most of which were now "on loan" to the Indian girls to wear to dances.

Sue was 25, energetic, smart, and exceptionally dedicated. She proudly asserted that she was a staunch Republican, voted for Goldwater in '64, and offered to produce envelopes full of clippings on Republican politics sent to her by her grandmother in Batavia, New York, who was also a staunch Republican. Sue had a brother in the Peace Corps, and claimed as her two best friends Sandy Lindsey and Betty Warnecke, two VISTA volunteers who worked in Spring Creek on the Rosebud reservation 45 miles away. I had met them on my earlier trip.

Sue planned to finish her year in VISTA, take a two-month vacation, and come back to Wanblee for another year as a Vista volunteer. "I wouldn't trade Wanblee for anything. I really had to fight to get here, and get away from the Old Folks Home, but it was worth it." She admitted she could use a raise in her stipend; she spent her money buying crayons, coloring books and other items for the children out of her own pocket. She didn't want her money back; just more money to buy sports equipment for her girls teams.

The minor but irritating struggle of volunteers like Sue and Jim Shepherd to break loose from the Old Folks home and get out on to the reservation resonated with me. On my return to Washington, I suggested in my report that "all training be reviewed to see if a certain minimum of independent decision about their work should not be encouraged in the volunteers .... To patiently bear with dishwashing for four months seems ... closer to the discipline of a cloistered convent than to the directed action desirable of a Vista volunteer."

***

The scenes and people I was encountering were teaching me how little I knew about the life of my country. But even as I began to understand how enduring was the legacy of long-ago wrongs, the country was undergoing new strains.

While I was visiting the Western Front in the Poverty War, the war in Vietnam and the opposition to it was escalating. U.S. planes were engaged in relentless bombing runs as part of "Operation Rolling Thunder." A 22 year old war protestor burned himself alive at the United Nations in New York. The North Vietnamese ambushed the 7th Cavalry in the Ia Drang Valley, killing hundreds of its men – a grim and perverse echo of the 7th Cavalry's own massacre of the Indians at Wounded Knee 75 years earlier.

Faced with ever-larger manpower needs, the Selective Service System began examining what effect OEO's programs would have on the national pool of young men available to be drafted for Vietnam. They needed OEO speakers to appear at training sessions for the military reserve officers who would run the system in the event of a large-scale draft. Having by now acquired a respectable experience in the subject, and having the virtue of availability, I was asked to take on some of the speaking engagements between field inspection trips. My first such assignment was to speak before

85 reserve officers at the Naval Air Station, Quonset Point, Rhode Island.

The modern draft had existed since the eve of Pearl Harbor. During WW II the Selective Service System drafted more than 10 million men, and later another two million for Korea. After that, although every man continued to be required to register with the System on turning eighteen, enough volunteers joined the armed forces to make activating the draft unnecessary. That was about to change. Lyndon Johnson was ordering troops by the hundreds of thousands to Vietnam. The draft was again moving to the center of military considerations.

My speech at Quonset Point was a cultural jolt for a former US Marine Corps Reserve infantryman like myself. The military does not run on democratic principles of equality, and certainly not in the infantry. Officers are, by act of Congress and the Commission of the President, "Gentlemen." Enlisted men are not. Involvement of the troops in decision-making is tantamount to heresy. To ensure unquestioning obedience to orders, the armed services segregate enlisted men from the officer class. The means are not subtle, and the differences can be graphic. Toilets in the officers "head" had individual stalls for privacy. Enlisted men were afforded no such gentlemanly touches. Six or eight men might squat on commodes all in a row, doing their business like so many cattle. There are rules against friendship ("fraternization" in military parlance) between enlisted men and officers, separate living quarters, separate bathrooms, dining areas, and so on. At the mess hall we grunts shuffled through the chow line and ate from metal trays on bare tables with paper napkins. Officers ate at tables in a separate section with tablecloths and cloth napkins. Such symbols of class distinction are considered necessary and traditional in the military, but, as Bill Mauldin's "G.I. Joe" cartoons from World War II humourously showed, they grate on the nerves of Americans raised to believe that every man is born equal. I have ever since avoided, whenever possible, dining without a tablecloth, place-mat or at least a napkin spread beneath my plate. An enlisted man must, on encountering an officer, salute him. It has been that way in almost every military service in the world, forever. In the Marine Corps Reserve I was an enlisted man, first in an infantry outfit until I was promoted to Lance Corporal and transferred to a Marine Fighter Squadron. In the infantry, officers were rare. Their living quarters were in what was called "Officer Country," from which enlisted men were barred unless going about specific duties. Quonset Point was officer country.

When I arrived to give my speech I was greeted by a Navy lieutenant in dress uniform and an ordinary seaman who took my bag. I was shown to a private room in the Bachelor Officers Quarters and invited to a pre-dinner reception for the assembled reserve officers. At the reception the glitter of silver and gold on the uniformed guests was impressive. In the crowd of a hundred or so there was not a single officer who was not a white man. There were no women.

People of color were present, of course. These were the Filipino stewards, men recruited by the Navy from the Philippines expressly to be waiters, cooks, and dishwashers. Here and there a black man could be seen carrying out the trash. Segregation between enlisted men and officers, while the sort of thing that could chafe, had at least a rational purpose in preserving the authority essential to leadership in combat. The racial segregation I saw that night had no such claim. President Truman had ordered the armed forces integrated as far back as 1948. In 1965 precious little progress showed. It was, even to the eyes of a civil rights neophyte like me, disturbing.

The officers were gracious hosts; friendly, interested in what I was doing, and made a good audience. My speech went well, although I could not escape feeling I was in a hundred-year time warp, addressing a dinner of Southern plantation owners while slaves in livery served the food.

There were 14 officers among the 85 present for my speech who were, in civilian life, members of the boards of their local community action agencies. They were interested enough in what I could tell them about involvement of the poor to stay around after the speech and ask me questions about what OEO was looking for in that regard. One colonel challenged the assumption that the poor could add any value to the decision making. I was met with stares of incredulity when I told them that under OEO's policy, the cooks and stewards of civilian life had as much right to sit on a community action board as they did. A few responsive souls spent a late hour with me discussing the very real problems they were encountering from their board colleagues when they pushed to involve the poor in their home towns. I assured them OEO would back them up and gave them Jack Williams's phone number.

Chapter 9: The Neighborhood Youth Corps in Appalachia

In the Appalachian hills and mountains of eastern Tennessee which I visited next, Knoxville's Youth Corps program was designed to enroll 210 in-school and 615 out-of-school kids. The Youth Corps was designed to put poor kids to work after school earning money while learning good work habits and helping various public agencies. The pay was $1.25 an hour. Working hours were limited to keep from cutting into study time. In Knoxville the program started late and was slow in recruitment. Only 105 of the 825 funded slots had been filled with enrollees. They were assigned to assist janitors, help librarians, work as nurses aides or park maintenance helpers. If they were still in school they were to attend regular classes; if they had dropped out of school they had to attend at least 8 hours of special classes every week.

I spent several days visiting the enrollees at their homes, many of which were located in rural sections of Knox County rather than in the City of Knoxville. Most were "shotguns", wooden houses that were only one room wide and ran straight through, so that if you stood at the front door and fired a shotgun it would go right out the back door. Few had any paint on the outside; the wood was weathered, splintered and often boards were missing. Front yard gardens were rare; back yards often featured a wooden privvy. Many homes had no telephone, so giving advance notice was not possible. Knoxville Youth Corps staffer Jack Sharp accompanied me, knocking on the doors first to see if the enrollees and their parents were agreeable to my visiting. In many homes, there was a strong contrast between the threadbare poverty that met the eye and the dignity of a mother in worn housedress welcoming us to her home.

Advice about applying for college scholarships, job-training programs, or post graduation employment was supposed to be provided by the state employment office. But because the employment office only came into contact with the enrollees at the initial recruitment stage, the NYC kids were on their own thereafter to find jobs, apply for schools and work out problems. NYC staffers like L. W. Hargis and Jack Sharp did what counseling they could.

The economy of Knox County was poor even at its best. In the rural areas, tobacco played a major role. Hargis made a point of showing me just how major. At his suggestion I met him one morning an hour before dawn. We got coffee and drove into the hills above Knoxville and parked overlooking a scene he thought I should see. In the darkness of the valley below were large warehouses. From their gates stretched a line of headlights, winding along the road as far as I could see – pickup trucks inching forward so slowly you had to watch carefully to be sure they were moving at all. As daylight grew I could see more details. The truck beds were loaded with bales of tobacco leaves as high as ropes could secure them. Entire families; man, wife, babies and teenagers, were crammed into the cabs. "Every family with any land at all grows tobacco," Hargis explained. "It's their cash crop. At harvest time they bring it to the auction down there."

Inside the gates the pickup trucks would stop for a buyer to examine the tobacco, decide on its quality and price, and make an offer by the pound. From there the truck would move to a weighing station where the tobacco was unloaded and cash received for it. The next stop was the market; large areas, some under tents and others in huge sheds, where new television sets, refrigerators, generators, clothing, furniture and tools were eagerly picked over by the families. I was so fascinated I took Hargis home, got more coffee, and returned to watch for another hour. The line of pickup trucks never ended. When, years later, public figures fought to limit the damage smoking was doing to everybody's health, against the determined opposition of senators and congressmen from Appalachia and the South, memories of that scene gave me a strong understanding of how much their tobacco cash crops meant to those small farmers and their families.

Some of L.W. Hargis's reports on his kids were gems: "Willie R was not on the job as promised yesterday. He made the boast that if anybody said anything to him he would punch them in the nose. So far we have not been able to contact him."

Another staffer, Jack Sharp, was a dedicated man of about 25, who had to leave his studies for the Episcopalian ministry for lack of funds. He gave up his Saturday and Sunday to accompany me to the homes of enrollees.

My visits convinced me the program was reaching the kids who needed it. Robert M, 16, left school in the fourth grade for lack of money. I listened as he related how, for as long as he could remember, he was doing odd jobs to bring home money for the support and education of his four brothers. His last job was as a builder's helper, where he learned to work with stucco on inexpensive houses. For the past three months, he had been working 20 hours a week for the Youth Corps, clearing brush and doing general park maintenance with the Knoxville recreation department.

The "enrollee record" was a Youth Corps form designed to compile the statistics of personal hardship, including family income, size of family, highest school grade completed, reasons for leaving school. What did not come through such statistics was a sense of the individual – the pride, independence, potential — or the lack thereof — in individual enrollees.

Richard K was black, 19 years-old, good-looking and articulate. His father worked as a janitor. His mother was a housewife. Their home was poor, but as clean as sweeping and hard scrubbing could get it. He dropped out after 11th grade to take a $200 a week job playing the saxophone with a traveling band. When he tired of traveling and sleepless nights, he gave it up and came home. There he worked at the general hospital as an orderly, got into an argument with a doctor and quit, then got the Youth Corps job. James told me he wanted to get his GED and go to college, either the University of Tennessee or Knoxville College. He wasn't sure how money for college could be raised, but felt his father could raise it if necessary. He had no objection to the eight hours of classes each week, but said they were boring. His counselor, Jack Sharp, explained that any one class might include youths of a wide range of education, from third grade dropouts to near graduates of high school. Sharp thought James's problem was compounded by his intelligence – that he had no problem with his classes, and would show up extremely well on any aptitude test. His ambition was to be a clinical psychologist, and Sharp thought he might well make it. James felt no friction because of his race, although he told me that while working in the commodity Center, a white worker had called him "nigger." He said he shrugged it off and learned later that two of his white buddies had "clobbered the guy."

There are other things which do not show up on the official forms or in the statistics – such as the distinctive stink of poverty — the distinct reek of coal, damp rotting wood, old beer, urine, filth, dogs, kerosene and other odors that thrive in houses where there is little heat and much dampness. Larry was a 17 year old white kid whose home was dank and dark and stank. The only light that penetrated the gloom was the glare of a black and white television set. Few of the lighting fixtures had bulbs. As in virtually every shotgun we visited, the front room was without furniture. All of the living was done in the middle room and in the kitchen, probably to conserve heat.

Larry worked on a park maintenance crew, but was not enthusiastic about it. He had medical problems with his ears, and was pale and anemic looking. During the interview, although he tried to make sense and understand my questions, he appeared to me to be half drunk. He bragged that he was a local hero to his buddies because he helped throw another NYC boy into the water, allegedly because the boy would not call one of his buddies "Sir."

We visited Chuck, a black 18 year old assigned to a park maintenance crew. He was the oldest of eight children. His father was dead, his mother on welfare with an income between $1,000 and $2,000 a year. His ambition was to be a doctor. His house, like Larry's, was dark and damp on a rainy afternoon late in November. On our way to the house Jack Sharp said that Chuck's mother kept him home as much as possible. Evidently he kept secret from her where he was working and what his plans were. During the interview she seemed suspicious that we were lining Chuck up for something she did not know about. She asked if the Youth Corps was part of the Navy. Chuck replied "Uh huh". After his mother left the room, Chuck's older sister commented that he bought food and clothing for the family, although he never channeled the money through their mother. In addition to his NYC work, he earned money running errands and cleaning backyards around town. I saw sitting in one corner of the dark room Chuck's younger sister, a thin girl about 14 years old. She was wearing a black sheath dress. Chuck remarked that his sister was okay and "made some money". He did not elaborate nor introduce her.

Our next visit was to Clarence, a cocky 17-year-old white boy. His mother was a housewife, his father a disabled veteran. There were four children in the house. Clarence told me he had completed eighth grade, but could not go on to high school for lack of money. His last job prior to joining the Youth Corps was as a dishwasher, which he said paid him 35 cents an hour, 70 or 80 hours a week. His desire in life was to join the Navy. When he talked about that, his face became animated and his speech speeded up. He took the Navy test once and failed it, but planned to take it again in December. He liked books and was currently reading Mark Twain.

There were 18 Youth Corps girls working 20 hours a week at Hillcrest nursing home, Knox County's home for the aged. They made beds, bathed patients, kept records, maintained essential supplies and sterilized instruments. The head nurse, a Miss Price, told me she was impressed by the program and thought it offered real hope to those girls who wanted to take it. Price was a capable, realistic woman, down-to-earth enough to control the girls and human enough to understand their needs. She helped those girls who wanted to take special classes in handling particular nursing duties such as care of the depressed, hygiene for incurable patients, and the like.

I interviewed Wendy, a self-confident black girl of 20 who thought the program was run by crooked politicians: "The county welfare commissioner and the county judge are rats." She was receiving counseling from a psychologist, although she said his attitude was "it's not so bad, being poor", to which, as she told me, she replied "the hell it ain't!"

Wendy said she did not encounter much discrimination because of her race, "except what you always get and you learn to live with that." She also felt that nobody, including "Sargent what's his name" and the President, knew what being poor was like and considered everybody who pretended to want to help the poor was phony. She asked why there were taxes deducted from her paycheck, noting that it was "kind of silly" for the government to give them a program and then tax their money away.

I met Minnie, an extremely shy and uncomfortable young woman. Although she was clean, she did not seem to have any idea of how to keep herself orderly. Her teeth were in bad condition, her complexion very poor, her ability to communicate almost nil. Jack Sharp and Miss Price explained to me later that Minnie had "improved 300%" since she had first joined the program in September. They said her home conditions were extremely bad, and that she originally came to work dirty and unkempt. Miss Price said that as far as she could tell, "the girl didn't know what a bath or a shower was." At the nursing home she now starts her day by taking a shower (under a standing order from Miss Price). Jack Sharp remarked that although Minnie's hair was uncombed when I met her, it was at least clean and a vast improvement over the "matted mess" it had been when she first arrived. Sharp told me about the day when, as was his practice to encourage new enrollees, he delivered Minnie's first paycheck to her at home. A member of her family shouted to her to come outside because a man was there to see her. She crept out. Sharp extended the check to her. Without a word she grabbed the check and ran back inside the house.

***

That Saturday night my budding career as a federal agent almost came to a farcical end. After a long day of home visits, I wanted a steak and a drink to go with it. Under Tennessee's liquor laws, beer could be sold almost anywhere up to 11 PM. But beer bothers my stomach, which ruled out most of the local restaurants. Mixed drinks could only be sold under special license at private clubs. There, however, they could be sold all night long. A friendly hotel clerk gave me the name of such a club and a contact to get me inside. It was a nice place; a dozen tables, a jazz combo playing smoothly in one corner; a cozy bar with 8 or 10 stools. After dinner I moved to the bar to listen to more jazz. Close to midnight two men in suits entered, flashed badges, went behind the bar, and took the bartender into the back office.

"What's going on?" I asked my neighbor.

"Beer raid."

"Beer raid?!!!"

"Yep!" he reached over the bar to put his beer glass down out of sight. "Not allowed to sell beer after 11 o'clock."

Although I wasn't drinking beer, all I could think of was the impressive set of credentials I was carrying in my jacket, with the big gold seal and "Executive Office of the President" emblazoned on the blue cover. I could see the headlines already: "White House Presidential Aide Caught in Raid!" My work took me no closer to the President than the statues in Lafayette Square, but Knoxville had gone for Goldwater the year before and I was taking no chances. My neighbor assured me I shouldn't worry. Prudence, however, dictated a fast exit out the side door.

***

Next to me on my flight back was a Milwaukee businessman who owned a small company specializing in the manufacture of machinery. He was a religious man whose pastor persuaded him to sponsor an OEO work-training program in his company. He told me about the experience:

"The kids we got were black, and really screwed up," he said.

"No fathers in the home, no sense of pride in their work, no education, and an attitude that put everybody's teeth on edge. My work force is pretty ethnic; white guys from Czechoslovakia, Germany, places like that where being a good mechanic is almost a religious duty. They hate Negroes to start with, and of course the colored kids didn't like them either. Then tools started to disappear. It was pretty clear the kids were stealing the tools, but it wasn't something that could be proved. Problem is, the tools don't belong to my company; they belong to the mechanic. Some of those guys still used the same tools their fathers gave them. Stealing them was like stabbing them in the heart."

"Sounds pretty grim."

"You don't know the half of it! I felt sorry for those kids — I came up the hard way myself. But some mornings I thought I 'd find blood on the floor."

"You had to fire the kids?"

"At first I thought I'd have to," he grinned, "then I got this idea. I bought every one of those kids a set of their own tools. But before I handed them out, I had them engraved with the kids' own names. You should have seen their eyes! Most of them had never seen their names in print for anything but bad reports, and here they had metal tools, built to last forever, with their names permanently engraved on them! They weren't about to sell those tools and, of course, once they had them they got curious about how to use them. Haven't had a problem since."

***

Chapter 10: Philadelphia

Three more field trips were lined up when I got back to Washington; one for an evaluation of the VISTA project in Philadelphia that was going sour. The volunteers were put to work by the City-sponsored Community Action Program with the initial mission of helping the adult poor learn how to function as low-income representatives and staff members on the local neighborhood community action councils.

While the VISTAs gave it their best shot, theirs was a bureaucratic chore from the beginning. The realities of big city politics stopped them cold. Political machines function on control; control of the way things get done, from fixing the streets to putting out fires to staffing the schools; control of jobs; control of votes and, most of all, control of its own organizational dynamics on which all else depended. In Philadelphia, as everywhere in the country, OEO funds was seen by the political machines as a two-edged sword. OEO's insistence on the "maximum feasible participation" of the poor in decision-making meant, to the aldermen, councilmen, and ward-heelers of the big cities, that somebody other than they might hand out the jobs OEO would fund. To avoid that, the machine politicians established the Philadelphia Anti-Poverty Action Committee. The Mayor's right-hand man was named its chairman. Two reliable political functionaries got the jobs of Executive Director and deputy Director. These were serious political operatives.

When the Office of Economic Opportunity people in Washington who were considering Philadelphia's various grant applications made noises about involving the poor, a Philadelphia writer of applications tried to meet their concerns by giving the VISTA volunteers the assignment of teaching the poor how to get involved. He did not seem to have grasped that the priorities of the poor, largely from the black community, might clash with the priorities of the political machine when it came to who got hired to do what.

As Bob Blundo, a 23 year old volunteer from the small town of Chamblee, Georgia put it: "It's bad. We're not able to get anything done. When they published attendance figures for PAAC's summer recreation program, we checked the files and found that attendance had been way below what they said it was. But when we mentioned it, they let us know that our coordinator would have it taken out on him if we let anybody know the real attendance. Hardy, our coordinator, told us 'Go ahead. If I lose my job, it's worth it.' But Hardy's got four kids. So we dropped it."

Philadelphia's heavy-handed officials were the focal point of discontent – on one occasion they ordered the volunteers to discontinue attempts to foster closer relations between the staff of the various neighborhood councils. The VISTAs grew so frustrated they resolved to finishing out their year "just to show them we have enough guts to stick it out." Other sponsors unaffiliated with the City invited the VISTAs to transfer to them where they could do useful work with the poor. This the VISTA office in Washington would not approve, even though one of its own earlier reports noted that "the project sponsor is in a sullen kind of way attempting to avoid the maximum use of the councils."

In Philadelphia, as elsewhere in my travels, I was meeting two Americas, and two types of Americans, both young. Kids in the Neighborhood Youth Corps were seldom younger than 16 or older than 19; the VISTA volunteers for the most part were between 18 and 24. One set was poor and glad to find jobs sweeping floors at $1.25 an hour; the other was volunteering a year of their lives to help the poor. The synergy was good; kids that never had a chance to see beyond their own poverty took to young volunteers who listened to the same music and understood their feelings better than did the middle-aged bureaucrats and social workers. But it was a two-way street; the VISTA volunteers also had much to learn.

In Philadelphia the volunteers gravitated to the neighborhood hangouts of the young black kids. One night I went along. The talk ranged from sports to music to movies and eventually to their environment. One white VISTA girl apparently got carried away with the social theories she had absorbed at the college training sessions. She challenged a black kid who described his dream of one day owning a big Cadillac. "Don't you think that's kinda materialistic?" she asked. "That's what's wrong with our society. It's all about luxury and things. It's sick!" The kid looked at her in amazement. "Oh, man!" he said. "If havin' a hot car and stuff is sick where you come from, I wanna go to your hospital!"

When I got back to Washington I stopped by the VISTA office to urge approval of the transfers requested by the volunteers. It bothered me to think of kids giving up a year and coming away knowing their year was wasted by bureaucrats and politicians.

***

Chapter 11: Kentucky and the North Country

From the problems of VISTAs struggling with the politics of the big city I returned to the equally intractable problems of impoverished Appalachian teenagers.

Floyd County, Kentucky was coal country, a collection of hills, hollows and shacks slumbering through the twilight of an Appalachian winter. The big coal mine operators had broken the back of the United Mine Workers union, partly through mechanization, partly through the use of subcontracting dodges exploiting the independence of the East Kentuckian, and partly through relentless opposition to the concept of organized labor.

With the gutting of the union locals, the men of Floyd County split into four major occupational groups. The smallest and luckiest group were those who remained employed in modern, largely mechanized mines owned by big steel companies. A larger group of miners worked as "independent contractors" digging coal out of unsafe and primitive "truck mines". The largest group were unemployed, disabled, or occasional miners. The last, inevitable group in the mountain counties were the men working for the county or townships. The heavy bulk of Floyd County's 443 Youth Corps enrollees were the children of unemployed, disabled, or dead coal miners.

For the kids whose homes I visited, geography was usually destiny. Their ages were the same wherever they were; their dreams often similar in the vagueness and uncertainty of youth; their spirits the same mix of hope, acceptance or defeat. What differed were the settings in which fate had placed them — settings which determined what they were up against; distance and poverty on the reservations; dead economies and poverty in Knoxville; bureaucracy and poverty in Philadelphia; man-killing coal mines and poverty in Kentucky. The Floyd County program was running well enough. It was the world in which the kids lived that the program could not change.

Almost every home I visited had its victim. James, 18, worked as a custodial assistant in the high school; his father was a disabled miner.

Patsenia was the 19 year old daughter of a coal miner disabled by disease. Loretta, 17, was the daughter of a man killed in a coal mine. Ralph, the 17 year old son of a disabled miner, had three younger brothers at home.

I wanted to know why fatal or disabling mining accidents were so commonplace. Many were afflicted with black lung disease — the terribly disabling result of breathing coal dust in the mines. The UMW fought for years to improve safety conditions, counting it a victory when the big mines issued breathing filters and improved the mine ventilation systems. There were no such luxuries in the truck mines.

Ignorant of what a truck mine was, I asked to see one. The father of an enrollee, with his arm in a sling, offered to show me. We drove up into the hills not far from his home, turning off the two lane paved county road on to a shale-paved track that wound its way up a slope barren of growth in the December cold. We stopped where the track ended. Saying nothing, the miner pointed at a hole in the side of the hill that was about three feet high by four feet wide – about the size of the top of a kitchen table. If you stood one on its side up against the wall, you would have an idea of the size of the opening into the mine.

He asked if I wanted to see the inside, clearly not expecting me to take him up on it. When I did he warned me not to go in too far. Going in was the hard part. Near the hole was a truck of the kind that gave "truck mines" their name. It was a small, flat piece of wood with steel wheels, much like the dollies garage mechanics lie on to slide under a car when they don't have a hydraulic lift. He helped me position the wheels on a rickety set of rails that ran into the mine. Wearing a helmet with a battery-powered light, I lay on my back and propelled myself into the mine – very slowly, and not very far. The ceiling of the mine was only a short reach above my face. After twenty or thirty feet – a distance that felt like miles – I had had enough. For the first time I understood what real claustrophobia felt like. If the mine caved you died or were crippled. If not, you followed the seam, breathing coal dust, filling your buckets and dragging the coal out behind you, trip after trip.

The truck miners didn't own the holes. The property – often the entire hill – belonged to the big companies, who leased it to individual miners and bought whatever coal they could chip and cart out of it. By treating the transaction as a lease of their property to an "independent contractor" the coal companies escaped any obligation to provide safety measures, pay wages, or provide health benefits or insurance.

Among the young, the attitude was less one of self-reliance than apathetic acceptance of the grim realties. One evening after a day of interviews and visits I went to an early movie near Prestonsburg. The theater was on a par with the Quonset hut of South Dakota – a cinder block affair built years before, with no pretensions to elegance or even comfort. The rows of wooden chairs had long since cracked and split; the movie's sound track bounced off the walls and the uncarpeted concrete floor. On the screen Burt Reynolds was roaring down a country road. The audience was made up of kids in their early teens, sprawled among the seats, smoking cigarettes and making out. At 14 or 15 years old, they already had an air of resignation about them – knowledge that their lives would not differ much from the lives of their fathers.

I headed back to my roadside motel, stopping to fill up at a lonely gas station on a road that crossed a hollow carved out by the quiet creek beneath my feet. The mid-December early evening was crisp. Far above the stars were beginning to come out in the twilight. Down in the hollow it was already dark. A light came bobbling down the hill on the other side of the creek. Out of the woods came the clear, halting voice of a boy singing a Christmas carol as he made his way downhill through the trees, carrying his lantern. "Si-I-lent night. Ho-o-ly night. All –is calm. All – is – bri-i-ght."

The boy behind that voice from the mountainside lived among dirty creeks, black, shaky mines, long trains of coal, and a stubborn, bypassed people scattered among lonely hills and hollows where youngsters walked miles along dusty roads to catch a school bus to a basketball game on

Saturday night. Up the road from the gas station where the twilight still lingered on the hilltops I parked for a few minutes looking down at the quiet hollow. Just below me a shack stood with no light welcoming. Two cows ambled down the slope toward it. The sound of their bells carried up the hill. An incredible peace. But the boys left in summer to find work in Cincinnati or Detroit, then returned to hibernate on unemployment in winter. Families were large, and intermarriage was frequent. Coal was cheap and there was electricity, but indoor plumbing was rare, and washing laundry was a major chore for the women. The mines closed down as quickly as the stars twinkled, throwing thousands out of work. The owners leased their hillsides to unemployed miners to use as truck mines, an "independent contractor" dodge letting the miners earn $8 for a 12 hour day, where before they earned $25 for 8 hours. Neither holy nor bright.

***

Our reports were winning a modest circulation at OEO headquarters. Just before Christmas I was asked to squeeze in a field check on the Neighborhood Youth Corps program in Plattsburgh, New York, an upstate town in the heart of the North Country, not far from the Canadian border. It was the chief community in a wintry land of frosted timber, frozen lakes, and prolific families. The area's economy was based on a Strategic Air Command base and Plattsburgh State College, with additional jobs and shopping money coming from nearby Dannemora State Prison and a Georgia and Pacific paper mill located in Plattsburgh proper.

Although the economy was limited, the families were not. Among the Youth Corps enrollees I visited, families with 8 or more children were the norm rather than the exception. Of 8 enrollees from Ellenberg, 5 came from families of 10 or more children, 2 came from families of 8 children, and the last was from a family of 6 children. I spoke with Betty, a 17 year old from Ellenburg who told me she had dropped out of school after completing her sophomore year. She said she was one of nine children in the house. According to her file, her father's annual income was slightly over

$1,000. Betty's Youth Corps assignment was to wrap and distribute Christmas packages in Plattsburgh's "Christmas Bureau," a non-profit group which collected, repaired, and distributed toys to the poor at Christmastime.

Audrey, 16, told me she dropped out of school to help her family pay bills the previous June after finishing 8th grade. Her father was an appliance repairman "if and when" as she put it, "he can get work." There were 9 children living at home. Audrey worked 32 hours a week at the Sacred Heart Nursing Home washing, ironing and folding clothes. She turned most of her money over to her mother to help pay bills. In the five months she had been in the program, she said, no counselor had talked to her either about going back to school or getting vocational training to realize her ambition to become a nurse.

I met Sue, an attractive 17 year old who dropped out of school after 8th grade, got married, and subsequently had the marriage annulled. She told me she had never seen a counselor. In truth, with no jobs available in that hardscrabble country, the only counseling that made sense might have been to tell the kids to go somewhere else and get an education – if education was not itself suspect. Many poor kids, like their parents before them, distrusted "book learning".

Carol, 18, was one of eight children. She made it through high school and was now getting training at a dentist's and hoped to get a job with the dentist at $1.25 an hour when her Youth Corps job ended "but I hope it doesn't end." The only school counseling she had received thus far came from "an old maid who is a teacher and wants me to go to college so I can be an old maid and a teacher." When I talked with her, she was equally unimpressed by the counseling from the State Employment Service, noting that she registered with them on graduation, and returned a month later to find "they hadn't done a thing they said they would, and when I showed up they hauled out my file and then started doing the things they promised they would do the last time I was there."

I met Barbara, a 17 year old high school senior working as a teacher's aide. There were 11 children in the family, 10 of whom were still in school. The 11th was two years old. She wanted to be a nurse and had applied to Champlain Valley Tech for a nursing course. Thus far she had saved $120 toward her nursing school, putting away $25 every two weeks and buying clothes and other necessities with the rest. She was also getting her teeth fixed. As for counseling, she explained: "We don't have a guidance counselor. If you want to be anything, you have to talk with the principal, and she tells you if you can be what you want to be." Barbara's words rang in my ears all day. "She tells you if you can be what you want to be." Not how, but "if." What kind of counseling was that to give a kid?

Brothers Gary and Mike, 22 and 19, worked at the Plattsburgh Airport clearing brush for a runway extension. They were likeable guys. Both dropped out after eighth grade. The brothers were 2 of 10 children in the family. Although both hoped to learn a trade, they were not being taught one in the Youth Corps, unless you count clearing brush as a trade.

Loren, 16, left school after the start of his freshman year at Plattsburgh High. Of 13 children, five still lived at home. His father was dead, his mother on Social Security. "Why should I stay in school?" he demanded. "It's okay and all, but it's so damn dull. Same thing, day after day." He had received no counseling from the Youth Corps.

And yet, against such pessimism about the value of education, there was an encounter that surprised me with its demonstration of hope in what education has to offer.

Rosalind was an exceptionally pretty, well mannered, clean and neatly dressed 17 year-old, the second oldest in a family of 13 children. Her father worked for the Street Department and earned $80 a week. She was perhaps the classic example of what the Youth Corps could mean to a poor family. A sophomore at Saranac High, she had been in the Youth Corps since July as an aide at the Plattsburgh library, working only Saturdays. Her good nature and quiet, hard-working manner impressed her supervisor, a quiet lady who told me they offered her more hours during weekdays after school, only to learn that Rosalind's parents objected on the grounds the extra work would take away her homework study-time.

Shortly before my visit, her supervisor told me, the electricity had been shut off in Rosaline's home. Her father — "a bit slow, but very nice" as the supervisor described him — had built his own house out in the woods and had been persuaded to install an electrical heating system in the roughly-built and uninsulated house. By early December – a time of bitter cold in the North Country – the family's electric bill amounted to $388. The electric company turned the power off and refused to turn it back on again until the family could come up with a minimum back payment of $250 and a promise of weekly installments thereafter, presumably to come out of his $80 a week after feeding the 13 kids.

After meeting Rosaline and listening to the supervisor, I visited the house. The family was living on heat from a bottled-gas stove, and from a rough open wood-fire set up on a corner of the cement floor with a home-made canvas smokestack poked through a window. The mother was a pleasant, slow-talking woman, remarkably young, who informed me that Rosaline was "not too good" in school, and might have difficulty with her grades if she worked more than seven hours a week. There was no mention made of the great relief that could be provided if the family took a chance on Rosaline's grades and let her work and earn more money. Nor was mention made of the lack of electricity, nor of the damp chill air of the house in the winter twilight, nor of the absence of Christmas ornaments and merry lights. Only the laughter of a horde of little children and their curious, mischievous stares — and the clear-eyed response that Rosaline's grades must not be allowed to fall, or else she might have to stop her education.

My interviews were completed by mid-day. My flight was booked for early evening to take me home to New Jersey for Christmas. But the interview with Rosaline's mother at their dark and snowbound home got under my skin. The thought of the electric company salesman who dealt with Rosaline's slow-witted father and had sold that poor bastard on electric heat for an uninsulated, drafty, cement-floored self-built house made me angry. Even more so did the fact that, having sold him on it, they cut the power off a few days before Christmas, leaving all those little kids shivering in the dark.

The cut-off men from the power companies were no strangers to me. In the constant struggle to stay in law school, feed the kids, and pay my own utility bills there were times when I had to choose between paying tuition and having the power cut off. A few years earlier — before I moved the family back home to New Jersey where life was less expensive and our families close by to help — the Dean called me out of a Constitutional Law exam one cold night to take an emergency phone call. The electric company had cut off our heat for being late on the bill and Maryanne had to let me know she and the kids would be staying with friends overnight. I went back in and finished the exam, then spent the next day scrounging money to pay the bill and get the electric turned back on. It sounds hard in the telling, but Maryanne had a pioneer spirit, and we both knew that if push really came to shove all I had to do was give up on law school and we'd be on our feet in no time. In Plattsburgh, Rosaline's family had no such options. I went to see the electric company about their situation.

The electric company guys offered a litany of helpless sympathy. Their first duty, they pointed out, was to their shareholders. If they gave away electricity every time somebody had trouble paying the bill, they'd be out of business. Yes, their salesman had perhaps been unaware the house was not insulated, and was poorly built, but they believed the customer was always right. Once the man ordered the electricity, it was their job to deliver it, and the rates were set by the public utilities commission. We lived, they said, in a capitalistic society. Hardship for some was inevitable. Without profit, there'd be no electricity available at all. Then where would we be?

Working with Bill Haddad's reporters had given me useful insights about the power of the press. With a ruthless Machiavellian canniness I never knew I had, I pointed out that while the profit motive was important to the shareholders of the electric company, newspapers were also in business to make a profit for their shareholders. They made theirs selling newspapers, and what sold more newspapers than almost anything else were sensational, heart-breaking, human interest stories — stories like 13 kids, many of them hardly more than babies, shivering in the cold because the electric company had sold a not-very-bright man on electric heat in a house most of their readers would have heated with wood stoves in a land where money was short but trees were plentiful. I offered a guess that stories making comparisons to Ebenezer Scrooge seemed likely — especially on Christmas Eve. God knows what the politicians would make of it when the story went public. Probably call for an investigation.

Suddenly it became possible that something could be done. After a call from its President — an electric company executive — the Chamber of Commerce agreed to pay the bill as a goodwill gesture, and pick up the tab to insulate the house. The electric guys grumbled something about being blackmailed. Before that conversation could develop further, however, I remembered I had a plane to catch and excused myself, wishing them all a Merry Christmas.

On the way to the airport I swung by the house. The lights were on. I half expected to see Tiny Tim tucking into the Christmas goose.

***

Chapter 12: Chicago and the Red Sequined Whirlwind

By mid-January of 1966 I was back in Washington between field trips. The OEO was again neck deep in controversy. This time the fight erupted in the fertile fields of California's San Joaquin Valley, where the harsh conditions of migrant laborers were being challenged by Cesar Chavez and his National Farm Workers Association, the NFWA. At the urging of Sanford "Sandy" Kravitz, OEO's Director of Special Projects, who was known irreverently within the agency as "Dr. StrangeGrant" for his willingness to fund controversial projects, Shriver approved grants to the NFWA for migrant education, day care, immigration counseling, citizenship classes, credit advice for buying cars and houses, and similar activities. With such attractions to offer, the NFWA's organizing success grew. That in turn brought protest and charges of "Communism" from the big farm operators and their local congressmen. Unfortunately for Shriver, the more the political clout of the agribusiness interests made itself felt in Congress, the more the charismatic Chavez and his NFWA became the darlings of Hollywood. The presence of movie stars and entertainment figures on the picket lines and as boycott leaders widely publicized the strike. The support of the big unions brought mention of the strike into almost every union paper and pamphlet in the nation. The active participation of various ministers and priests ensured that Shriver's decisions would be discussed in the religious press all over the nation.

Assigned to do a telephone check into the charges of communist influence, I spent several days and found the only alleged "evidence" of communist influence came from unsupported statements of a Deputy Sheriff known for seeing communists behind every bush. My recommendation was of little weight in so large a controversy, but for what it was worth I pushed to keep money flowing to Chavez.

***

Not every front in the Poverty Wars drew Hollywood stars or prompted dramatic headlines. For every grape-picker's strike or civil rights march, thousands of people trapped in poverty shuffled along the bureaucratic treadmills of traditional government programs. Welfare bureaus and unemployment offices had done much in their day to relieve the effects of the Great Depression. But their day was increasingly remote. With the passage of decades they had settled into encrusted bureaucracies. The children of many of their client families were the third generation to depend on welfare checks for food and shelter. Neither welfare bureaus nor unemployment offices could make good on the goal of getting people off welfare and onto payrolls.

In recognition of the problem, Congress included a "Work Experience" experiment in the Economic Opportunity Act. It included programs designed to wean people off welfare and introduce them to the benefits of earning their own livelihood. Funds were available to help welfare recipients with on-the-job training, transportation costs, wage supplements and education – almost anything to bridge the gap between welfare dependency and the self-respect of a job.

I was sent to Grand Rapids, Michigan to see how one such program was working out. For a week I interviewed welfare and employment office bureaucrats, welfare recipients, and the managers and supervisors in the public agencies where they were placed for work.

Grand Rapids prided itself on being a big-thinking city. Its furniture manufacturers were being drawn away by lower wage rates in the Carolinas, but automotive parts plants, metal works industries, and firms producing jet-age instruments had created one of the better employment pictures in the nation. Unfortunately, subsidized jobs in private enterprise, which could offer sophisticated training and strongly encourage companies to permanently hire Work Experience trainees, were not provided in Grand Rapids' program because the local director mistakenly thought such training was unauthorized. In fact, it was both legal and desirable to place the trainees in private employment. That was, after all, the whole purpose of the program. That it did not happen was the result of OEO's failure to get good information to the field. The result of the mistake was what I found on the ground; a program that trained welfare recipients for jobs as parking lot attendants, furniture movers and other dead-end jobs. For example, one job at a county warehouse where surplus food was distributed involved breaking the contents of 50 lb. bags of flour down into 5 lb. bags – a job that took about 10 minutes to learn. The local program staff did the best it could, given the misapprehension under which they were working. Searching for any possible employment for which they could train older workers, they learned that fifty county welfare recipients were expensive patients in the county hospital awaiting transfer to the less expensive county nursing home. But the nursing home beds were filled with other welfare recipients who could be cared for even less expensively in their own homes if only there were health aides available. The Work Experience program used its funds to train home health care aides, which freed up the nursing home beds, in turn taking the pressure off the hospital, saving the county money all around.

It was a good effort. But other home-grown inconsistencies endured. The director of the project told me he ruled out accepting candidates with large families. As he saw it, a family with eight kids would be entitled to a "full needs" budget of $800 a month, which worked out to $9,600 a year. The sticking point with that was that the average caseworker in the county welfare department was paid only $6,827 a year. The director said he avoided the problem by refusing help to large families. When I pressed for examples, however, the policy turned out to be more theory than fact. He had one family enrolled which had 11 children.

To his credit, he did a strong job of encouraging welfare mothers to further their education, by persuading local civic groups to provide tuition scholarships while his program paid for their books, transportation and other costs.

I sat in on a class with several welfare mothers. Their enthusiastic instructor assured me he found them a refreshing change from his regular students. These were adults eager to learn, even if they had not been in a classroom for years. The downside was that many women had not or could not take such classes because they had no babysitters, no appropriate clothes and, far too often, neither self-confidence nor hope. Visiting such dispirited women in their homes left me disquieted at the pervasive sense of defeat I found.

After months of seeing poverty all over the land I was angry at the difference between the Hollywood version of America I had naively expected – an America of courageous people fighting their way to a better life — and the real America I found. Seeing the lives of the poor close up in what Michael Harrington had called "The Other America," I felt like one of those disaster investigators who prowls through the sites of tragedies, noting the charred beams that mark where a factory or apartment house stood before the fire, or the twisted wreckage of trains and planes crashed in remote forests. Had I seen such conditions in another land I would have thought how lucky I was to be an American. Yet here I was traveling in the heart of the greatest civilization the world had ever known, finding despair and poverty in every corner. I never knew there were so many welfare mothers in the country. Streets full of children, welfare mothers in the house, and where the hell were the men? A one-legged society. Not gay divorcees, nor seductive housewives — just plain women with the gloss worn off, the paint peeling on dingy walls. Watching the kids in those houses I thought of Churchill's poignant comment while campaigning in a Manchester slum: "Fancy living in one of these streets — never seeing anything beautiful — never eating anything savoury — never saying anything clever." After enough walking up and down dingy staircases asking how's life among the poor, America the Beautiful sounded more like a real estate ad than a national song of celebration.

***

When John Daum drew the assignment to do a field check on Chicago, he asked me to join him. Daum was a lanky Yale honors grad with a New England accent and a shy manner that did not quite conceal a brilliant mind. He had played a decisive role in dissecting a multi-million dollar grant application from Los Angeles so thoroughly that Shriver refused to sign off on that or any other grants until they were vetted by the Office of Inspections — a major victory in our constant efforts to keep OEO's programs true to their mission. Since then Daum, like me, had been moving around the country on inspection trips.

As in Los Angeles, the Chicago application for community action funds was a multi-million dollar bundle of programs designed from the top down. Unlike L.A., however, Chicago's legendary Democratic Mayor Richard J. Daley, truly the most powerful of the old style big-city political bosses, had an iron grip on his city and on every federal dollar that came to town. As it happened, Chicago was also Shriver's home town, where as Joe Kennedy's young son-in-law he had managed the Merchandise Mart, the vast and world-famous Kennedy-owned department store, while also serving as President of the Chicago School Board.

With the Watts riot still fresh in the public mind, everyone was conscious of the coming summer. There was little doubt that rioting was likely in the major cities once the weather grew hot. In Chicago it was taken as a virtual certainty. Martin Luther King had already announced the South was not alone in racism; he was shifting his focus from Alabama and Mississippi to the northern cities — and most intensely to Chicago.

It would be an understatement to say we were greeted at the airport by representatives from Mayor Daley's office. We were greeted by two impeccably-tailored black giants who glued themselves to our sides from the moment we got off the plane until we arrived at City Hall. They were polite, efficient, and obviously there to keep us from straying off on our own to see what was going on in Dick Daley's Chicago.

At City Hall, the giants escorted us to the office of a high-level guy who politely offered us coffee and promised the full cooperation of the city. What, exactly, did we want to know – and why? Tell us the information you need, and we'll get it for you. You can use one of our conference rooms for your interviews. You don't mind if my assistant sits in? The Mayor wants to be sure you get absolutely everything you need. The two aides you met at the airport will drive you around to visit any site you need to see and make sure you get everything you want. How long will you be staying? Four days? Great! Where are you staying? Terrific. We'll have you picked up there first thing in the morning. 8:30 sound good? And we'll try to get you in to meet the Mayor before you head back to Washington.

John Daum and I listened to this plan with silent admiration. The KGB in Moscow couldn't have done it with smoother control. Mayor Daley's men were not about to let us poke into Chicago's civic closets and run back to Shriver with trouble-making reports. When at last we checked in at our hotel and met to compare notes free of our minders, John and I agreed something had to be done. How we could get loose of the giants was not immediately obvious. For starters, however, we saw no point in allowing ourselves to be waltzed around town together. By splitting up, we doubled our chances of actually talking to anybody. We parceled out between us the programs we thought we might cover, and agreed to meet at dinner to exchange information.

Fortunately, Chicago itself came to our rescue in cloak-and-dagger style worthy of a John LeCarre spy novel. A muted after-dinner rap on my door announced the arrival of a contact from the Chicago underground. "Jamar," as he introduced himself, was a young black guy who looked around the hallway and over my shoulder before giving me his name.

"You the guy from Washington?"

"Yeah."

"Here to check on the OEO stuff?"

"Yes."

"You ain't gonna see nothing if the Mayor got anything to say about it."

"That's the way it looks."

"Wanna find out what's going on?"

"Hell, yes!"

"OK. Let's go."

I put on my coat and went out into the Chicago night with Jamar. We went to a "blind pig" – in Chicago, as in other cities, the street name for a bar with no liquor license. Jamar guided me down an alley to a side door that opened into a dimly lit nightclub. I followed him through the all-black crowd of dancing couples to another door at a back corner. At his knock the door opened. He motioned me in to the club owner's office. A desk, chairs, sofa and a filing cabinet. Three black men – one wearing a cartridge-filled ammunition belt that crossed his chest bandolier- style from shoulder to waist – looked me over. The only white man besides myself was a young Irish priest complete with clergyman's suit, roman collar, and dull red hair. The bandolier was comically theatrical, but I felt no urge to laugh. It took no great imagination to envision a shoot-out with the cops if the place was raided.

Brian, the priest, did such introductions as there were. The Irish priests of Chicago were no cloistered bunch. They'd involved themselves in the civil rights movement, which gave them street credibility and made them unwelcome at City Hall. There was a Father Michael Dempsey of Our Lady of Lourdes church; Father McAteer of the West Side Center, and others, including "Father Brian", who introduced the men by first names only. The bandolier-wearer mentioned, with intended emphasis, the defiant-sounding name of a black revolutionary group, although it wasn't a name I'd heard before. I was put through the same cross-examination John Daum and I had endured at City Hall. Why were we here? Who did we want to talk to? Why? Who would we report to in Washington?

I satisfied them with the truth; that what we wanted was simple and straightforward: to size up the programs and talk to the people involved in them. After a four-way conversation among themselves, the revolutionaries drew up a list of program sites we should insist on seeing. We would at least get the feel of the thing, they said, even if there was no hope of hearing anything worthwhile at the sites. They would set us up to talk with the program participants, away from the sites, next night and the night after. Jamar drove me back to the hotel. Next morning I filled John in on the events. We decided he would cover our diplomatic flanks by visiting the sites suggested by our minders, while I would work the list given me by the black power guys.

When I informed my driver-minder that I wanted to see sites that were not on his approved itinerary, he balked. When I insisted, he called City Hall for instructions. When he still resisted, I left him in the hotel lobby. That was the last I saw of him or any other representative from City Hall. The Irish priest had given me his phone number. A call to him resulted in my meeting a large and cheerful black guy who served as my unofficial guide for the next few days.

The sites I visited were, for the most part, small programs where the influence of the black underground — thoughts of the French Resistance in occupied Paris came to mind – was stronger than fear of Mayor Daley's minions. Although there was no question of outright opposition to Daley's control, with the help of my guide I talked with people who conveniently forgot to check in with City Hall until after I left the site.

One work site for teenage drop-outs presented a vivid scene, although it seemed prudent not to include it in any official report. We drove through potholed streets of abandoned houses and broken-down cars with smashed windows and missing tires to a large trash-filled lot strewn with the debris of inner-city poverty – rusted old shopping carts, busted milk crates, weather-rotted children's dolls, broken wine and beer bottles everywhere, discarded drug needles, tipped-over trash cans spilling their contents wherever they landed, and unwanted furniture whose upholstery had long since burst under the onslaught of rain, snow and prowling cats and dogs.

On the lot a dozen teenagers were working at a furious pace to pick up the trash, carting it to an old dump truck that looked like it deserved a place on the lot for itself. All were black, although the complexions varied from very dark to very light skins. They looked in age from 12 to perhaps 16. A thin girl, perhaps 15 years old who was dressed in spiked heels and a tight red sequined dress set the pace. She tirelessly went after one piece of trash after another, picking up what she could carry alone and bringing extra muscle to move bigger pieces. She had leadership. When she told somebody to give her a hand, it was more order than request, and promptly obeyed.

The straw boss of the extraordinary crew was willing to talk with me, once he was assured by my guide that I was trustworthy. My question was obvious: how in the world did he get those kids to work so hard and so fast?

He pulled out a wad of bills that would choke the proverbial horse. "Simple! I pay them cash." he said. "Ain't nothing like cash! When that lot's clean, they go home with the green. No waiting, no bullshit about filling out forms. Just cash – right now and enough of it to do something with. Oh no, I ain't got no problem getting them to work. See that girl over there?" he nodded at the red-sequined whirlwind. "This the only chance she got to make money different than what she got to do every night. She'd be here every day if I had more money." I longed to ask where he got the money, but there are things a federal agent is better off not asking. From general comments and a few broad hints from my guide and later from the priest, I gathered that the straw boss had a pipeline to one of the Chicago programs where payroll padding and kickbacks were accepted as part of the game. Progress had to be made in case anybody checked, so enough cash was diverted to persuade the kids to show up. The lots got cleaned, the kids got cash, the straw boss got his cut, and the less City Hall knew, the better.

The tattered remnants of my budget analyst conscience tried to rally and failed. It was illegal, of course, and I had no business turning a blind eye to it. Those kids had no social security taken out; no insurance if they stepped on a nail or a needle; no training in skills they could market elsewhere; no educational courses and no counseling. Almost every single thing a dozen well-intentioned programs and laws insisted upon was ignored. But having seen the dead-end lives of the coal miner's kids, the defeated welfare mothers of Grand Rapids and the apathy of the Indians on their reservations, I thought of the energy and zeal of those kids attacking that trash, and especially of that red-sequined girl so furiously fighting her way up, and let it go. No welfare worker or office bureaucrat could teach her what she already knew better than they did.

Besides, I rationalized, except for the straw boss whose name I hadn't learned, nobody had actually said time sheets weren't being signed and payroll deductions made; I had assumed all that from the circumstances. I had no last names, no proof whatever except a clean and empty lot. Just in case, however, I thought it fair to keep my colleague John Daum out of the loop on the matter. One dubious conscience seemed enough. I salved mine a bit by asking Father Brian to see what could be done to get that girl into a more hopeful setting.

The irony of it hit me as I fell asleep that night. What that straw boss had done was what I in my job at the bottler's lobby had viewed critically as the racist treatment of black driver-helpers by the white driver-salesmen when they paid their black helpers in cash with no social security, worker's compensation or other paperwork. I objected to that, yet here in Chicago that black straw boss was doing almost the same thing to those black kids at the trash lot. There was a difference in the two situations, but not one you could over-simplify.

On the second night of my after-hours meetings with those working in the programs, my guide took me to a nightclub on Chicago's Near North Side to meet a black musician who worked days in a community center. We had to wait until he finished his set at midnight. He was willing to talk freely if we came along while he kept a promise to visit another musician's act. It was a long night. Chicago's liquor laws were something like Knoxville's. Licensed nightclubs were supposed to close at midnight, unless you bought a higher level of license. If you paid an extra $1,000 you could stay open until 1 A.M.; $2,000 kept you open until 2 A.M. and so on. It was the habit of musicians working clubs that closed at midnight to move on to another that closed at 1; pick up their musician friends there and move on to the next that closed at 2. Some of the troupe were a bit reserved at first until I told of being marginally involved with the "It's What's Happening, Baby" show. Then I was temporarily admitted to the fellowship. By the time the rolling party ended I had picked up useful insights from a variety of musicians and black revolutionaries — including a few of Mayor Daley's lower echelon people.

Daley's approach to OEO funds was to take the money and ignore the community action philosophy it was intended to encourage. The idea of encouraging the poor to find a voice and organize themselves was poison to the existence of his political machine. As Father McAteer of St. Agatha's on the West Side told John Daum, the OEO-funded community reps could get action from the City better than the poor on their own, but "the precinct captain is still the fastest route."

Chapter 13: The Deep South

When I was sent to the Deep South to evaluate more Work Experience programs, I half-expected to step into the racial cross-fires Jack Gonzales' Head Start inspections had encountered. What I met instead was apathy. There was little in the Work Experience programs themselves — programs designed to help welfare recipients make the transition to employment — that differed in Alabama and Mississippi from the one in Grand Rapids. Among the adults in the welfare-to-work programs life stayed largely in the worn tracks created over generations of slavery and its aftermath. Everybody knew there weren't any jobs available anyway, and that such jobs as might open up would follow the traditional racial pecking order: light work and front counter jobs for the whites; heavy-lifting, dirty or back-of-the-house work for the blacks, whether the work be in factories, restaurants or retail stores.

I spent days driving up and down back country roads, meeting and talking with the participants in and around Greene County, Alabama, and eastern Mississippi. What differed from the programs I visited elsewhere in the country was the sense of surveillance and suspicion that followed me everywhere I went.

The roads I was traveling — the back roads of western Alabama and eastern Mississippi – from Eutaw in Greene County, Alabama to Philadelphia, Jackson and Meridian in Mississippi, were in the heart of such Ku Klux Klan horrors as church burnings, night riders and murder. In the spring of 1964 civil rights activists had mounted a campaign to register black voters in the South. Northern volunteers were recruited. My interest in civil rights had been minimal at the time but my curiosity was aroused by a notice on the Law School bulletin board. I attended a recruitment meeting in Washington in the weeks just before OEO was created by Congress. The combination of being broke and having a family to support, and my uninformed indifference to civil rights, ruled out even a slim chance that I might participate. Others were more in tune with the times. Late in June three civil rights workers in their early twenties, Andrew Goodman and Michael Schwerner, young white men from New York, and James Chaney, a local black youth from Meridian, were followed down a lonely road near Philadelphia, Mississippi by a Deputy Sheriff and arrested, allegedly for a traffic violation. While they were held at the jail, arrangements were made for their murders. En route to Meridian after their release, they were forced to stop on a lonely road by two carloads of white men. All three were shot and killed. Their bodies were buried in a nearby earthen dam. Their station wagon was torched and abandoned in the woods.

There were indications of foul play early on; indications so strong that President Johnson personally involved himself, forcing a reluctant FBI Director J. Edgar Hoover to dispatch large numbers of federal agents to a massive search. When the charred chassis of the station wagon was found, pressure from public opinion and from the White House resulted in over a thousand US Navy personnel being ordered to assist in the search. When the boys' bodies were finally unearthed, Mississippi was subjected to the most intense murder investigation in memory. Federal agents covered every mile of the roads, interrogated every conceivable suspect, pressed every possible informant. In October the case broke when a Ku Klux Klan member revealed that he had witnessed the murders. The search for and trial of the murderers eventually led to the 1988 Oscar-winning film "Mississippi Burning" starring Gene Hackman and William Dafoe.

Over the next two years, the full strength of the federal government was brought into play to prepare the case for prosecution of the murderers. By the time I was sent to evaluate the completely unrelated Work Experience programs nineteen local men, including the Sheriff and Deputy Sheriff of Neshoba County, were under indictment awaiting trial. Federal agents were relentlessly continuing their efforts to nail down every scrap of incriminating evidence and testimony they could find. As irrelevant as my work was to that great drama, to white Southerners no outsider bearing federal credentials could be seen as anything other than a hated and feared federal investigator.

By then I had outgrown my rookie's fascination with credentials, and rarely displayed them nor needed to. But the fact persisted that they weren't just federal; they were credentials stamped "Executive Office of the President." When I had to satisfy the car rental agency's request for extra identification by producing the credentials along with my driver's license and Government Travel Request the clerk at the rental counter summoned his manager. The two examined them, and me, with close attention. Whether or not it was justified, from then on I felt like a marked man. Too often for coincidence I noticed a sheriff's car trailing me as I drove through back country pine forests and remote cotton fields to ask black participants and white politicians how things were going. At meals in small town restaurants and crossroad cafes the Confederate-flag-and-pickup-truck crowd were often joined by the local cops, who knew who I was and where I was from and didn't bother to lower their voices when they told others at their table that I was "a fed'ral." Suspicious stares in my direction followed. I was never directly threatened nor even challenged, but I stayed in lighted places after dark. I thought back to evenings in Washington listening, over drinks at the Embers Lounge, to the stories of racial hatred the Head Start guys had reported. For the first time in my life, I felt what it was to be surrounded by an air of muted menace — a mild example of an intense evil that black people had to live with every day.

Even two weeks of that is a long sentence, and I was facing a third week of it. I called Washington for permission to pack it in and come home. Bob Martin, our Southern regional director suggested I drive down to New Orleans for the weekend to lift my spirits. Never having been to New Orleans I took him up on it, although I saw no relief in going to what I thought would be just another southern town. My expectations of New Orleans, shaped thus far by Mississippi rednecks and Alabama crackers, were low.

It's a long drive to New Orleans from Meridian; down pine-bordered highways that lead past Mississippi towns like Laurel, Hattiesburg and

Purvis to Louisiana's Lake Pontchartrain. A long causeway carried me across the lake to New Orleans and my hotel in the French Quarter.

I discovered that traveling from central Mississippi to New Orleans is only technically traveling from one part of the South to another. It is more like transporting yourself to a different planet. This became clear when I went down to the hotel lounge, which ran along Bourbon Street in the heart of New Orleans. The room featured a long bar that stretched along the back wall and a series of tiny round tables hardly big enough to hold the high heels of the girl who danced on it while a small jazz band got the afternoon going. Large French doors opened out onto Bourbon Street where in late afternoon the tempo was picking up. I ordered a drink and sat back to celebrate being out of Klan country. A cheerful girl put her hand on my shoulder and stepped up onto the opposite chair, and from there to my table. Other girls were dancing on tables in different parts of the room, adding a conviviality that was sorely missing in Mississippi and Alabama.

I was not, however, completely out of Mississippi's orbit. A big beefy guy with a creased red neck came in; the kind of farmer whose sunburn ends where his John Deere cap begins, above which he is pasty white. He was a few beers beyond mellow. With him was a teenage black girl, who stoically chewed gum as he caressed her neck, shoulders, hips, and any other part of her anatomy his hands could reach without getting too far from his beer. Eventually, he headed for the elevators with her in tow. I made some comment to the table dancer as she climbed down. "Oh, yeah," she said, "They bring 'em down 2 or 3 times and leave them here when it gets embarrassing back home."

Bemused, I wandered out onto Bourbon Street. As evening approached the lights grew brighter and the Friday night tempo increased. The police put up traffic barricades at the cross streets, converting Bourbon Street into one big walkway for the night. In late afternoon the people walking on it were obviously tourists; gawkers, geezers, and a few young families broad-minded enough to let their kids take a peep at the wild side.

There were teenage girls out for giggles, cops keeping a bored eye on the scene, and squads of beer-bellied delegates from whatever convention was in town. By mid-evening, the families were gone. The teenage girls morphed into young women out for fun, the cops doubled their attendance and sharpened their lookout, and the middle-aged conventioneers mixed in among burly young men swigging beer from plastic go-cups, eyeing the strip and sex shows. Naked dancing girls could be glimpsed from the street, which certainly didn't happen in Mission, South Dakota or Plattsburgh, New York.

Still, I had seen that kind of honky tonk as a young Marine Corps reservist loose in Tijuana on a Saturday night. What I was unprepared for was the art and beauty of the French Quarter's Royal Street, which parallels Bourbon Street a block closer to the Mississippi river. For every bit of music, drinking, and partying on Bourbon Street, Royal Street offered an elegant and quiet counterpart. It's filled with art galleries, furniture galleries, jewelry galleries, rug galleries and window after window of brilliantly lit and colorful displays of art. Old carriageways open invitingly into courtyards discreetly lighted to display paintings and sculptures of every description. New Orleans awakened something in me. It restored my faith in the good things in life enough to let me get through another week of Southern suspicion in Mississippi.

Chapter 14: The Wretched and the Righteous – Skeel's Allotment, Ohio

It's a thousand miles from the French Quarter in New Orleans to Skeels Allotment in Ravenna, Portage County, Ohio, and even further from the burning cities, war protestors and black power revolutionaries that generated the headlines and gripping TV footage of the day. Ravenna was the last place anybody would look to understand what was going on in America. Skeels Allotment and its nearby neighbor McElrath Park were "target areas." They were the two worst areas in Portage County, a fair-sized county in the center of the rust-belt triangle that ran from Pittsburgh on the east to Cleveland on the north and Akron to the southwest.

"It's bad," Jim Brenner told me when we discussed my next assignment. "If I was a prosecutor in that county I'd ask a grand jury to indict somebody!" This from a mild-mannered Republican lawyer not given to extreme statements. He did a field check on the planning grant awarded to the community action agency in Portage County in September of 1965, making serious recommendations for change. Seven months later, it was my job to see if things had improved enough to warrant funding of the main grant. "Whatever you do," Brenner advised, "don't make up your mind until you see Skeel's Allotment and McElrath Park."

The problems Brenner had found months earlier were rooted in misinformation, an outsized personal dispute between an insurance executive and a history professor on ego trips fighting for control of the program, and local communities so desperately poor it shocked the conscience.

> *(Author's note: It's been a long time since the events I describe. Probably both the insurance executive and the history professor are dead. But I thought their conduct so reprehensible that, like Jim Brenner, it seemed almost criminal. Rather than burden their descendants with that long-ago scandal, I have replaced their real names with "insurance executive" for the one and "history professor"*

for the other. JTW)

For months the insurance executive used Robert's Rules of Parliamentary Procedure to tie the community action agency's board in knots while his adversary the history professor tied his knots using the fine print of the board's constitution. The result was confusion, delayed applications, staff turnover and lost opportunities to help the poor. The only gleam of hope was a HeadStart program begun and run independent of the Board by Mrs. Ritchie, an active college-educated black woman who had grown impatient at the infighting and took charge of getting funding for HeadStart and running it when funds arrived.

For a year and well into the following Fall the ego fight went on. Meanwhile winter closed in, and in the shacks of such target areas as Skeels Allotment and McElrath Park the poor waited for the promised progress. Late in November, the insurance executive took it upon himself to hire an Executive Director— Kenneth Bliss, a 27 year old substitute teacher. Bliss lasted until mid-January, at which time his resignation was accepted by the insurance executive the day before Bliss tendered it. Still no program for the poor. And on and on it went.

Following Jim Brenner's advice, I familiarized myself with the two main target areas; Skeel's Allotment and McElrath Park. My interviews of the participants and tours of the communities involved showed me how important it was that the wrangles cease and programs get underway— and how dim were the prospects of any end to the parliamentary battles. Among those I met was the Reverend Benjamin Saddler, a black clergyman from Skeels Allotment. Skeels was technically part of Ravenna Township, but lay outside of the city. Its government consisted of three trustees who were elected from the city and did not reside in Skeels. As Rev. Saddler wryly remarked; "They're usually bankers from downtown."

Skeels was one of the seven target areas in Portage County. It had open-ditch sewerage, unpaved and ungraded roads, and neither sidewalks nor running water. Fires were common in Skeels, and often fatal. The houses generally had a 1,000 gallon water tank, but filling them cost money and when the water was used up the houses burned down. Two blocks from Reverend Sadler was the house of a mother of five children. She had nine until a fire the previous November destroyed her house and claimed her four smallest children. Sadler himself was burned out the following January.

Racial discrimination was high in Portage County, particularly in employment. Saddler named specific stores which refused to employ blacks, and asked whether under the anti-poverty program a store could be built right in Skeels. "Right now it's three-four miles' walk to buy goods. We are taking up a collection among Skeels, five dollars each, to buy some flour and sugar and stock it. Then, if we make any money, we'll expand and put in some more store goods. Can OEO help us on that?" The insurance executive had advised establishing a committee to study whether such a store could be started, but never actually appointed the committee.

I interviewed the insurance executive in his home, a comfortable brick dwelling featuring wall to wall carpeting, plush-covered chairs, stylish furniture, and a new Chrysler in the driveway of his landscaped yard. It was not an opulent mansion – just the spacious and solid suburban residence of an American executive secure in middle-class affluence and stability.

The man had been described to me as paternalistic in his manner and a difficult man with whom to carry on a discussion. He was. When I asked him to describe the present CAC situation, he bridled: "I do not have to answer your questions. I am not a paid employee. I don't have to justify to you what I do!" Eventually he agreed to answer some questions, although he first wanted to know how long the "investigation" would last, who had been interviewed thus far, who was going to be interviewed, and who sent me. Since the news of his latest resignation as Chairman had appeared in headlines the previous day, I asked him what his future relationship would be with the Board. He replied, "Oh, I will be very active indeed. I think the professor is trying to take over this program. I'm not going to let him do it. The poor people do not want him to dictate what is going to happen." Throughout the interview, he repeatedly referred to his rights under Roberts Rules of Order. A well-worn copy of the Rules lay on a nearby table.

After leaving him I met with Andrew Howard, an aged black man retired from thirty years in the federal service. He was easy to like and hard to rattle. Howard had little use for either the insurance executive or the history professor, and was enthusiastically in favor of Mrs. Ritchie, not only for Head Start but as the person who should be running all of the community action programs. His enthusiasm stemmed from his experience driving a bus for the children in Mrs. Ritchie's Head Start. He told me a story about Mrs. Ritchie's insistence on integration. "I was driving and she was riding. Suddenly she got up and went back and stared at the kids. Then she made me stop the bus and she rearranged the kids, so that there wasn't a bunch of white kids and then a bunch of colored. The kids wasn't so sure at first, but by the end of the summer they got along real good. There's a lot of people don't like her. My, oh my, what a temper she <u>has</u>! But she still gets more done than those men squabbling downtown."

I toured Skeels Allotment in company with Howard. An accurate description is difficult to write. Some families lived in old, pre-World War II trailers. Some lived in lean-to shacks. Many houses used coal or wood stoves and a few used bottled gas. Lack of running water and the primitive heating arrangements made insurance unattainable, even if people could have afforded the premiums, which they clearly could not. Some of the houses stank of rotting filth and excrement. It was difficult to believe that nine miles from Akron, Ohio, such wretched conditions existed. A line from Jim Brenner's earlier report of was appropriate: "For a governmental agency to permit such conditions to exist indicates a deliberate disregard of public trust."

Howard pointed out a house in which two children died in flames the previous December. "Their mother went out to get drinking, and left them there alone. Time she got back, they was dead. I know she shouldn't drink, but if we could pay some old granny to watch little kids and maybe teach them something in the daytimes, their mothers might get drunk or even get jobs someplace without the kids being left alone. Why should them little babies pay for somebody else's mistakes?"

The determined pursuit by the insurance executive of personal triumph over his adversary was bad, but neither was there much in that adversary, the history professor, to inspire confidence among the poor. A former CAC Chairman, former CAC Executive Director, and at the time I interviewed him a CAC board member and history teacher in Ravenna, he referred to himself as a "gentleman farmer" and "an interested citizen working in the War on Poverty." He disagreed thoroughly with OEO's congressional mandate to encourage "the maximum feasible participation" of the poor in designing and running anti-poverty programs. "I certainly think the poor should be involved," he insisted, "but the poor have no technical competence — they can't put together or run programs. You must understand. This anti-poverty program was meant to be set up by the educated — by people with technical competence, and even though the poor should know what's going on, the decisions have to be made by those with ability — not by the poor."

A year and a half earlier I might have agreed with him. But that attitude changed considerably on my first field trip, to Boston, and had been changing even more strongly on every trip I'd made since then. It changed even more when I heard the history professor talk after seeing Skeel's Allotment. The poor could hardly do worse than the teacher or the insurance executive, and had every chance of doing a good deal better.

That the exclusion of the poor from decision-making often meant the exclusion of blacks on a racial basis did not trouble the history professor. He freely admitted that a Head Start program run by the CAC was not likely to include any minority teachers. "But that's not racial. There just aren't any qualified Negro teachers in our school system."

It was a convenient coincidence for him that being able to jump back and forth between being on the CAC board and on its payroll fit his teaching schedule. In the course of the interview at his home, his wife mentioned that her husband was thinking of resuming the post of Executive Director during the coming summer. "It fits in just right with his teaching vacation."

He defended his half of the running parliamentary debate with the insurance executive on the grounds that "He's out to run this program like a dictator. I don't think he should be allowed." Eventually even the newspapers covering the arguments and counter-arguments lost track of the score. Meanwhile the poverty that lay so open to view festered while the funds to do something about it went unsought.

Alfonzo Robinson lived in McElrath Park, another target area not far from Skeels. He was black, had nine children, and was one of the three community coordinators hired by the CAC. Robinson and his family were living in the basement of a store in McElrath. The rooms were damp and not furnished in the usual sense. There were several beds, a rough table, one chair, a bench, and a great many boxes. A pot-belly coal stove heated the room. The house stood on ground that was lower than the road passing by.

> "The sewer is that ditch out there, and when it rains it gets pretty messy in here. That ditch don't take much to overflow."

Robinson was unimpressed and unafraid of either the insurance executive or the history professor: "Those guys are fat. Nice cars, nice houses — why hurry?"

The insurance executive had instructed Robinson to "slow down" in his efforts to tell the poor about the availability of anti-poverty programs. "He says I will get the poor excited promising them programs," Robinson said. "Hell, that's not me. That's the Economic Opportunity Act that makes the promises. All I do is make the poor aware of them."

Robinson wanted to know if a separate community action agency could be started in McElrath Park, and how they could raise the 10% local share. No one had told him OEO could waive that 10% matching requirement in extreme cases. As for the insurance executive's accomplishments as Chairman, Robinson said: "He keeps telling us how he hired three Negroes from poor areas to work, instead of college kids like the other guy did. But you can't stop there. What's three jobs? Right here in McElrath we have two hundred families to reach. It's going to take more than just three jobs. Folks out here just aren't interested in arguments about Robert's Rules or the CAC constitution. We want results, and we're not getting them."

Touring McElrath Park with Robinson we passed several burned out homes. "That's my old house there," he pointed to a pile of ashes. "We were lucky because my youngest woke up and cried. We all got out safe. That house over there, they weren't so lucky. Woman lost two kids in that fire and one died next day. Probably just as well, because he had all ten fingers burned off in the fire. What chance would he have in life?"

Mrs. Robinson's pet project was to set up day care centers for children, and to train mothers in entry-level skills so they could get local jobs. "The stores say they don't hire Negroes because there are none qualified. Well, I'd like to get a job school going for three months; then we'd show them who was qualified!" Mrs. Robinson's outlook on Mrs. Ritchie was similar to Andrew Howard's. "We had all colored classes, and she made us go out and get white kids to join them. Said she'd close down our classes if we didn't."

Melvin Mitchell was a black foreman at a General Motors plant. He lived close to McElrath Park, but in a new, split level home. He was Secretary of the Community Action Council and, simultaneously, Vice President of Mrs. Ritchie's Citizens Committee. He held both the insurance executive and the history professor in low regard. "We should have a brand new CAC. What we have now is a lot of scar tissue. No matter what we do, those guys will still be lining up people for and against each other and holding up programs." He was happy OEO had funded Mrs. Ritchie's Head

Start rather than the CAC proposal.

During the interview, Mitchell asked what could be done about the bad housing conditions in the area. He produced a set of blueprints he had obtained from various sources, all of low-income housing. One of them was for a low-income community center, another for inexpensive housing units especially designed to be built in areas that had neither sewerage nor running water. "These are what the people need. But those dam fools spend all their time raising points of order. We just can't get programs going. I'm fed up with this damn nonsense, and I'm ashamed to look my own people in the eye when they ask me what help the program is giving the poor. I do think we could come up with a new CAC, with some of the old CAC and some of the Citizens Committee, and some new blood, if we could just get around that 10% requirement of OEO. That's what the insurance executive holds over our heads, that 10%." I told him OEO had discretionary power to waive that 10% requirement and gave him a few appropriate telephone numbers.

David Low and John Peoples, both black, were members of the CAC. They knocked on my motel door early Sunday morning and asked to talk about "the mess we're in." According to Peoples, neither the insurance executive nor the history professor was "anything but a headache. We go to meetings, and one walks in with his nose in Roberts Rules, the other comes in waving the CAC constitution, and we can't find a way out. The poor just aren't being helped. We don't claim to represent the poor. We are Negro, but we both have good jobs and we eat well. When all this started, we took part because we were invited to by the Interfaith Council of Ministers. For a year, we just let the power structure run the show, thinking because they were executives they knew how to get things done. But they don't. There are real problems here. We need programs that give people motivation, especially the young. A white boy, or a middle-class Negro boy, usually has some tentative plans by the time he's halfway through high school. But in some places here, the boys don't even get through high school. What's worse, they don't care. They can't see any future."

In fact, the only positive achievements in the Portage County programs had come from Mrs. Ritchie, who had foreseen the failures of both the insurance executive and the history professor, and seized the initiative to start her own Head Start program. She told me that her original intention was to work through the Community Action Council — "But it got all bogged down between those guys, so I decided to go it alone. They still don't look like they're doing much, do they?"

The final interview I did in Portage County summed up with unintended irony the problems of the entire CAC. Victor Biasella, Chairman of the Board's Personnel Committee, was charged with the task of finding a new Executive Director. "We have a committee including three professional personnel men and a poor woman," he proudly informed me. "We have only been in operation about three weeks, but I don't think we'll have results within the next month. Maybe longer. I know we don't have any programs, and I know that a year has been lost. But I am not going to stand up and say to the Board, 'Here is the man I recommend' until I find the right man. Perfection is called for, and that's how I intend to perform. No matter how long it takes!"

Back at OEO, I recommended that we terminate the existing Community Action Council and encourage formation of a new agency with a clear proviso barring the present and past chairmen of the CAC from participation. It was a recommendation that went the distance. As Ed May wrote to Shriver, "The attached report is a case study of bungling ... this kind of program should be shut down, the money returned to OEO and no further funds expended or provided until a new, viable ... group is created .... it is high time that OEO begin to admit that in some counties in this country the shakers and movers don't want to see the program succeed and that the minority in these counties which does, doesn't know how to make it so."

My report came back with Shriver's handwritten endorsement: "I'm ready to shut down a few using whatever authority I have."

Chapter 15: The Migrants of Washington's Yakima Valley

My next assignment sent me to the West Coast, to the State of Washington where the newspaper clippings revealed that a community action program was reportedly bogged down in a turf war between local Democratic Party leaders and labor union officials frm the Central Labor Council over who would represent the poor — or, more accurately, who would get to decide who represented the poor. Each side claimed a historic right to speak on behalf of the poor — and, consequently, the right to name their own delegates to the community action board to fill the seats reserved for the poor and so control the jobs. Reports indicated the poor themselves were not consulted by either the labor leaders or the Democratic Party leaders.

The chief labor figure was Larry King, President of the Central Labor Council. I met with him and his colleagues at his home, and learned too late how important it was to keep your guard up when tangling with union leaders, or young newspaper reporters. As was becoming standard procedure, King demanded to know who sent me, who I was talking to, what I was finding out, what my recommendations would be, and to whom I would report. When I politely declined to be cross-examined, King refused to continue the interview and showed me the door.

Over the next few days I interviewed the other players. Nobody in the dispute struck me as entirely right or wrong. On balance I thought the labor guys were more likely to involve the poor than were the politicians, although I did not get back to King with that conclusion.

The controversy between King's labor group and the politicians had boiled over in the papers for weeks before I arrived. When a local reporter asked to interview me, I realized that a "no comment" might result in another in a rising trend of editorials then appearing around the country that blasted OEO and Shriver for keeping secrets from the press about the problems of local programs. Foolishly thinking that by some process of osmosis I had learned how to handle the press from the seasoned reporters I'd worked with in Haddad's office, I decided giving a local reporter the inside story would pressure the labor guys and the political types to step aside and let the poor have a chance. After getting the young reporter covering the feud to agree that whatever I told him would be off the record, I filled him in on the details. The resulting story was on the desks back at OEO before I checked out of my hotel in Richland. The reporter may have tried to keep his promise of keeping me "off the record", but his editor had no such scruples. The next edition of the *Tri-City Herald* headlined a page one story:

"RIVAL POVERTY GROUP THREATENED IF CAC FAILS TO MAKE CHANGES".

> "The Benton-Franklin Community Action Committee may find itself supplanted by a rival 'War on Poverty' organization unless it makes sweeping changes in its membership, informed sources disclosed today," the paper declared. "Joseph Wilkins, Inspector from OEO who visited the Tri-Cities last week and this week investigating complaints by the Benton-Franklin Central Labor Council refused to comment on his findings. He did admit that he was directed to the Tri-Cities to look into organized labor's representation on CAC and alleged irregularities in the hiring of the executive director."

For those who still hadn't figured it out, the rest of the story hung it around my neck every other line, with such evasions as:

> "Wilkins said he is filing his report this week with Sargent Shriver, head of OEO, but that his conclusions and recommendations must remain confidential until acted upon by OEO .... Informants predict Wilkins' report will

> recommend changes in CAC bylaws .... The report is expected to suggest .... 'Right now', the source explained, 'the impression is....' .... regarding the hiring the source said investigation revealed five facts: ;... But Wilkins' report will make no recommendations on the hiring procedures, the informant added .... Sources said the report will express the belief ...."

As I was learning, labor leaders knew how to fight Washington-style. The article had been faxed to OEO's headquarters, where it won wide circulation. It was a long trip home, knowing I was heading into what would be a critical reception. The hoo-rah from the reporters still working in Inspections would be bad.

"Gee," reporter Jack Williams said with a straight face when I got back to Washington. "Wonder who the informed source was?"

"No goddam comment!" I snarled. There are some lessons you only learn when your teacher has a baseball bat. I didn't realize it at the time, but the lesson came just when I needed it. I was about to spend a long few years up to my ears in newspaper controversies back home, which eventually lead to one Member of Congress threatening me with a charge of contempt of congress for quoting, of all people, Mark Twain.

***

Back in Washington finishing up my report and getting ready for the next field assignments, I ran into Clint Bamberger, national director of OEO's Legal Services Program, then in its first year of operation. Bamberger, a successful partner in a Baltimore law firm, had answered Shriver's call for help establishing OEO's program setting up legal services for the poor, to be run by local non-profits dominated by lawyers but still complying with the Economic Opportunity Act requirement that the programs include the "maximum feasible participation" of the poor. Meeting that goal ran squarely up against the legal profession's strong insistence that there be no middleman between client and lawyer – a time-honored way of insuring the lawyer represented only his client, without any outside influence or interference with the lawyer acting in his client's best interest. How, then, to allow the poor to participate if they and not the client were controlling the lawyer's pay?

When he learned what I had been doing for Inspections, and that I was a law student myself, his interest quickened. He invited me to stop by his office for a chat. I did and we talked about what I had learned on my field trips and the thorny problems he faced. He and Earl Johnson, his deputy and eventual successor, were looking for somebody who could make sure the poor could get on local Legal Services governing boards and not be shut out by the often conservative local Bar Associations. They were looking for a young lawyer already admitted to the Bar, which initially left me out. But my experience fit their needs better than they expected. From my point of view some, but not constant, field trips would be needed, and the scheduling could be flexible. It seemed an ideal way to make my living and still get back to law school. I agreed to think it over and talk again on my return from my immediate assignment. There was no direct job offer, but he strongly hinted one could be mine for the asking, inspecting local legal services programs to make sure the poor were being involved as much as possible. It was an exciting prospect.

It is a cliché but often true that, as they say "It never rains but it pours." I was reviewing the files for my next assignment, this time returning to the West Coast to check out problems with the migrant programs in the lush Yakima Valley farming district when I received a call from Paul Porreca. He was a young lawyer in Millville, New Jersey who in 1962 was the Democratic candidate for Congress in my home district, New Jersey's 2nd Congressional, on which my long-term hopes to get to Congress were pinned. After narrowly losing to the Republican incumbent in 1962, Porreca had turned his energy to his law practice and his duties as the elected Commissioner of Parks and Public Property in the City of Millville. He played a key role in establishing a local community action agency covering

New Jersey's Salem, Cumberland and Gloucester Counties — three farming counties bordering the Delaware River and Bay. It raised high hopes among the rural poor throughout the three counties, especially in the rural black communities that lay among the ruins of a once prosperous oyster and shellfish industry on the small tributaries that fed into the Delaware Bay. Those hopes, easily raised, were soon frustrated by OEO's inability to process applications with reasonable efficiency. After nine months of delays and false starts, limited funds finally came through in April of 1966. But much damage had been caused by the disappointed early hopes. Tensions grew into arguments; arguments into controversy, controversy into factional battles, and the whole mess erupted in the headlines. An executive director hired late in November was fired in May. Searching for a replacement, Porreca called to see if I would take the job. Suddenly faced with two welcome but very different prospects, I told him I'd get back to him on my return from the West Coast.

I now had much to think about on my flight west. For a year and a half I had been immersed in the War on Poverty, in its efforts and controversy from the inner dynamics of its grant-making at the Washington end to meeting the poor and their would-be saviors all across America. I had seen poverty firsthand, from the coal mines of Appalachia to the Indian reservations of the far West; in backwoods towns of the Deep South; the cold of the North Country; and in the slums of the cities.

The process had changed me — had taken me from a world of comfortable budget bureaucrats with clean desks to places where teenagers hustled for $1.25 an hour to help their younger brothers and sisters eat. I had dreamt of a life in politics without fully thinking through what I would do if I were ever elected. Now I knew. Government programs were no longer abstract theories for me, accepted as parts of a political creed inherited from the prior generation. I now realized they meant work, schooling, hope and dignity to the Americans at the bottom of society. I also had learned something of the limits of such programs and the need to keep them responsive to the times and to the lives of their intended beneficiaries.

But a political future required a law degree, and the same assignments that took me around the country were keeping me from a return to law school. I was still a dozen credit hours short of graduation. I would have to move quickly if I intended to re-enroll in the Fall semester. Carrying a course load, even in night school, would be impossible if I had to spend my weekdays traveling on assignments around the country.

Here was a tough decision. I was caught between two tempting prospects; either working for the National Legal Services program in Washington, D.C., or running a local anti-poverty agency in South Jersey. Weighing the choice gave me a lot to think about on the long flights to and from the Yakima Valley. I was not used to thinking analytically about my career. Thus far I had had no time for such sophistication, having expected to just put my head down and bulldoze my way to get my law degree and go into politics, meanwhile supporting my growing family. That had carried me so far. Now it was time to think more clearly about where I was going, and how to get there.

The Washington job had a powerful pull. It would inevitably bring me into contact with the national leaders of the Bar – the kind of men who could give a young lawyer strong support in his career, including recommendations of clerkships for federal appellate judges; perhaps even to clerk for Justices of the United States Supreme Court; and certainly to promising positions in the U.S. Department of Justice. From any of those, a distinguished career could be launched. There were other advantages. Finishing law school, which was located near DuPont Circle and just a short walk from OEO's offices at 19th and M, would be a snap if I didn't have to travel too much on weekdays. I could bring the family back to live in Washington. We could raise the kids in a city that was, in my eyes, the center of the world. Universities and bookstores were everywhere; the White House was just a few blocks away; Congress and the Supreme Court a short taxi ride down Massachusetts Avenue.

Taking the job in New Jersey would lead in a very different direction. For one thing, distance would clearly be a problem. I'd be able to live at home in Brigantine with Maryanne and the kids, but it was a 40 mile drive from Brigantine to the community action agency's Millville headquarters. Even assuming I could transfer my law school credits from Washington to a law school in Philadelphia or Camden, that would add 45 more miles at the end of the day and a 60 mile drive home from school every night. Three hours of driving a 145 mile round trip every day wrapped around an active work schedule and the rigors of law studies was a daunting prospect. More to the point, a move back to South Jersey was unlikely to advance my legal career after I won my law degree. It was, by any measure, a backwater.

Maryanne, I knew, would be in my corner and would support whatever decision I made, so long as we ended up near good schools for the kids.

It did not take me long to decide where to go — nor to reverse that decision, and then reverse it again — and again. I could think as coldly as I wanted about the advantages of Washington over South Jersey, but something in me resisted that choice. I boarded my flight to Seattle with indecision running rampant in my mind.

***

From Seattle I caught a commuter flight to the Yakima Valley. We flew low enough to see the majestic snow covered peak of Mt. Ranier at eye level from the plane. My eyes were on that scene, but my mind was on the decision I'd have to make when I flew the 3,000 miles back to the other side of the continent.

Realizing this would probably be my last field assignment for OEO, I put aside my thoughts on which job to take and forced myself to pay attention to the job at hand. I was to report on a dispute between the statewide migrant program and the local community action agency over who would control anti-poverty funds for migrants. The Yakima Valley is apple country, sixty miles of irrigated bottomland in Eastern Washington replete with apple and fruit orchards, hops, sugar beets and peas. The valley is divided by a ridge through which the Yakima River slices at Union Gap, allowing room only for a road, a railroad track, and the river itself. In the upper valley fruit orchards predominated. There, the more desirable stand-up work of picking apples, peaches, cherries and other orchard crops went to the Anglos who floated out of the migrant stream and became seasonal farmworkers residing year-round in the area. In the lower valley, stoop crops were left for the Hispanics and blacks to bend their backs and pick.

One of the problems in dealing with migrant poverty was the relative unpredictability of their work. A shortage of labor on the coast might draw migrants away from Yakima for most of the summer. A frost or drought on the coast could mean a surplus of migrants in Yakima. The decision to shift a day care center from Yakima to the coast or vice versa would necessarily call for a sponsoring agency large enough to make broad scale decisions and to coordinate moves. The trade off was that it was harder to give the poor a meaningful voice in state-wide programs. In the ideal world envisioned by OEO, representatives of the migrants in the Yakima Valley would be given seats on the local community action board, and funds would flow through that board to programs operating in the migrant camps. It was not, however, an ideal world.

The prospect of federal money to address the problems of the migrants provoked, as was all too usual with OEO's programs, a turf fight between competing agencies; this time both of them creatures of OEO planning grants. The resulting friction led to local charges against the statewide program of waste and of what was more alarming, kickbacks. That sort of abuse was easier to spot than almost anything else. Veteran reporter Jack Williams had taught me to look for what he called the $10 ashtray syndrome. "Go into the top guy's office and look around," he said. "If you see expensive furniture, good carpeting, and stuff on his desk you wouldn't buy for your own, start digging. You can bet that a guy who treats himself to a $10 ashtray is looking after himself first and the poor last."

There were no $10 ashtrays in the migrant programs, nor unwarranted use of rental cars, nor kickbacks. Mrs. LaFramboise, a voluble and energetic Mexican-American mother of eight who was active in promoting migrant care contemptuously dismissed the charges of kickbacks: "You think I'm going to work my fingers to the bone raising money, and then see a kickback? Ha! Show me this kickbacker! I'll fry him like a tortilla!"

Far in the back of a camp in the lower valley, where the stoop labor migrants were sheltered, I sat around a fire one evening with old timers who had sharp insights into the limits of programs designed by social workers and do-gooders. "Ain't no sense talking about job training," one man said, poking the fire. "Folks got more immediate problems like beans and beds. Families come in here late nights after being on the road further down, they got no money, no food, no place to stay. Most of all, they got no work, because next day they gotta register and get to the shape-up, and that's for work the day after. So it's gonna be least two nights before they get any money. What we do," he nodded at another old timer, "we put up the first night's rent and give them food. Then next morning we take them with us to wherever we got work lined up. They get a better shot at working right away, and we get our rent money back at day's end."

The talk around that campfire nourished in me a skepticism about programs designed from the top down. I was becoming convinced the drafters of the Economic Opportunity Act were right; there was no substitute for letting the poor have a say in the design and running of programs.

Dining at a Yakima Valley crossroads restaurant the last night of my trip, the offer to run the program in South Jersey was much on my mind. On a small atlas I carried with me I picked out the places I'd been since joining the Office of Economic Opportunity; places like Mission, South Dakota; Prestonsburg, Kentucky; Plattsburg, New York; Ravenna, Ohio; Greene County, Alabama; Jackson, Mississippi; Sparta, Michigan and Chicago. There hardly seemed a type of poverty I hadn't seen, nor an anti-poverty idea

I hadn't watched somebody try.

***

The late night flight from Seattle to Washington, D.C. had few passengers. Unable to sleep with thoughts of the choice facing me, I sat quietly reading. Across the aisle, also reading late into the night, was Senator Wayne Morse of Oregon. It was the second chance meeting I had with Senator Morse; the first had been in August of 1964 when Lyndon Johnson, having declared War on Poverty and after signing the Civil Acts Act in July, decided to set himself up as a War President in the style of his own hero, Franklin D. Roosevelt. The closest thing he had to a war was Vietnam, where thus far America's presence had been limited to thousands of "advisors" not technically authorized to take part in the actual combat between the North Vietnamese and our allies in South Vietnam.

Early in August President Johnson insisted there had been an unprovoked communist attack on US warships in the international waters of the Gulf of Tonkin. The night was foggy, no ships were actually hit, and the sonar reports were ambiguous as to whether there was any hostile action at all. Johnson was said later to have admitted, "for all I know, what those sonar boys heard could have been a whale fart" rather than a torpedo attack. But the incident served his purpose and he seized upon it. He demanded a resolution from Congress authorizing him to use whatever force he thought necessary to protect the interests of the United States — in effect, a blank check to wage war without the formal declaration of war that might trigger hearings into the whys and wherefores.

When the Gulf of Tonkin resolution was debated on August 7, 1964, a few days after the alleged incident, I was in the Senate Visitors Gallery watching the show. Two senators were suspicious of Johnson's claim; Wayne Morse of Oregon and Ernest Gruening of Alaska. Both had served with Johnson when he was the arm-twisting Senate Majority leader. Neither trusted him. Morse, who had been in turn a Republican, an independent, and now a Democrat, demanded proof that the US destroyers, the *Maddox* and the *C. Turner Joy*, were in fact fired upon as alleged — and that they were outside of Vietnamese territorial waters when the incident occurred. "Produce the ship's logs!" he demanded — only to be shouted and hooted down by his fellow senators. My ambition to be a US Senator suffered a setback that day as I watched the Senators' taunting response to a perfectly reasonable request. I stayed to watch the Gulf of Tonkin resolution pass by a vote of 88-2. Morse and Gruening remained adamant to the end in opposition.

After the vote, I headed for a lunch of Senate bean soup and a sandwich at one of my favorite Washington spots — a hideaway restaurant located just off the Senate floor along the magnificently tiled and frescoed hallway near the Senate chamber.

Waiting for my sandwich, I looked up from my paper to find Senator Morse standing at my table, crowded out of the Senatorial section and anxious to have lunch before his next committee meeting. I waved him into a chair and offered him my newspaper. He accepted the chair, declined the newspaper, and ordered lunch.

"I just came from watching the Gulf of Tonkin debate," I told him after introducing myself. He still had steam coming out of his ears.

"They ought to know better than to trust Lyndon Johnson," he sputtered. "The man is a goddamn liar, as corrupt as they come. Always has been, always will be." He then treated me to his entire arsenal of objections to the Gulf of Tonkin resolution.

When we met again in 1966 on the flight back from the West Coast to Washington, D.C., I reminded him of our lunch in the Senate restaurant the day the Gulf of Tonkin Resolution passed. He had insisted that the Tonkin Resolution was a blank check for Johnson to involve us in a disastrous military adventure. The nearly two years since then proved him right. 7,000 American troops died in those two years; another 35,000 were wounded in action. The count of the "body bags" used for our dead was climbing daily. Since the day the Tonkin Resolution passed over Morse's objections President Johnson had ordered over 429,000 troops into combat in Vietnam. He was keeping American planes bombing the Viet Cong relentlessly in Operation Rolling Thunder. Even as war correspondents questioned whether we were losing the war "for the hearts and minds" of the Vietnamese people, American generals boasted of body counts of enemy dead and of "seeing the light at the end of the tunnel." The draft was re-activated. Massive protests against the war roiled the country and divided hawks and doves into bitter conflicts. It became clear that Johnson's insistence that we could afford "guns and butter" was nonsense; the funds for the War on Poverty were already being swallowed up by the War in Vietnam.

As we flew across the country in the wee hours of the night I told Morse my own dream of being a United States Senator. He nodded approvingly. We discussed New Jersey. I told him of the offer to run a community action agency, wondering whether in my Republican district a job so controversial would cripple my chances for elective office someday. He encouraged me to take it. I mentioned how I admired New Jersey's Senator Clifford Case, a moderate Republican known for such signs of personal integrity as riding the public bus daily from his apartment in Washington to the Senate. "He's not that moderate," Morse commented as he snapped off his overhead light and lay back to sleep. "When you're ready, give me a call. I can tell you how to beat him." It would be years before I could run for office. Still, it felt oddly comforting to have my personal dream taken at face value by a United States Senator.

As he slept I finally realized what had been bothering me about taking the National Legal Services job in Washington. If I took that job and it led on as I expected, I would be choosing a life where what I could accomplish would be decided by whoever might appoint me to various positions along the way. I might have power to do good, perhaps even eventually shape policy. But that power would always be dependent on other individuals. If the Administration changed, I might find myself suddenly with no horse to ride, and no quick way to earn a living or accomplish anything worthwhile. Worse, I could find myself in some dead end job, serving out my time until I could retire — in effect I might end up looking out the window of a government office hoping for snow so I could go home early.

Compared to the New Jersey job an appointed job in Washington offered little prospect of leading to elective office. And of one thing I was sure; a man who had a seat in Congress was, in the long run, his own man. Appointed officials come and go. Presidents change every four or eight years, and their appointees get replaced. The odds of getting to Congress were long — after all, half of the candidates who run for Congress lose. The odds were a lot longer for a Democrat like me in the solidly Republican district in which I lived. But if I could build up to a seat in Congress, my fate would be in my own hands, subject only to the will of the voters every few years. Those who made it had, in my eyes, the best chance to make a difference in the world. It was worth the chance. Running an anti-poverty agency in South Jersey was a great deal less glamourous, and my future would be far less promising. But it seemed to me that the more time I spent working on the problems that existed in the district, the more effective I could someday be if I were to ever get to Congress.

I decided to let Washington go, and take the New Jersey job, not at all sure I was doing the right thing.

I shall be telling this with a sigh
Somewhere ages and ages hence:
Two roads converged in a wood and I,
I took the one less traveled by.
And that has made all the difference.

"The Road Not Taken", by Robert Frost

Chapter 16: Running a Community Action Agency

August 1, 1966 was my first day at work as Executive Director of the community action agency for the three rural Southern New Jersey counties of Gloucester, Cumberland and Salem. In my life, it was a day to mark with a white stone.

Nearly 3 years had passed since the assassination of President Kennedy ripped through my idealism and my political hopes. Working for Bill Haddad and the OEO had taught me much. It gave me an invaluable sense of the lofty ideals of public policy and the practical difficulties of bringing them to life in the rough and tumble – and apathy– of the real world. It felt good to be given a challenging responsibility and the authority and potential resources to meet it.

On a personal level, two years of steady employment had made a big difference in our finances. With four small children to feed and another expected we were not out of the woods, but things eased enough that on my new salary of $12,500 we were able to get a mortgage and buy our first house, a 3 bedroom, 1 bath $14,900 rancher in Brigantine. Maryanne, who gamely put up with a half dozen moves from apartment to apartment while going through four pregnancies and now on her fifth, largely on her own and stretching far too few dollars to cover far too many expenses while I was bulldozing ahead on college and law school and sudden job changes and constant trips, came into her own at last. Life now at least offered her own house and the stability of a home where all of her supportive family and mine were within a few blocks, and where in summer she could take the kids to the beach every day. While my life was filled with challenging and exciting events, she had missed most of it, loyally sacrificing her own education to see to it that our growing family grew up in a happy and loving environment. She never complained, nor pointed out how my single-minded pursuit of my goals left her doing the heavy lifting of raising the kids. Far beyond that, she became the center of love and support for her, and my, younger brothers and sisters as they grew up in Brigantine.

The move to Brigantine let me see more of my family, but still required an eighty-mile round trip to work every day. Our youth made it easier to handle all that was going on in our lives, and at work I and my new staff had plenty of energy to meet the challenges. At 27, I was only a year or two older than the staff I was to direct. We did not seem unduly young to ourselves. The soldiers heading off to Vietnam – and the ones coming back in body bags – were even younger than we were. The blacks coursing down the streets of cities calling for violence and rebellion were our age. H. Rapp Brown was 23; Stokely Carmichael 25. Among those preaching non-violent protest John Lewis was 26; Julian Bond was 26. Heavyweight champion Muhammad Ali, banned from boxing in America for his religious convictions and refusal to serve in the Army, was 24. The flower children of Haight-Ashbury and the drug culture were of our generation. So were those who sang of the times: Paul Simon and Art Garfunkle, at the top of the charts with "Sounds of Silence" were 25; of the Beatles, John Lennon and Ringo Starr were 26; Paul McCartney 24, and George Harrison 23. Jerry Garcia of The Grateful Dead was 24; Mick Jagger of the Rolling Stones 23; Diana Ross of the Supremes 22, Cher, whose 1965 "I Got You, Babe" was the first of her many hits, was 20. In the world of movies, Robert Redford was 29; Jane Fonda, his co-star in "Barefoot in the Park" was 28. Among the young activists of the day "Don't trust anyone over thirty!" became the catchword.

As Wordsworth wrote about another time of upheaval and challenge:

Bliss was it in that dawn to be alive.
But to be young was very heaven!

The sense of challenge John F. Kennedy brought to public affairs had not died out among our generation. From civil rights protests to farmworker's boycotts to break-through music to rebellion against the misdirected authoritarianism of the Vietnam debacle, there was in the air a heady mixture of youthful idealism, of commitment to causes larger than one's self. I remembered Kennedy's use of the Greek definition of happiness: "The full use of one's powers, along lines of excellence, in a life affording them scope." My challenge was on a humbler scale, but still thrilling.

***

A "community action agency" for those uncertain of its definition, was a new creature in public affairs; a locally-organized and operated entity usually but not inevitably a non-profit corporation which could be recognized by federal agencies such as the US Office of Economic Opportunity as qualified to receive and disburse federal funds by direct grant or by contract in pursuit of federal policies. Grants and contracts could follow a universal design, such as HeadStart or the Neighborhood Youth Corps, or could be unique and experimental so long as the funding agency found the activity consistent with its own authorized goals. It differed from government bodies such as school boards, employment offices or police departments in that the public was invited and encouraged to help design and operate the community action agency and the grants and contracts it administered. A major difference from government was the legislative requirement that community action agencies involve the poor to, as the Economic Opportunity Act mandated, "the maximum feasible extent," preferably as members of its governing board.

The community action agency whose Board had hired me and I was now to direct spread over three sizeable counties in Southern New Jersey. The area of my new responsibilities stretched 55 miles from Shellpile on the Maurice River northwest to Westville, across the Delaware River from the Philadelphia International Airport. An estimated 350,000 people lived in the 1200 square miles of the three combined counties. The chief towns; Woodbury, Salem, Glassboro, Vineland, Bridgeton, and Millville — were farm towns of long standing, some older than the United States itself.

Woodbury had personal significance for me. My ancestor John Wilkins arrived there with a group of Quakers in 1677 as an 8 year old indentured servant bound to work until adulthood to pay for his passage and his keep. By the time of the Declaration of Independence in 1776 his descendants had established the Wilkins Inn in Woodbury, a building which still stands across from the Quaker Meeting House.

All six towns were market centers for their surrounding farms – proud of their histories and slow to either recognize or accept change. Counties in other states call their elected officials commissioners, or judges, or selectmen. In New Jersey they are called "Chosen Freeholders", historically meaning they owned their land free of debt. That was no longer a requirement for office, but the historical title still reflected local attitudes towards the thousands of dirt-poor farmworkers who owned little more than the shirts on their backs.

My new office was at the Millville Airport, a collection of concrete runways and wooden World War II buildings far out in the pine woods that served as a training base for flyers during the War and was given to Millville as surplus property afterward. Paul Porreca, as Millville's Commissioner of Parks and Public Property, arranged free space at the airport for our headquarters. We had four buildings and could have had a dozen. They were one-story wood-frame affairs used as barracks, classrooms and offices when thousands of student pilots trained there during the War. They were neither well heated in winter nor air conditioned in summer, but they were clean and had plenty of windows that opened to the breeze and lots of parking. Best of all, they were free and counted toward the 10% matching "local share" of the costs we were required to come up with as conditions of our grants.

Much but by no means all of the poverty population consisted of farmworkers, both migrants and the stay-behinds. Our chief communities each had its own problems of unemployment, under-education, and poor housing. Salem and Woodbury had been favored by a long tradition of hard-working farmers and a heavy influence of Quakers. There was poverty, but it was masked by the greenery of summer. In Glassboro and Millville wide streets shaded by generous old trees standing guard over trim lawns, carefully tended shrubs and solid houses with wide, inviting porches gave way to shabbier yards and broken fence gates and eventually to smaller houses whose paint had weathered off, and soon to potholed roads leading to trailer parks and shacks with dismantled cars perched on cinder blocks in their front yards. Vineland and Bridgeton offered more urban scenes. Even there, however, the tallest buildings seldom reached six stories. Each town boasted its own daily newspaper, although most carried only local news and sports with a passing nod to the larger world.

Opening on a minor point, my first decision was to change our name. I knew from having so often searched the clippings files at OEO for troubled programs that everything we did – the good and certainly the bad – would be grist for the headline writers, especially in South Jersey, which had no major league teams of its own, no celebrities, and few local scandals sensational enough to amuse newspaper readers. For months the local papers had run stories of the controversies plaguing the organization I now directed. But headline writers have no room for stuff like "Southwest Regional Economic Opportunity Corporation is Plagued by Troubles." They preferred a space-saving acronym, as in "SREOC Fights Erupt," which fit neatly atop the story. I had no wish to go through my days as the director of something pronounced "Schwree-Ock." Clearly a new name for the organization was in order. JFK's remark about "a life affording scope" was on my mind. Fighting poverty in South Jersey was as much scope as my life had thus far offered. "SCOPE" had the right ring to it, so my first step was to change the name of the organization to the "Southwest Citizens Organization for Poverty Elimination," on which no editor would waste precious headline space when he could shorten it to "SCOPE." It wasn't perfect but it was positive-sounding, quick and cheap.

Believing the bright promises of the early days of the War on Poverty our Board President Bob Shaffer, an active and involved young Presbyterian minister, had organized local community action councils in the six larger towns. Money was borrowed from local banks and offices were opened in storefronts and other space donated by local governments anxious to support anything that promised new jobs in town. Each had a staff person lining up work assignments for the limited number of funded Neighborhood Youth Corps slots we expected, and planning for the long-delayed funding of larger programs expected to come through any day from OEO.

Three young educators had come aboard in anticipation of running the programs for which early planning money had trickled through. Patricia D'Augustine, a teacher, had a matching talent for practicality and plain speaking, coupled with a commitment to social justice — although she would not in a hundred years put so serious a label on so obvious a motivation. Pat coordinated our migrant farm worker education programs. Rosemarie Russo, a high-school counselor with a quick and keen mind, had a gift for organizational detail and planning. She headed our Community Services activities. The third member of the trio of educators, Martha Woodward, had a gentle disposition and a dedication to the children of the poor. She was a natural to direct our Head Start programs. Together they formed a team that never missed a chance to move the program forward.

It happened that my first days on the job came at the peak of the migrant farm worker season. Our three counties drew more than half of all the migrants who worked New Jersey's fields. It was necessary, for the brief months while the migrants were at work, that they have places to live convenient to the crops they picked. Far off the roads, out of sight in the remote reaches of the fields, were the shacks which housed them. The farmers provided housing with the barest of amenities. Few had running water or flush toilets. Electricity was often carried over a dangling line strung from the nearest pole.

Driving to and from my initial meetings with our Board members in the long summer evenings I was immersed in scenes of growing crops coming into harvest season. Southern New Jersey is essentially produce truck-farming country. A wide variety of crops grown there were trucked to nearby cities for sale to the supermarkets, or sold under contract to local food processors such as Campbell Soup or Bird's Eye Frozen Foods, or sold direct to consumers during the season at outdoor roadside farm markets. Fields lush with snap beans and beets, blueberries and broccoli, cantaloupes and cucumbers, parsley, peppers, sweet Jersey corn and succulent Jersey tomatoes surrounded me on every side. Their scents drifted into my car at every crossroad stop sign. But those plants and vines had to be tended and harvested by the hands of migrant workers who stooped to weed, cut, pick and place the harvest into baskets before storms or pests could ruin it. After that was done, however, they were unwanted and unwelcome.

Not all farmworkers fit the same description. Puerto Rican men were recruited through contracts arranged through the farm lobby under the nominal supervision of the Puerto Rican government. Those men were expected to tough it out in whatever housing was arranged. They brought no families with them. The most wretched farmworkers were the coastal migrants. These were black families who followed the harvests from Florida fields picked in early spring up along the eastern seaboard through the summer to Maine's potato harvests of the fall, bringing their babies with them in decrepit old cars or run-down school buses. Some stayed in the area year around, although they were so poor that getting through the winter was a major challenge.

Numerous as they were, farmworkers were not the whole of the population of poverty in the three counties, even during the harvest season. One in five families in our area lived on less than $50 a week. Unemployment was high; low educational levels the norm; substandard housing common.

Nor, except for the farmworkers, was such poverty predominately black. I had seen this for myself on my trips to Appalachia, the North Country, and the migrant worker camps of the Northwest. Whites were the majority, had the media realized it, of the poor.

But the media did not realize it. Perhaps because of our vigorous fighting for civil rights as the Head Start programs in the Deep South got underway, the Poverty Wars became so identified with the civil rights revolution that OEO's efforts were seen almost exclusively as programs designed for blacks. Anti-poverty programs could be and easily were painted by white conservatives as giveaways to blacks — a distortion reflected in the coded but virulent racism that rose to oppose anti-poverty programs which were, in any true light, statistically far more beneficial to poor whites than to poor blacks. It was a mis-perception shared equally by the media, by poor whites, and by newly-empowered African-Americans determined to claim their place at the table. At the national level Martin Luther King, Jr. saw the trap. He was beginning to argue that racial injustice should be seen not as somehow in competition for resources with the needs of the poor, but as part and parcel of the larger economic deprivation that afflicted the poor of all races. The media ignored him in favor of covering the fiery younger black leaders who were jockeying for leadership through sensational demands for "Black Power." Such posturing brought new life to the Ku Klux Klan, whose activities promptly increased. Overall, such coverage made it easy for the white public – and much of the black public – to perceive the poverty war as a black man's battle. The coverage had obvious internal contradictions. When they weren't showing angry blacks and whites in threatening pictures, news stories, television specials, and magazine photographs of the day commonly featured the suffering faces of black people, usually in settings of personal tragedy and hardship. Images of that sort were easy enough to find among the poorest black families. Almost 20 years after Ralph Ellison's powerful "Invisible Man," blacks who were first stereotyped as happy cotton-picking slaves, then as shuffling darkies, and later as murderous criminals, were now stereotyped as poverty's woebegone victims. Except for athletes and entertainers few African Americans were shown as successful, confident and self-reliant. Bill Cosby reached TV in 1965 as part of the "I Spy" series, but it wasn't until 1968 that NBC risked having Diahann Carroll play a doctor's nurse on the NBC series "Julia", the first casting of a successful black professional in a series.

***

To their credit my predecessor, and the Board, had recruited a good staff. With local offices open and people looking forward to the long-delayed programs, in essence the organizational plumbing was in place but we were receiving only a trickle of funds. The hiatus in the program's administration before my arrival left several grant applications languishing in the OEO pipeline. My first priority was to get the money coming in. In that effort I knew I could count on help from my Washington contacts. OEO's grant-makers had learned how hard it is to take the spirit behind a policy and apply it to reality on the ground. Having someone with my understanding of the agency's goals take charge of a local organization was, from their point of view, a chance to see their theories tested under the most favorable conditions for which they could hope. On these I was able to get fast action. By mid-September we had won enough funding for a Neighborhood Youth Corps program to put 135 kids to work, and to hire a full time director, full time counselor, and a secretary-bookkeeper to manage the payroll. A newly enthused board and staff set out to find jobs for those kids as secretarial aides, hospital aides, mechanic's helpers and similar assignments. Of the funded slots, 75 were for kids who had dropped out of school; the other 60 for those still in school. The influence of teachers like Pat, Rosemarie, and Martha insured a heavy commitment to getting the drop-outs back on the school track wherever possible.

While we organized the new programs, I was learning that, as D'Toqueville noted, Americans are great for joining organizations. In our small towns civic clubs and groups like the Lions, Elks, Jaycees and Chambers of Commerce thrived. I spoke at their weekly luncheons to explain what we were about; using the occasions to ask employers and local officials to give us a hand finding training positions for the kids we were enrolling. At first I tried to explain the theory of community action, but small town businessmen were not much interested in theories of community action. Talking about getting drop-outs and poor kids into the world of work was a different story. Attention focused and ears perked up. It was a rare speech when I didn't come away with a scrawled list of contacts to pass on to John Johnson, a big, bluff, African-American with a background of teaching and coaching we hired to run the Youth Corps program. Johnson was a down-to-earth kind of guy from Glassboro who could reach the kids and their parents – of whatever race — in plain language.

The difference between Washington theory and local reality soon hit home. Pat D'Augustine burst into my office one day: "Joe," she declared, "we have to teach these kids about birth control! Some of these girls are on their second pregnancy and they're not even 18!" I knew she was right. We had money to hire community aides, people from among the poor who served as outreach workers, letting their friends and neighbors know about our programs and encouraging them to take advantage of them. One of these, whom I will call "Mary Sue," had originally signed up as a participant in our Neighborhood Youth Corps program. She was 17, barely 5 feet tall, perhaps 100 pounds soaking wet, with a high, squeaky voice, blond hair and bright, bird-like blue eyes. A 7th grade dropout, she was on her second pregnancy and had never traveled more than 30 miles from home. Dirt poor and conscious of a wider world only because it appeared on TV, there was still a sparkle of curiosity in her eyes; something that offered hope she was tough enough to keep going no matter what. Her enthusiasm made her a natural for outreach work. Rosemarie Russo put her on the payroll as a community aide, and arranged for her to attend classes with the enrollees so she could work toward her G.E.D. When I had to deliver a grant application to New York on deadline, I asked Mary Sue to take it by bus from Millville, and let her take a girlfriend with her for safety. When she came back from the wonders of the Jersey Turnpike, Lincoln Tunnel, New York Port Authority and Manhattan taxicabs, I asked her what she thought of it all.

"It's all one piece!" she exclaimed. "It looked like you could start peeling back one street and the whole city would roll up like a carpet!"

When Pat D'Augustine raised the problem of birth control advice, it was Mary Sue who came to mind. There was, of course, no way Mary Sue's sex life or that of any of our enrollees was any of our business. For all I knew, she might be devoutly religious and opposed on that ground to any such activity. Or she might resent any prying into her personal life, or might simply be too shy to discuss the subject. I did know, however, that in the larger sense Pat was absolutely correct in her concern that unplanned pregnancies would have a tremendous effect on the girls in our programs.

I had no ready answer to the dilemma Pat raised. It might be an invasion of their privacy to foist birth control discussions on them, but it would be a dereliction of our duty not to make information available for those who sought it. The public was coming to the conclusion that birth control offered a reasonable chance for married couples to plan how fast and at what intervals they would have children. Condoms were readily available in local drugstores. "The Pill," available by prescription for several years, was reportedly used by almost one out of four couples, and President Johnson saw to it that OEO had legislative authority to fund family planning programs. But the issue was far from decided. The Catholic Church, a potent political influence in the Northeast and Mid-Atlantic states, saw sexual abstinence and the dubiously effective "rhythm method" as the sole acceptable means of avoiding pregnancy — a teaching that had little appeal to the unmarried young, for whom sex was seldom postponed pending discussions of family planning. The Church opposed not only the use of contraceptives, but the furnishing of information about their very existence. In Massachusetts it was still a felony as late as 1966 to sell contraceptives to unmarried couples. It had been only a year since the Supreme Court struck down a Connecticut law which made criminal the use of contraceptives by married couples.

What we had in our Youth Corps were by no means married couples. They were teenagers who were for the most part ignorant of modern means of birth control, certainly among the girls. Dispensing birth control information as part of the Youth Corps program was likely to generate a great deal of controversy, especially among Catholics, who showed promise of being strong local allies in the rest of our anti-poverty efforts.

Fortunately, the spirit of Pope John XXIII inspired a renewed commitment among religious people of many faiths, and decidedly among Catholics, to work toward social justice. Two of my most recent appearances had been before Catholic groups; one a seminar on poverty sponsored by the Camden Archdiocese that brought in priests, nuns and lay activists from all over the mid-Atlantic region; the other a gathering of nuns interested in what they could do to involve themselves in the anti-poverty effort. Many of the religious who worked with the poor were caught between the Church's hard line against birth control, and the evidence of their own experiences that the largest families were the poorest families, and that kids were having sex and were having it with no knowledge of how to avoid pregnancy.

The religious aspect of the question made little difference to me. On matters of religion I believed in the separation of church and state. Like many American Catholics I decided for myself how much attention I paid to Rome's preferences on how I lived my life – an anti-clerical tendency probably strengthened by my educational history. From kindergarten through law school I had never spent a day in a school not run by the Catholic Church. The experience left me skeptical about the Church's more rigid doctrines. Still, as the father of four children, with a fifth due come February, I could hardly preach what I so obviously didn't practice.

Of more immediate relevance was my near total ignorance of the subject. The Catholic school systems I attended did not deal with birth control except to condemn it without describing it, and the schoolyard jokes of boyhood were no help. My formal education about the use of condoms consisted of stern lectures from grizzled Marine Corps sergeants urging the troops to wear a rubber when having sex in Tijuana. Since part of my single night there at the age of 18 was spent in the Tijuana jail, the advice was of limited use. And not even the saltiest Marine would dare discuss birth control in a marital context. They made it clear condoms were to avoid catching the clap from prostitutes. They considered a Marine's relations with his wife were sacred and private. Nor had I any idea how dispensing birth control information to girls would work in a practical sense. Except for Marine Sergeants telling us to use condoms, the closest anyone ever came to explaining the female part of the human reproductive process in my hearing involved men who muttered about "female problems" while disclaiming any knowledge of "female plumbing."

"Do what you think best," I finally answered Pat. "I'll back you up whatever happens."

It was not the most informed decision I ever made, but was the best I could think of at the time. Happily, no controversy followed.

Chapter 17: The Fight in the Fields

In September potatoes and squash, leeks, watermelons, tomatoes and eggplants filled the fields in every direction, obscuring the bent backs of the migrants who moved along the rows picking them. Most migrant families were housed on the farms where they worked. Some arrived in old school buses painted blue or red — ramshackle affairs filled with black families and many babies, organized by black crew chiefs. Everyone old enough to pick, picked; those too young were locked in the cars and trucks. Tragic summer stories came as regularly as the crops themselves about the deaths of babies and little children left in migrants' cars with the windows rolled up to keep them in while their mothers worked the fields.

The VISTA program's Washington office recognized the traveling-circus nature of the migrants' lives, sent VISTA's to Florida in June to travel with the migrants as they followed the harvests north through the summer and fall. Although there was not much the volunteers could do in the traditional way, they were able to scout the communities near which the migrants worked for day care centers, health services and other programs available through churches and community action agencies like ours and to link the migrants to such efforts.

To South Jersey's farmers the VISTA volunteers appeared as union organizers — there to foment protest and strikes at their most vulnerable moment; the short window of time when the crops had to be harvested. The VISTA's weren't labor organizers, but almost everything they did to alleviate the misery of the migrants posed a threat to the farmers' control of their labor force. The farmers, relying on their ownership of the migrant housing, of the fields surrounding that housing, and of all access to that housing from the roads across their land, posted "no trespassing" signs and ordered strangers off their land as soon as they sighted them. Geography, the law, and the appearance of the occasional shotgun-toting farmer combined to isolate the migrants. Even where less drastic means were used, there was no hiding the fact of the volunteers' presence as they drove up dusty tracks to the migrant shacks – a presence that resulted in farmers telling the migrants that if they welcomed such visitors they would not get work and must leave.

Because the farmers could not be everywhere at once; it was possible now and then to get to the migrant housing. Soon after I started as executive director William Blakely, the leader of the VISTA volunteers then working with the migrants passing through our three counties, invited me on a tour of the farms that he considered offered the worst conditions.

Technically there existed a governmental agency, the State Migrant Labor Board, which was charged with overseeing the conditions of migrant labor. But it was dominated by farmers who relied upon that same migrant labor. Prodded by news accounts critical of migrant conditions, the Migrant Labor Board agreed to hold a public hearing at Trenton. Ronald Sullivan of the *New York Times* covered the hearings, at which a social worker from Monmouth county testified about a migrant family with small children who had nothing to eat but potatoes for a week. I passed on accounts I heard from migrants on the farms of incidents of intimidation and threats of eviction by farmers, and of unjust treatment by local law-enforcement authorities. Several civil rights and labor leaders at the hearings demanded the resignations of two of the Board's members, including Louis Pizzo, a prominent Cumberland County farmer who, referring to migrant laborers in one of his fields, shouted to a *Times* reporter and a group of Vista volunteers:

> "See them people in the field? Well, they're nothin', I tell you, nothin'. They never were nothin', they never will be nothin', and you and me and God Almighty ain't going to change them. They gave me the bottom of the barrel, and I'd fire them all, clean them from the fields, if you'd get me someone else."

This from a man appointed to a Board meant to help migrants. Pizzo and his fellow board member-farmer Edward B. Fogg, each had records of migrant housing violations on their farms.

The Director of the State Health Department's Division of Preventable Diseases testified that a premature infant born to a Puerto Rican migrant couple died in Underwood Hospital in Woodbury. The couple, who had no money, sought local assistance to help with the burial costs.

> "According to Samuel Mopsik, a Traveler's Aid Society official working in South Jersey under contract to the State Health Department," the *NY Times* reported, "and Miss Sarah Dougherty, a Gloucester County nurse, the East Greenwich welfare director, Benjamin Leonard, refused to give the couple any funds. Mr. Mopsik quoted the welfare director as saying that 'Puerto Ricans should practice birth control.' Mr. Leonard reportedly was persuaded finally by other officials to bury the infant, who had died on a Tuesday. The infant was taken from the hospital on Thursday, buried on Friday, and the couple, who had thought that the child was still in the hospital mortuary, were not informed of the burial until the following Tuesday. Miss Dougherty said she met them in the fields and informed them."

Such facts argued powerfully for immediate reform, but the head of the state Migrant Labor Board was not a man to rush such things:

> "The Board," noted the *NY Times*, "adjourned without voting on recommendations submitted to it for improvements. The chairman, John Seabrook, said he and other members wanted to confer with the Governor and to have the State Labor Department study the proposals."

John Seabrook was a prominent name in Cumberland County. Seabrook Farms was the main source of the crops that found their way into Bird's Eye Frozen Foods. It was also the place, near Bridgeton, at which several thousand American citizens of Japanese ancestry ended up after the U.S. Government drove them from their homes and farms in California in the panic after Pearl Harbor and put them on trains bound for camps thousands of miles away. One of the children brought east to work at Seabrook Farms was Vernon Ichisaka, who remained in the area when the war ended and he grew up. He was the chairman of the board's personnel committee – and a man who never shrank from supporting efforts to improve migrant conditions.

Angered by the ineffectiveness of the State Migrant Labor Board, our board chairman Bob Shaffer sent a telegram to New Jersey's Governor Richard J. Hughes urging him to create a special commission to study migrant labor conditions. The Governor, stung by *NY Times* critical stories about New Jersey's farmworkers, agreed. One of his first appointments to that special commission was Bob Shaffer.

Even with that appointment, waiting for the state to take significant action was a losing game. With Shaffer's involvement Al Federici organized a Farmworkers' Conference, made up of 25 migrant workers and 20 seasonal farmworkers — migrants who had eventually put down roots in the area, working the farms as of old during summers, and finding what work they could when winter came.

Federici was a returned Peace Corps volunteer and a native of Margate, New Jersey who spoke Spanish. I met him at the Archdiocese's seminar on poverty. With strong expectations of funding for migrant programs and a belief that you can't go wrong hiring a returned Peace Corps volunteer, I recruited him to direct our farm worker programs. It was not an easy sell; two years in the Peace Corps had left him skeptical of organizations in general as compared to direct personal involvement with people in need. He finally agreed to give it a try. He was steady, he was determined, and he moved comfortably among scenes of rural poverty of the sort which, while shocking to me, he had seen throughout his two Peace Corps years in Peru.

Bob Shaffer, in his capacity as a Presbyterian minister, brought Mrs. Lonnie Allen, a migrant who one year had stayed behind with her large family, to the Presbyterian Synod that year in Ocean City, New Jersey.

There she told a respected and influential audience of how she had become President of the Farmworkers' Conference, only to be evicted by Maurice Uhland, the farmer for whom she and her family had worked. Mrs. Allen, a grandmother and head of a family of 15, had lived in a dilapidated house on the Uhland farm for more than three years. The *NY Times*, in a follow-up interview, caught the flavor of life for Mrs. Allen and her family on the Uhland farm.

> "Asking 'Are you white or colored?' before talking to a reporter in a telephone interview," the *NY Times* reported, "Mrs. Uhland conceded that a major factor in Mrs. Allen's eviction was her anti-poverty activity. 'Why should I house those kind of people?' she asked. Mr. Uhland, a prominent Cumberland County farmer, was fined $50 Monday by the State Migrant Labor Board for conditions at the Allen home, which included an overflowing cesspool and gross rat and roach infestation."

Our efforts were bringing harsh attention to the plight of the migrants, but resistance to improvements was deep-seated and stubborn. As I had seen on the Indian reservations of South Dakota and among the open sewage ditches that served the burned-out families of Skeels Allotment in Ohio, the continuance of such conditions on the farms of Southern New Jersey was no accident. They were shielded and in part enabled by government oversight designed and implemented by those most likely to benefit by violations. Getting even minimal changes was going to take all the energy, money and public outrage we could bring to bear.

***

One personal consequence of the great effort led by Bob Shaffer and Al Federici to change things was that my hoped-for September return to night law school in Camden or Philadelphia, had to be put off even further, and any dreams I had of someday getting elected to Congress were dimming fast. Republican farmers and Democratic officeholders were too often the inevitable targets of our attacks on intolerable conditions. Neither were likely to forget the role I was playing; their enmity was a highly predictable price I knew I would have to pay if and when I got into politics.

In any event, I had left the national Office of Economic Opportunity with the regretful belief that I was turning my back on Washington, the focal point of my dreams for the future. I could not hope to return until I had finished law school in Camden or Philadelphia, established myself as a lawyer in Atlantic City, and gone into politics. Even then, the only way I saw myself getting back to Washington would be if I were, on some far distant day, elected to Congress – an increasingly unlikely event.

My absence from Washington, however, lasted only about six weeks. It became obvious that our chances of success in the local fight against poverty were heavily dependant on winning not only substantial funds from OEO, but in having flexibility to interpret how those funds could be used. We needed money and room to try new programs with fresh approaches to fighting poverty. Most of all, we would need support from OEO when our adversaries, already concerned at our championing of the poor, tried to cripple our efforts.

The real force for change were the horrific events of migrant life that were coming to light as the result of active and dedicated news reporters and their editors. Stories of unburied babies and granite-hearted officials were shocking the conscience of the public. I understood how quickly local interests would react to such developments by pressuring OEO to put us on a short leash. Nor would opposition come only from the conservatives and Republicans. My experiences around the country showed we had as much to fear from our traditional Democratic friends as from our adversaries. The unions were inherently suspicious of any job training programs they didn't operate; the educators viewed with alarm Head Start and any other education programs they didn't control; even Governor Hughes, a highly respected and liberal Democratic national figure and strong supporter of President Johnson, was caught between our efforts on behalf of farmworkers in Cumberland and Salem counties and his hope to save the seats of the Democratic state senators and assemblymen from those counties, who depended on the votes of their farmer-constituents.

To give our cause a fighting chance to live up to its promise, I realized I would have to spend time in Washington nourishing contacts on our side and searching out funding – a search that was growing increasingly competitive as other community action agencies around the country were hunting for resources already diminishing under pressure from the costs of the war in Vietnam.

In that effort I had two strong advantages. First was the personal contacts I had made in my time working for OEO, and the second was the easy travel distance from Millville to Washington, a drive of less than 3 hours. I made it my habit to show up at OEO's Washington headquarters at least one day a week to prospect for funds. It was my theory that Thursday was the best day to strike gold in Washington. Congress is cynically known as the "Tuesday to Thursday Club" because its members go home on weekends to politick. The rhythm of leaving Washington on Thursday afternoon and returning late Monday dictates the congressional schedule, which in turn sets the pace of government offices throughout Washington. Thursday morning's coffee-break marks the shift of gears. Catch a grant-making bureaucrat late on a Thursday morning and you have your best chance of finding out what he's looking to spend, and for what. By then, all his priority stuff for the week has either been handled or kicked elsewhere. He's looking forward to the Friday night poker game and the plans for Saturday night dinner. Over coffee on Thursday mornings I could learn who had grant money he had not yet committed; who was frustrated at the unimaginative or impractical grant applications that crossed his desk, and who might be delighted to tell you what his ideal application for funds would look like if only he had his druthers. After that it was no work at all to weave his ideas into our next grant application, and give him a heads-up that it was coming his way. In Washington, Thursdays were priceless.

By late October I could report to our Board that we had, in addition to several hundred Neighborhood Youth Corps kids at work throughout our three counties, 53 low-income adult students taking special courses, 68 little kids in our Migrant Day Care project; and 90 unemployed and almost unemployable men and women receiving on-the-job training under our Manpower Development Training Act grant. That was for programs still gearing up and accepting new enrollees. More applications were in the pipeline, for funds to put 50 low income senior citizens to work in our service centers; to pay college students to set up reading programs for those whose illiteracy rendered them almost completely unemployable; to establish a Foster Grandparent program whereby 20 senior citizens would work with retarded children in a special school; another to put 70 seniors to work on beautification programs. Much more was to come as we planned to expand the following summer's Head Start program to 1,700 small fry, and the child development program for slightly older kids to 600. It was gratifying to report progress like that.

It was even more fun to try new ways to break out of the rut of traditional government programs. I remembered the lesson of the small manufacturer I'd met on a flight to the West who, confronted by Neighborhood Youth Corps kids stealing the tools of his older mechanics, hit upon the idea of giving each kid his own set of machine tools, but first having them engraved with the name of the kid, which gave them such pride they quit stealing other's tools and started to learn how to use and care for their own. I called that sort of approach the "druthers method." If you want to make things happen, take the people aside who really work with the poor, and the poor themselves. Ask them what they'd "druther" do with the grant money if there were no rules, no regulations, no government-imposed red-tape. One idea that came from asking such questions had to do with clothes; another with cars.

One of our goals was to put welfare mothers to work, using on-the-job training contracts, special education classes, and counseling. It was working, but often missed a beat until a community aide at a staff meeting burst out with "It's their clothes! These woman hate going to a new job wearing whatever they have in the closet. If I had my druthers, I'd give everybody a new pantsuit or something for their first day at work." I couldn't find money in our government grants, but Nadine Newcomb, one of our staff, spoke to a woman's group, and suddenly our woman enrollees were showing up in decent clothing donated by local women. Traditional government regulators might look down their noses at such a free-wheeling approach, but it reminded me of the straw-boss in Chicago who paid cash. It was unorthodox, but it worked.

"I'd buy them cars,"another community aide said, "Could be old clunkers, but at least they could get to work on time. The way it is now, by the time they get the kids on the school bus and then catch their own bus to work they have no chance of being on time." Gib Tateman, a gray-haired portly guy who ran our Bridgeton office, contacted an employer who had given jobs to several of our trainees. He arranged used car loans for 2 or 3 enrollees, and reported immediately improved morale and attendance. We couldn't always get government money for such ideas, but when we tried them on a small scale, they worked.

The most exciting change was the active involvement of the poor. Our community action agency was becoming a force for change. For the first time in anyone's memory there was a vigorous organization of citizens from all walks of life, including the poor as equal participants, ready, willing and able to attack the root causes of poverty in our communities. We were introducing changes that were essential if the cycle of poverty was ever to be broken.

Chapter 18: Cross Burnings and Flush Toilets

"The times, they are a'changin" Bob Dylan sang. The accelerating pace of social changes, from the militant civil rights movement to the emerging feminist movement to a disenchantment with all authority centered on an unpopular war in Vietnam, was upsetting to the middle class. People who grew up proud of America's ideals, its strength, and the hope it offered to the world were confronted with challenges to their values, their pride, and their way of life.

The educational community – teachers and school principals, district superintendents and school board members, was solidly in the middle of that middle class. They were professionals, proud of their mission and dedicated to it. A core value for which most of them fought was to keep politics out of the classroom; reserving the vital function of educating the young to those who qualified themselves for it by hard work and study. Their effort was against difficult odds. School budgets were paid for out of the local property taxes – a system which pits retired homeowners living on fixed incomes against higher teacher salaries, music and art classes, special education for disadvantaged or gifted children, counseling, class trips and almost every other innovation the educators knew would get the job done.

If the educational establishment had fought hard for the children of the broad middle class, it had not done nearly enough for the poor. Whether white, black or Hispanic, poor kids did not show up well in the school systems. In many cases, they did not show up at all.

Poverty followed as strong a pattern of inheritance as did wealth. Parents who were themselves drop-outs had little trust or regard for schools. The poor seldom came to PTA conferences, or contacted their kid's teacher about schoolwork. There were always the exceptions that inspire all who heard of them; hard working mothers who saw to it their children got to school on time, properly dressed and their homework done; prematurely old men in factories and coal mines who did without so their sons or daughters might have a chance to get book learning. The failure of the education system was that such people were the exceptions that proved the rule.

It is a truism that education begins in the home. Yet in home after home low income parents felt, too often rightly, that they were looked down upon – were members, if they could have expressed it, of a permanently depressed class of people who could trace their cultural ancestry back to the peasants of the dark ages. The councilman's daughter had status even in first grade; the trash man's son, however high sounding the platitudes uttered by politicians, did not. If we were going to find a way to hook up the families of the poor to the engine of education, it had to start by encouraging enough self-respect and self-confidence among the poor to let them deal with the world of teachers and schools. Until we could deal with that, little progress could be expected. We dealt with it by retrieving control over the Head Start programs from the schools and setting up committees of Head Start parents who would have the power to hire the teachers and aides for next summer's programs. It was, I knew, an idea that would guarantee increased funding from OEO's grant makers, for whom involvement of the poor in hiring teachers was a defining ideal. It was also an idea bound to bring us into direct conflict with the educators, for whom losing control over the patronage of summer teaching jobs was a bad dream. Aside from that loss of summer patronage, there was the inherent challenge to the old order of things. It was one thing for a new college graduate to work under a Principal who had a Master's or a Ph.D. It was quite another to have the trash collector or the cleaning lady do the hiring. And yet, as revolutionary as the idea seemed to them, in essence it was nothing but a return to a concept of self-government, applied now to the poor. The educators could hardly voice opposition to that without revealing deep prejudices of class and race many of them did not know they had.

Once I assured them OEO would back us up, Bob Shaffer and the SCOPE Board were heavily in favor of the idea . We announced the change in November when we submitted our Head Start application for the summer of 1967. Rosemarie Russo, Pat D'Augustine and Marti Woodward, all experienced and qualified teachers, glanced at one another with shock at my naiveté when I explained what we were going to do. They knew how strong the reaction would be once word got out. And they were right, although the first news coverage was as innocuous as a baby's gurgle. "Approval was given SCOPE," reported the *Atlantic City Press* about our Board meeting of October, "to develop a proposal as the applicant agent for a summer Head Start program to service approximately 1700 children." That was the entire 21st paragraph of a 22 paragraph story on our activities. Very quickly, however, the Head Start controversy came to dominate the headlines and front pages of the local newspapers – accompanied by stories of our equally controversial involvement in fighting for better farm worker conditions and to provide lawyers for the poor. It was a controversy that fit neatly into the context of the late 1960's.

***

Although I was a very partisan Democrat in my political beliefs, as Executive Director I never asked and seldom learned the political affiliation of those with whom I worked. We were covered under the federal Hatch Act, and in any event I felt strongly that it was unfair to ask employees to take part in partisan politics as part of their employment. But with my growing involvement in local controversies, it was impossible to kid myself that leadership on public issues would advance my political hopes. I was moving steadily to the Left while the country and my congressional district were just as steadily moving to the Right.

The mood of the country was uneasy. Americans had been jolted from the calm of the Eisenhower years by the civil rights movement, energized by Kennedy's youthful vigor, stunned by his assassination and tumbled about in the wake of Johnson's legislative initiatives and programs that put the muscle of the federal government behind civil rights, voting rights, the anti-poverty program and a long agenda of other changes.

There were plenty of changes that gave the conservatives of the Goldwater wing of the Republican party ammunition for their campaigns.

“End bloated government!” had long been their rallying cry. They had only to point to Lyndon Johnson and his programs to rouse their faithful. But the times had gone beyond such ordinary politics. After President Kennedy’s assassination events moved so dramatically and swiftly that what once was a political landscape of cities and suburbs and farms with distinct and varying interests had now become a land of emotional volcanoes, of which the two most explosive were the civil rights movements and opposition to the war in Vietnam. Each challenged the very essence of authority. Police were angrily confronted on one side by anti-war marchers and on the other by black protesters.

Out of all this came a cry for a return to “Law and Order.” While useful on the stump, the slogan ignored the underlying cause of the upheavals. Without a commitment to social justice, law and order became euphemisms for oppression and suppression. But it was a great sound bite.

Like a storm crashing through a forest, the Johnson landslide in November of 1964 had pruned the Republican party of its congressional deadwood, toppling 36 vulnerable incumbent Republicans. Two years later, however, the mid-term congressional elections offered no presidential coattails to carry the weakest Democratic incumbents. For Republicans, it was payback time.

My home Congressional district, the 2nd New Jersey, included four counties; Cumberland and Salem, both of which were in our area; plus Atlantic County, where I lived in Brigantine; and Cape May County, the home and long-time base of a nasty voiced right-wing religious demagogue and radio personality, the Reverend Carl McIntyre.

McIntyre’s audience was national in scope, and very strong locally. Out of the rural electorate in Cape May County that he dominated came Charlie Sandman, a Republican lawyer with an ambition to be Governor of New Jersey. Given McIntyre’s influence, Sandman had neither the ability nor inclination to be anything other than aggressively right-wing in his politics. The public persona he presented was that of a snarling malcontent railing against liberal policies. In person he was a man of intelligence, charm and considerable political talent. He saw service in Europe during World War II, went into politics and rose to be the majority leader of the New Jersey State Senate in 1964 and 1965. He was stymied in his quest for the governorship because, among other factors, his home county of Cape May had the smallest population in the state. He saw running for Congress as a way to broaden his constituent base in anticipation of an eventual try for the governorship. Running on a Law and Order platform offering harsh criticism of Lyndon Johnson's Great Society, the anti-poverty programs, and the civil rights movement, Sandman beat our weak Democratic incumbent freshman congressman Tom McGrath without breaking a sweat. Come January of 1967 Charlie Sandman, strongly opposed to the programs I was running in the western two counties of his district, was to be my new congressman.

Our third county was Gloucester, where John Hunt, another right-wing freshman, was elected to Congress from New Jersey's 1st District. Hunt was the prototype of the Law and Order Republican candidates in 1966. He joined the New Jersey State Police as a State Trooper in 1930 at the age of 22 and served 30 years, except for the War, during which he saw combat in Europe. He ended the war as a highly decorated Major. Returning to the state police after the war, he stayed active in military intelligence in the Army reserve until 1963, rising to the rank of Lieutenant Colonel. When he retired from the state police he successfully ran for Sheriff of Gloucester County, and was re-elected until he ran successfully for the New Jersey State Senate, where he served for two terms as a colleague of Charlie Sandman. Now he was the newly elected Congressman representing one of our three counties.

If you had to pick a pair of new congressmen most critical of what we were trying to do, it would have been hard to find a match for Charlie Sandman and John Hunt.

The off-year election in November of 1966 did not come close to costing the Democrats their long-term entrenched majority, but it did boost the Republican side by 47 seats and brought in many other freshmen "law and order" Republicans who were fierce critics of OEO and its efforts. Another who came in on the 1966 tide was a freshman Congressman from Houston named George Herbert Walker Bush.

Before the 1966 Congressional elections, the main opposition to the anti-poverty programs came from Democratic figures who, whatever their complaints, historically favored programs that helped the poor. From and after the 1966 elections a much harsher opposition came from Republicans who, comfortable beneficiaries of the existing order, tended to see the poor as deserving their misery. To them, OEO's attempts to break the cycle of poverty was fertile soil for future campaign targets. There was an added benefit to their viewpoint: given the drift of Southern Democrats toward the Republican party in the wake of Johnson's insistence that blacks be treated with equal justice, attacking the poverty program served as a convenient mask for appeals to racism. Such racism made moderate Republicans uncomfortable, but it drove Republican success at the voting booth.

African-Americans reacted by insisting on racial justice with growing impatience. The riots in Watts had happened; in Birmingham Police Commissioner Bull Connor's electric cattle prods and high-pressure fire hoses had been turned on peaceful marchers; club-wielding police and attack dogs had been loosed on unarmed women and children. Murders had been done. Martin Luther King, Jr. was losing control of the forces he led in the "non-violent protest" which had brought into bright light the authoritarian brutality on which racism depended. It was difficult to restrain the angry young. King's disciples of non-violence such as John Lewis, Chairman of SNCC, the Student Non-Violent Coordinating Committee, were shouldered aside by younger black leaders who saw nothing heroic in being beaten with police clubs and attacked by police dogs. Stokely Carmichael, then 25, took over from John Lewis as chair of SNCC in 1966. A few weeks later, James Meredith, the first African-American admitted to the University of

Mississippi – albeit by force of federal marshals – was shot in the back by a sniper. Carmichael marched in protest, was arrested, and on his release gave a speech calling for "Black Power." The phrase caught on immediately, gaining support from the blacks while exciting the primal fears of white police and politicians. Within a year, Carmichael was succeeded as head of SNCC by H. Rapp Brown, who openly scorned King's non-violent policy with the proclamation that "Violence is as American as cherry pie!" The Black Panthers and cries of "Burn, baby, burn!" captured television attention everywhere. "If America don't come around," Rapp Brown vowed, "we're gonna burn it down!"

As 1967 opened and political attention turned to the presidential campaign to come in 1968, the war in Vietnam was growing; protest against it was growing; the civil rights movement was growing. Established authority was challenged everywhere, and established authority was fighting back. The reaction was necessarily piecemeal, because the Democratic Party that dominated the country for almost two generations was badly divided. As Finley Peter Dunne's fictitious Irish bartender Mr. Dooley said of an earlier time: "The Dimmycratic Party ain't on speakin' terms with itself!" Never was that insight more true. The black community, once considered strong for the Democrats, now marched against Southern Democrats, big city Democratic mayors, and goaded the Democratic President for being too slow to change. College professors and their students, long dependable champions of liberal Democratic policies, came out vigorously against the war in Vietnam – with chants outside the White House of "Hey, hey, LBJ! How many kids did you kill today?" Older Union workers were angry at having to admit blacks to their ranks, angry at the sight of the American flag being burned, and angry at the rest of the Democratic Party for abandoning them in favor of peaceniks, black power revolutionaries, and long-haired hippies who smoked marijuana and marched in the streets. Younger soldiers and Union workers grew even angrier when the prettiest girls seemed to side with the long-haired, free-love hippies. As 1967 opened OEO, and our local agency, were heading for a controversial year. It started with our application for funds to open a legal services program.

***

One of Shriver's pet projects at OEO – he being a lawyer himself – was Legal Services. The law always proclaimed more equality than it delivered – a dissonance which leading lawyers tried to address by setting up Legal Aid Societies for the poor staffed by volunteer or low-paid lawyers. Although it was a commendable effort, it was not and never could be enough to handle all of the legal problems of all of the poor. Except for places like New York that could raise money to hire staff attorneys, Legal Aid Societies handled only civil matters that involved volunteer lawyers spending a few evening hours giving advice or drafting simple letters. Routinely fighting injustice in the courts was beyond volunteer resources.

In our area, the Cumberland County Bar Association had put together an application for funds to strengthen the local Legal Aid. It was a limited application; along the lines of paying rent on a small office and providing a secretary who could arrange appointments and type the letters dictated on the one or two evenings a week when volunteer lawyers would be available. Brashly assuming that if they liked a little the Bar Association would love a lot, I worked my Washington contacts. Discarding the original proposal, I was hot on the trail of serious funding — a chief attorney, six lawyers, six secretaries, everybody full time, working in each of our six larger towns, with a seventh lawyer riding circuit in a mobile office to reach the smaller towns in the three counties and handle farm worker cases. A full law library and all the trimmings. All this was to be run by a new, non-profit corporation on the board of which representatives of the poor and other community figures would sit, along with lawyers. I sent in the new application, sending a courtesy copy to the Bar Associations. Compared to getting money for Head Start, which was in demand everywhere, this was far easier — particularly since my friends at OEO headquarters in Washington assured me I had a lock on the Legal Services money.

What I did not have was any semblance of approval of my vastly expanded plans from the Cumberland County Bar Association. The chairman of its Legal Aid Committee, a Bridgeton lawyer named Warren Lummis, was particularly outraged. Lummis was a white-haired old lawyer who practiced on a quiet side street. At first I assumed he was miffed because I had not consulted with him before sending in the proposal. It had not occurred to me that the Bar Association should have a veto over such a program, nor control of it. The county Bar Association was made up of lawyers whose clients often included, along with respectable homeowners and small businessmen, slum landlords, farmers routinely cited for violating migrant labor laws, and finance companies who thrived on questionable lending practices.

It was the prospect of a vigorous legal services program capable of challenging such practices that triggered Lummis's opposition. He objected vehemently to my version of what legal services was to be, and fired off letters to me, to the three county bar associations, to the state bar association, and to Governor Hughes.

I was not in the Governor's good graces. In his efforts to lead the way among the states in the Poverty War he had created a cabinet-level post to direct it in New Jersey. To that post he appointed John Bullitt, well-connected son of FDR's pre-war Ambassador to France and a blue-blood society type from Philadelphia. Bullitt, a man of inherited wealth who accepted the highest salary in New Jersey's cabinet at a time when the conservatives were in search of examples of what they called "poverty plutocrats", was a man with impeccable social credentials and the anti-poverty instincts of Marie Antoinette. We clashed over whether programs for migrants should be run locally, or from the state capital in Trenton. His first application was for money to "study the problems of the migrant workers," which problems had been infamous since at least 1939 when John Steinbeck published "The Grapes of Wrath", and 1960 when CBS broadcast Edward R. Murrow's "Harvest of Shame", and could be discovered anew by visiting a farm, or by reading the morning newspapers. My public criticism of Bullitt's application evidently shamed him into staging a photo-op visit to a farm in Cumberland County. He arrived on the farm in a long, black limousine driven by a State Trooper, part of a four-car motorcade filled with aides and reporters he invited along for the tour. The closest he got to a migrant was when he stopped so appropriate photographs could be taken. I raised public hell, about the visit and the application for funds, and was joined by Irene Smith, long-time leader in the New Jersey NAACP. The resulting stories in the *New York Times*, the *Philadelphia Inquirer* and other papers of wide circulation sank Bullit's application and led to his eventual departure from the state cabinet. Using my contacts, I was able to get OEO to re-rout the funds to us, where Al Federici put them to useful work actually dealing with farmworkers' problems. After this public embarrassment of the Governor's highly-paid "Poverty Czar", Bob Shaffer and I followed up by roundly and publicly damning the Governor's Migrant Task Force for including among its farmer-members men who continually violated the state's farm labor laws — more juicy stories that broke in the *New York Times* and other papers.

After all that, the arrival of an angry letter from the Cumberland County Bar Association protesting our legal services application landed on the Governor's desk with my name in prominent mention. As with the migrant programs, the state government's approach to legal services programs was to centralize them in the state capitol under a statewide director, where the inconvenient poor could be safely neutralized. Since the state had OEO funds for the operation of a "technical assistance" program theoretically designed to help us local incompetents get our applications in order, they were in position to carry out that policy. Aside from that consistent dynamic, Governor Hughes had been a widely respected judge for 13 years before being elected governor. He understood how the legal profession works and was not about to ignore either a protest from a bar association or a complaint about the outfit that was becoming a constant pain in his ass. He sent his new State Director of Legal Services, Howard Kestin, down to meet with Warren Lummis and me to see what could be worked out – and, I suspected, to see how the state's program might benefit at our expense.

***

We met in Lummis' Bridgeton law office – a pleasant office in a pleasant house on a pleasant street. Bridgeton is in the heart of the migrant area of South Jersey, and was the center of a large black population of seasonal farmworkers. It is the county seat, with the county courthouse and the customary inn and restaurant across the street, and nearby the offices of lawyers whose practices revolve around the courthouse. It is a South Jersey town in which the word "South" is more descriptive than the "Jersey".

Lummis was a frail old gent carefully dressed in crisp white shirt and perfectly knotted tie, comfortably seated behind a neatly organized desk in an office into which we were shown by a fusty secretary. The Governor's man, Howard Kestin, was about 6'3" and moderately bulky. Between Kestin and me we crowded the office. Lummis cleared his throat a bit nervously as he started. None of us had ever met before so we opened up with frivolities and the sort of chit-chat that lets you size up the other guy and decide how to handle him.

Kestin, hoping to assume the role of impartial moderator, asked Lummis whether it would help if he explained the legal services program in detail.

"Oh, I fully understand how it would work," Lummis said. "What it will do is pay lawyers to get divorces for all these colored women."

After a moment of stunned silence, Kestin realized that we were dealing with an unexpected and highly unwelcome racial attitude. Keeping his composure, he asked Lummis if he thought legal services ought not to handle divorces, or if there was a question as to how poor a woman had to be to get a divorce through legal services.

"I don't mind their handling divorces," Lummis said. "Although I can't see what that has to do with poverty. No, it's these colored women that worry me. Colored women are very promiscuous, you know. They have children all the time, and once they have legal services lawyers to get them free divorces, they'll be back again and again."

Kestin glanced at me to see if I might pick up the fight and hammer Lummis so Kestin could slip into the role of peacemaker. It was one of the rare occasions when I had the sense to keep my mouth shut. After a long pause, Kestin gave up. "Well, thank you, Mr. Lummis," he said as he rose. "I'll convey your concerns to the Governor."

Kestin returned to Trenton, Lummis returned to his practice, and I returned to the Head Start fight while OEO processed our legal services application.

***

The educators angered at our decision to let low-income parents hire the teachers for Head Start had only one weapon in their arsenal and that was to deny us the summertime use of classrooms under their control. We had clear control of the funds and would be hiring only teachers certified by the state's educational processes. That left the local superintendents in the position of refusing to let the children of the poor use the schools. It was, they claimed in justification of their action, a matter of principle. The real issue was that we were stripping the school superintendents of summer patronage jobs.

We planned to run Head Start programs in 29 school districts throughout our three counties. Church halls of every denomination had adequate facilities in most towns. But the schools were our preference. Ever an optimist and hoping to ease their concerns and win their support I embarked on a tour of every school board that had rejected our initial request to use their facilities. The odds were not in my favor. In almost every case in which I addressed a school board, the faces of their members were set in stone. In effect, I was asking them to overrule their own entrenched superintendents.

By February the newspapers were covering the Head Start story as if it were a sport; keeping a running tally of games won and lost. As the *Vineland Times Journal* reported; "... the School Board, allegedly confused by SCOPE's demands for Head Start reorganization, has balked at again providing classroom space.... Elsewhere in the tri-county area this controversy has been more heated as SCOPE's explanation ... has been met by school administrator's charges of an anti-poverty "power play" and "takeover." .... Wilkins received guarantees of support from only 10 of the 29 affected school boards. .... The Director, however, expects no difficulty in securing facilities from some church or agency in each of the proposed Head Start areas."

I was, in fact, whistling past the graveyard about those "alternate facilities", at least in Vineland. Seeing little hope of persuading the Vineland superintendent to do things our way, and even less of persuading his Board of Education to overrule him, I asked Pat D'Augustine to contact one of the Catholic churches in Vineland. She was a certified teacher and a Vineland native who was raised Italian Catholic and married to another Italian Catholic. I was sure she could persuade the Italian pastor of an overwhelmingly Italian parish to let us use his parish hall for the kids. This particular pastor was locally famous for two achievements; playing the clarinet at the annual Christmas play, and organizing travel groups to take tours to Rome, the Holy Land, and wherever else he could sign up enough pilgrims to win a free trip for himself.

It seemed a brilliant strategy. Unfortunately, I ignored the possibility that the clarinet-playing, trip-organizing priest wouldn't want to anger his audiences or paying customers by taking sides in the controversy.

"That son of a bitch!" Pat fumed when she got back to the office. "He says the kids would put too much wear and tear on the linoleum. The freaking *linoleum*!"

***

Knowing our legal services funding would come through, I thought it prudent to mend whatever fences I could with the Cumberland County Bar Association. As with the educators, I decided to go over Warren Lummis' head and directly ask the Association' membership to support our approach. Paul Porreca accompanied me to the monthly dinner meeting. Lummis was there, but did not bring up any business concerning our program. Bob Halpin was also there, a Democrat and State Assemblyman from Cumberland County who, as Speaker of the Assembly, served as Acting Governor whenever Governor Hughes was out of the state. It happened that Hughes was on vacation with his wife Betty when the Cumberland Bar dinner came around. Halpin, a likeable lawyer, showed up at the dinner with two uniformed State Troopers as his driver and bodyguard. I worked the dinner making all the contacts I could, explaining the Legal Services program to any who would listen, determined to counter Lummis's objections. The lawyers all made me welcome. Lummis left early. Acting Governor Halpin invited me to sit in on a friendly poker game after dinner, where he and several other Bar Association leaders and a judge or two took what little money I put on the table with good-natured chuckling. Poker was illegal in New Jersey at the time; a law cheerfully ignored by everyone present, including the lawyers, the judges, and the two State Troopers who stood by making sure nobody stole the pot except by traditional means.

Meanwhile, Howard Kestin had completed his report on the three-way meeting between himself, Warren Lummis and me. As that report wended its way to Governor Hughes and on to Washington, Lummis wrote more protest letters — including one to Clifford Case, New Jersey's moderate Republican U.S. Senator. In it, Lummis racheted up his protest against our legal services application by claiming that the Cumberland County Bar had found me "personally obnoxious."

I wrote to Senator Case in response to Lummis' letter:

> "I will not discuss," I wrote, "the need for a legal services program in this area, replete as it is with mass evictions, cross-burnings, harassment of the poor through

unconscionable contracts and the like.

"I was a guest at a regular meeting of the Cumberland County Bar Association and had an opportunity for the first time to converse with many of the members of that fine organization.... I was invited to no less than seven different luncheon engagements by members of the bar, and I devoted a considerable portion of the evening to fending off offers of drinks made, presumably, by those same people who hold such 'strong personal feelings' against me. Mr. Lummis was in attendance at that meeting."

That, I was convinced, should settle Lummis' hash. It didn't. He had an ally in the person of a lawyer named Benny Bardfeld, whose practice included garnishing the wages of people who got behind on their debts. Bardfeld was a colleague of Lummis and was then serving as Secretary of the County Bar Association. He received a copy of my letter to Senator Case, and took it upon himself to prove how reckless and uninformed I was. What drew his particular ire was my reference to mass cross-burnings in the area.

"I do not believe," he wrote to Senator Case, sending me a copy, "that there have been 'mass cross-burnings' in this area. I believe there have been one or two incidents of a cross-burning which have been by and large frowned upon by the majority of our responsible citizens..."

Before Senator Case could reply to Bardfeld's allegations, the *New York Times* ran a story that saved him the trouble:

CROSS-BURNINGS STIR JERSEYANS
300 AT RALLY PROTEST 15 SALEM COUNTY INCIDENTS

Salem, NJ April 8. More than 300 Negro and white marchers paraded through this city's main street today to protest 15 cross-burnings in Salem County since early last December.

.... When the first of the cross-burnings occurred December

> 4, Salem County residents .... passed it off as a prank. But the fiery crosses multiplied and with each burning there was a flood of hate pamphlets. A typical throw-away said 'The White Knights are here. We will never yield to integration of the black and white race. Join! Help us fight Black Power.' Posters later appeared announcing another group called the "White Crusaders for God and Nation."

The protest march was peaceful, but tense. 'Scores of state and local police lined the route of the march,' noted the *New York Times.* I was glad to see them there as we marched. In New Jersey, unlike marches in Mississippi and Alabama, the cops had a fair sprinkling of black officers and what is known as "command discipline", meaning even those white cops who held strongly racist views knew they had to keep order. No New Jersey politician was going to risk television coverage of peaceful demonstrators getting beaten or clubbed while policemen stood idly by as in Alabama.

That did not ensure that we were safe from harm. The cross-burnings had at last drawn public attention, and the route of the protest march was announced in advance. Threats circulated throughout the area that the White Knights would have shooters ready to fire into the march as we passed this or that tavern or roadhouse. The heavy police presence was a result of those threats. It certainly helped, but nobody knew whether a whacko might take the risk and shoot. This was gun country, where shotguns, rifles and handguns were easily purchased and in plentiful supply.

In addition to the White Knights and the White Crusaders, the march drew Philip Savage, director of the National Association for the Advancement of Colored People's tri-state operations in Pennsylvania, New Jersey and Delaware. Savage showed up wearing an expensive silk suit, heavy gold rings, and driving a new Cadillac. At the church meeting where the march was forming up, he let it be known he was carrying a gun and fully intended to shoot back if anybody fired at us. This was a troublesome prospect in a march filled with the elderly, young kids, and all sorts of peaceful demonstrators.

The president of the Salem N.A.A.C.P. was Mrs. Clara Matthews, an elderly black church lady of bulky figure wearing a plain dress, straw bonnet with small flowers on its brim and plain black shoes. Her ankles swelled over the rim of her shoes and looked like a source of discomfort to her as she walked. There is a tradition in churches of the black community known as "the amen corner," where the most respected ladies of the congregation lead the response to the minister's sermons. I had seen the power of the amen corner in communities around the country; if you had them with you, much could be done. If they were against you, you were in for a lot of quietly stubborn opposition. Besides being president of the local N.A.A.C.P., Mrs. Matthews presided over the amen corner of the church in which we assembled.

Phil Savage should have known better. Hardly had he finished puffing his chest and boasting about his gun when Clara Matthews walked over, stood between Savage and the congregation with her back to Savage and firmly declared, "There will be no guns in this church or in this march! We are going to link arms and walk in the grace of God. If Jesus decides he wants us to come to him today, then we will abide with him. *But there will be no guns!*"

Savage sheepishly agreed to lock his gun in his car. As we marched, he started to drift behind the front row, presenting less of a target. Clara Matthews was having none of it. She linked her arm with his and other church friends to form the front row and off we marched. We all took turns in the front row, joining Clara and her new friend Phil Savage, who kept looking nervously into store windows as we walked. She never let go of his arm, and he walked that whole route in the front row, right in the cross-hairs with her.

There was no shooting. By the time we reached the steps of the county courthouse Savage regained enough composure to make a strong speech, demanding the state outlaw the burning of crosses as symbols of racial hatred. It was a good speech and a sure winner, since every local politician had already endorsed the idea. The anti-cross-burning law passed the New Jersey legislature not long after. It was the first such "hate-crime" legislation in the country.

***

The controversy over having parents rather than school boards run the Head Start programs became a recurring feature of the local headlines. Of my speaking tour of recalcitrant school boards the *Philadelphia Inquirer* reported I had "run into a wholesale revolt against boards over the operation of Head Start" and that I was "scouring the area for facilities." I had received support from only 11 of the 29 school boards. Most of those whose opposition was adamant were in towns where racial discrimination ran strong; places such as Maurice River, Fairfield, Commercial and Lawrence Townships, and the city of Bridgeton. "Educators," reported the *Atlantic City Press*, "view the program as an educational one for culturally deprived children and feel the control should rest with the school boards and school authorities."

Too often such words of principled concern were used to defend institutionalized racism. Eleven school boards had agreed to try things our way. I was determined to keep trying with the others.

The day came when I was to make my pitch to the Commercial Township School Board. I had gone home early for a PTA conference for my daughter Jeanne-Marie in Brigantine, and drove back in the afternoon to attend the school board meeting.

Driving west from home I came to the fork in the road where U.S. Route 40 veers northwest to the Delaware River Bridges at Wilmington and the left fork, the road I took, continues straight ahead to Millville. It is a country road, crossing at grade the single-track railroad at Milmay where a blinking red light marks the intersection that divides the tavern on the left from the tavern on the right. From there across the Cumberland County line to Millville the road is thickly bordered by pine and oak trees, occasional farms, chicken coops sitting off in the fields, and dirt roads that turn off to the sand quarries that made Millville's world-famous Wheaton Company and other glass-making factories possible. For long stretches the houses are separated from each other by a mile or so of woods, into which deer hunters eagerly fan out from their pickup trucks each season. Not much changes until you come into Millville, a small, proud town struggling to outdo its more populous neighbors of Vineland to the north and Bridgeton to the west. Running south from Millville the Maurice River divided the impoverished Maurice River Township on its east bank from the even poorer Commercial Township on its west. It is estuary country — wooded land in which the sand and gravel pits gradually give way to the marshlands and flat salt meadows of the delta until you come to the last dry land on the way to the great Delaware Bay.

Commercial Township, until 1958, was a thriving community, especially just south of Port Norris in the small and busy communities of Shellpile and Bivalve. Port Norris boasted of itself as "The Oyster Capital of the World." Shellpile and Bivalve were where the actual work took place. There the oyster boats docked head to stern, fifteen or twenty boats in a row and three abreast where the river comes in through the marshes and the oysters could be toted over the docks to the shucking and packing sheds a few yards away.

Oysters were worth money; lots of it. In the tiny towns distant enough from the smell and noise of the docks and sheds the owners and captains built their mansions. There the architecture of money showed in proud Victorian mansions, wide streets, noble trees and gracious lawns.

In Shellpile and Bivalve the oyster shuckers and packers lived in shacks and cabins only a few steps from the packing sheds. The shuckers and packers were descendants of rural, southern, uneducated blacks who had picked cotton for generations and eventually found their way north to Shellpile to work in the sheds and shacks of the oyster trade. Oyster shucking and packing was hard work. Money was minimal. The men who hauled the oysters from the boats to the sheds were powerful and could be violent. The women who worked at the shucking tables were no shrinking violets either. Drinking was heavy, prostitution and rape were common. A veteran state trooper remarked to me that, on Saturday nights, Shellpile was "the meanest town in the whole goddam state." Fights that erupted in angry moments often ended in murder by shucking knife.

In 1958 a virus wiped out 90% of the oysters in the Delaware Bay. When the oysters died, almost overnight Shellpile died, Bivalve died, Port Norris died, and the paint began to weather and peel on the mansions further inland. Those with enough money moved out; those with less got by in slowly declining circumstances. The shuckers and the packers were stranded, left to live among the ruins of a dead industry in shacks built on the sun-bleached discarded shells of bygone years.

There was what was referred to as "the colored church," the "colored houses," and the "colored school", above whose door was lettered "South Port Norris Public School." All were within a two or three minute walk to the packing sheds and the docks. This was the school that had been offered to us for our Headstart classes, over the protest of our staff that it was unsuitable.

The school at Shellpile was a one-classroom wooden building, painted white on the outside and complete with flagpole and something of a steeple. It was built on low ground, within sight of the packing sheds. The first floor of the school was three wooden steps up from the roadway. There was no sidewalk or playground other than a small empty field that gave way to the marshes. In summer the strawberry flies, mosquitoes and fiercely biting greenhead flies were everywhere. The schoolhouse had no running water. To your right as you entered, a door led off to the toilet – a room the size of a walk-in closet with a four-hole board for the kids to go to the bathroom, with a window whose rusted screens had holes and sags that made them useless against the flies. There was a divider board between the two holes for the boys and the two for the girls. That was it for privacy. In the building's single classroom with the windows open and the doors open a cross-breeze was possible and made the room tolerably comfortable in summer, except for the flies. The screen doors opened inward, which meant that if a fire started in that old wooden building, little kids would have trouble getting out.

I stood looking at that four-hole privy for a long time. It was 1967 in one of the most prosperous states in the most prosperous nation in the world. America was getting ready to send a man to the moon. We were spending billions bombing thatched huts in a far- away country. Yet we could not build a new school with flush toilets for those kids.

It wasn't true, of course. A new school stood in the township, complete with air conditioning, fire safety standards, good lighting, drinking fountains and up-to-the-minute toilet facilities. Although it was commonly referred to as "the white school," it was named after a man named Brown, providing an irony much enjoyed by local wits who never tired of pointing out that the black school was white and the white school was Brown.

I went to the meeting of the township school board to ask their consent to use the new school for our Head Start program. As with most school boards in the three county area, there was resentment because we insisted the poor should have a voice in hiring teachers. In Commercial Township, the resentment had a more vicious twist.

"What's wrong with the colored school?" a burly farmer on the school board irately demanded, his scalp and forehead gleaming white above the deep red tan of his face and neck. "They been usin' that for years."

"It's not safe," I replied. "There's no running water, there's no fire extinguisher in it, and the screen doors open inward."

"Ain't gonna be no fire in summer," he said. "And if there is, they can put it out with a bucket brigade. Ain't that far to the river."

I had come prepared to argue the case – the ideological case – of why the poor should hire the teachers. Finding an official on a school board who was publicly defending that school building threw me off balance for a minute. Then I lost my cool and let the son of a bitch know what I really thought.

"That building's a disgrace!" I charged. "It's unsafe, it's unsanitary, and instead of flush toilets all it has is a four-holer!"

"What, now they want flush toilets? Flush toilets?" he barked. "Lemme tell you somethin'! Them (coloreds) don't know how to use flush toilets! They'll go in front of them, they'll go alongside of them! The only time they'll use flush toilets is if you put wine in 'em, and then they'll use them for a drinkin' fountain!" He didn't use the word "coloreds", but the "N" word he used was worse.

The quote wasn't considered fit for printing by the local family-oriented newspapers, but I made sure the raw version got to the Governor's desk. Dick Hughes was not a man to tolerate either that kind of school or that kind of school board. Port Norris was soon the focus of visits from more state officials and inspectors than they previously knew existed.

In Bridgeton our opponents tried a more sophisticated approach. When our local community action council was planning their Head Start program the superintendent of schools called the chairman of the local Community Action Council and asked to speak at their meeting, in hopes of convincing the parents to let the school board run the program. The parents, mostly black with a smattering of whites, listened politely as he explained the years of education required to become a teacher, the constant "in-service" training they received, and the monitoring of teacher quality the school administration carried out.

"Mr. Superintendent," one lady asked when he finished, "my question is, since whatever teachers we hire have to be certified just like if they worked in your schools, why shouldn't we get to hire them? They're just the same, aren't they? We'll probably hire some teachers who already work for you. What's the difference if they work for you or us, so long as they're qualified?"

There being no difference the Superintendent could point to, he fell back on the training and monitoring arguments.

"We got that covered," the woman smiled. "SCOPE's setting up three days of training for all the teachers and the teacher's aids over the whole three counties just to deal with Head Start. We've got trainers coming in from Glassboro Teachers College and from Rutgers University just for that."

"You're forgetting," the Superintendent tried again, "how important it is to monitor their classroom performance."

"We ain't forgetting nothing," said another mother. "First off, it's only an 8 week program, so there's not so much to monitor. Second thing, we can tell every day how they're doing. All you got to do is ask them when they get home and on top of that, the teacher's aides are our friends and they'll be working for us. We'll know plenty about what's going on."

"Well," the Superintendent persisted, "I don't know how to convince you how important it is that professional teachers should only be hired and supervised by professional school administrators. I'm sure you mean well, but unless you have a professional education, it just won't work."

"Mr. Superintendent," a white-haired old black man rumbled, "I'm raising two of my grandchildren myself. If they get a toothache, it's up to me to decide which dentist is best for them, and I never got out of grade school myself. If they get sick, I'm the one has to figure out what doctor to take them to. Now if I'm qualified to decide about professionals like dentists and doctors, how come I'm not qualified to decide about teachers?"

The old man's question left the Superintendent nothing to do but make as graceful an exit as he could. But he wasn't graceful enough to let us use the classrooms.

The presence of public officials on the boards of community action agencies like ours was often considered a threat to the involvement of the poor. They represented the established agencies of government which often ignored the poor in the running of their own shops. Bob Shaffer's personality and his ministry gave him an ability to see beyond those immediate concerns to the strength and experience public officials could bring to our efforts once they concluded those efforts were worthwhile. He made sure our board included a fair representation of such people and that paid off in the Head Start fight. In rural counties like ours, the personal relationship between county officials is often long-standing and mutually supportive. The County Superintendents of Schools in all three counties were strongly opposed to what we were doing. In Cumberland County, the County Health officer sat on our board — a competent, friendly and low-keyed man who stopped by my office at the airport one day to go over plans for medical examinations of the Head Start kids. Chuckling, he told me he and his wife were at the supermarket over the weekend and ran into the County Superintendent of Schools and his wife, everybody doing their Saturday shopping. The couples saw a lot of each other and sometimes vacationed together.

"He knows I'm on the SCOPE Board," the Doctor said, "and got me cornered by the meat counter, bending my ear for ten minutes about how bad an idea this is. Then I told him I was all in favor of the parents hiring the teachers." This with a mischievous grin. "For a second there he was wondering if I'd turned communist on him! Then our wives joined in and even his wife told him those parents should have the right to hire teachers. 'You've been complaining for years about some of the teachers that get hired by those rural school boards,' Mrs. County Superintendent apparently said. 'This may be a chance to get new blood into those schools!'

After my encounters with the school bureaucracies in 29 school districts, realizing we were getting through on personal levels like that was heartwarming. A few days later the *Atlantic City Press* carried the happy headline: "Wilkins Expects Head Start Program Funds Wednesday"

The fight was not over. The early weeks would be taken up hiring teachers and aides, training them, recruiting and screening the kids and parents who would participate, and setting up the round of field trips for the kids that formed part of the Head Start experience. Meanwhile, I had more school boards to deal with, the legal services funding was coming through, the migrant farmworkers were arriving to pick the early crops, and the cross-burnings had not stopped.

Several public officials were still trying to dismiss the cross-burnings as "pranks." I felt obliged to counter that nonsense, pointing out to readers of the *Press* that police reports showed:

> "the crosses were pre-made, hinged for folding in the car, wrapped in braided rugs, which had been soaked in kerosene, and then ignited by cigarettes."

Some prank.

Chapter 19: Food Stamps and Race Riots

We were trying to inform thousands of people spread over 1200 square miles about programs that could help them, and had no television or radio resources at our disposal. Newspaper coverage of cross-burnings and migrant housing lent strength to our efforts for reform. But news coverage based on controversy is necessarily limited both as to time and focus. Little of the good stuff we wanted the public to know was getting into the newspapers.

The *Atlantic City Press* had a Cumberland County bureau, where reporter Joyce Vanaman covered our activities with a professionalism a big city paper might envy. The problem was that to get in any significant copy from Cumberland County, she had to compete for space with the paper's preferred coverage of news in its home areas of Atlantic City and Atlantic County. In Salem County the *Press* had very limited circulation, and even less in Gloucester County.

The *Philadelphia Inquirer* enjoyed widespread circulation in all three counties, especially for its sports coverage of the Phillies, the Eagles, and the 76'ers. When it came to news coverage, however, the *Inquirer* only covered our controversies, especially when we raised hell about farmworker conditions. It left unreported almost everything else we were about. The *Philadelphia Evening Bulletin* rarely covered New Jersey to any significant degree and even then their coverage centered on the State government in Trenton. The *New York Times* carried the kind of clout that made Presidents, Governors and Senators sit up and take notice, and had the ability to shine a bright light in dark corners whenever it chose. Except for the New York metropolitan areas, however, the *Times* didn't cover routine local matters.

In each of our six major towns a daily paper was alive and well. They kept small staffs and relied on spoon-feeding from syndicated news and feature services. They covered our activities some of the time, but a fire on Main Street or an overturned tractor-trailer out on the Pike took everything they had in the way of reporting resources. The result of all this was that our doings usually reached the public only in direct proportion to our value as a source of controversy. This was not a good thing. What we were trying to do was important and at its heart demanded a public that knew more about our work than punch and counterpunch.

Fortunately, about fifteen smaller townships in the three counties also managed to have a weekly, filled with ads for the local hardware store, church news, Little League scores, and photos of the latest home run or of happy politicians in hardhats posing with shovels at groundbreaking ceremonies. For other copy they relied on canned jokes, cooking recipes, and police reports of juveniles caught stealing bicycles.

Those weekly papers fascinated me. No matter how thin their news coverage, you could count on two basics; when the local team won or the eighth grade graduated, the name of every kid involved would be in the paper; and that paper, every week, would be on the kitchen table of every family in its community. If I wanted to get our story out in enough context to explain what we were all about, there was no better soapbox than those weeklies. Best of all, to my way of thinking, was that they'd print nearly anything, so long as it was free and avoided sex and cuss words. I decided to write a column, send it to all the weeklies, and see what happened.

I called it the "Community Action Report", and sent it out over my byline with the statement the opinions were my own. About 15 papers carried the column in the average week, although it varied. Almost every paper ran it uncut – most of them on the front page. Instead of being at the mercy of space-grudging editors and sensation-hungry headline writers, I now had the luxury of explaining in my own words what we, and the War on Poverty, were all about.

I started slow and tame, with statistics of poverty and announcements of new programs and grants received. Census figures came in handy to make the point that in our three counties $48 out of every $100 went to the "haves" while only $2 went to the "have nots."

But a soapbox is a tempting thing. Before long I was hammering away at the moves in Congress to eliminate the Office of Economic Opportunity and transfer Head Start, our most popular program, to the new Department of Health, Education and Welfare. As the expense of the War in Vietnam started to force cuts in social programs, I wrote that Vietnam cost more in three months than the federal government spent in an entire year for education, manpower training and anti-poverty programs combined. LBJ insisted we could afford both war abroad and social programs at home; that we could have, as the phrase ran, both guns and butter. The fallacy of that position was becoming evident to everybody except the White House. Watching OEO compete for funds against the Pentagon was disheartening.

Our side of the legal services controversy, the migrant battles, and the Head Start controversy came easily to my pen. After months of giving speeches and interviews that might or might not make it into the dailies, it was pleasurable to be able to get it all out there.

OEO Director Sargent Shriver sent a copy of my early column to various congressmen, including Charlie Sandman and John Hunt, the two new right-wing congressmen in whose districts our programs were located. As Shriver proudly pointed out to my new congressmen:

> "This, as you will see, is a report by SCOPE director Joseph T. Wilkins on the community action being taken against poverty in the Millville area and represents, I feel, an effective way of getting across the local orientation of the economic opportunity program."

That letter came back to haunt Shriver, but meanwhile there were several unanticipated benefits from my column. One was that the larger papers, which did not run the column in full, nonetheless cherry-picked it for news they did run. When I announced approval of the legal services grant in my column, for example, it was picked up by the *Inquirer*, the *Bulletin*, the *Camden Courier Post*, and the *Atlantic City Press* and was run as straight news, with little or no mention of the controversy over our Legal Services program. Another benefit was the echo effect. The weeklies had differing deadlines, which meant that one column might appear in a weekly in Gloucester County and two or three weeks later in another weekly in Salem, keeping our activities constantly in the news. A third benefit was prophylactic; it kept the editors and reporters in the six major towns from distorting the stories about us in order to pump up the controversial elements.

That benefit came in handy when my campaign to persuade the recalcitrant school boards led a superintendent in Gloucester County to try a new tactic. The Deptford School Board denied us the use of its classrooms, which seemed to put them in the public position of opposing education for kids. To fend off the resulting adverse publicity, the superintendent announced the school board had reversed its position and would "conditionally approve" the use of its facilities by SCOPE for Head Start. "We believe in Head Start and are only too willing to offer our facilities and services," they announced.

The conditions were, however, that we would turn the Head Start funds over to the school board, which would hire the teachers and run the program. The announcement was meant to project the illusion of cooperating with us while defeating the central thrust of our policy of having the poor hire the teachers. This we rejected, which lead to headlines such as "SCOPE Rejects Deptford Bid" and "SCOPE Nixes Offer." However, since my column reached those papers right away, my response was quoted within the story in my own words, which were that the School Board's actions were "a rejection of the democratic voice for the poor in Head Start... The imposition of such conditions can only be taken as a conscious and deliberate denial of school facilities for children of the poor." We were able to make the point that the Deptford School Board was not acting in good faith when it tried to impose such conditions of approval.

Another example of the column's usefulness dealt with the food stamp program.

A popular joke taped to doors and walls and much admired in the OEO offices in Washington was the saying that "When you're up to your ass in alligators, it's hard to remember your initial objective was to drain the swamp!"

The federal Food Stamp program struck me as one of those genuinely good ideas that should attract no alligators. It provided food coupons having a dollar value which poor people could buy at a discount and redeem for food at full face value at the grocery store and supermarket. The food stamps couldn't be used for liquor, cigarettes, or imported meats or foods. Otherwise, the program enabled a poor family to put $100 worth of groceries on the table for $60.

This remarkable program was not an OEO project. It sprang from the staid old U.S. Department of Agriculture, which saw it as a way to help American farmers and food producers increase their market. It was an innocuous program. Yet still the alligators attacked – this time on behalf of a local trucking company owner who allegedly had the contract to haul surplus food to distribution points, which was reportedly at risk if food stamps replaced the surplus food distribution scheme.

The surplus food program dated to FDR's day, when farmers were stuck with excessive produce in a time of falling market prices. To keep the farmers afloat, the government subsidized them by buying what crops they could not otherwise sell. Rather than let the surplus food rot, the government gave it to the poor in burlap bags and gallon-sized cans. The available food varied according to the surplus profile and had to be picked up by the poor at county distribution warehouses. One month there might be potatoes, lard, and green beans; another month powdered milk, powdered eggs, and onions. It was a good program as far as it went, and offered the extra benefit that politically connected local trucking companies could get the contracts to haul the food from the government's regional warehouses to the county distribution points.

The advantages of Food Stamps over the old Surplus Food program were obvious from the start. A mother trying to feed hungry kids on lard and potatoes had a tough job trying to come up with balanced meals. Armed with food stamps, however, she could go to her local store and buy food the kids would actually eat and that might even be good for them.

The Cumberland County government had rejected the food stamp program the previous year. The program came up for another review just as we were growing in influence. Before the county Board of Freeholders was due to consider it again, we sponsored a rally of representatives of the poor to generate support for the food stamps. The initial rally drew more than a hundred low-income residents of Cumberland County. As I reported in my next column, the U.S. Census revealed there were 5,000 families in the county eligible for the program if it were activated.

> "Salem and Atlantic Counties both have the Food Stamp program and it seems to be working out very well. At our meeting last week two Salem County women told of their experiences under the program. One mother of five children, living on $232 per month income, related how her children had to subsist on "powdered milk, tomatoes cooked every which way, and lots of hamburger" before the food stamp plan went into effect. Now, she said, 'my kids drink six or seven gallons of fresh whole milk each week, and eat balanced meals.' She reported that all had received substantial increases in school grades since she started using the food stamp plan."

When the Cumberland County Welfare Board met to consider the Food Stamp program again, we packed the room with almost 200 people – the kind of crowd that makes local politicians look for merit in whatever the crowd wants. To loud applause, the county welfare board this time voted unanimously to sponsor food stamps.

The surplus foods programs survived, because they remained the best way for the government to subsidize farmers without destroying the surplus food. But now mothers had a better option than to show up at the warehouses, declare themselves paupers and haul home lard and potatoes or whatever else was surplus that month. Grocery store managers griped about the extra paperwork until it dawned on them that food stamps effectively increased their sales to the elderly and other poor people by about 40%.

***

By mid-spring of 1967 Gloucester County's new right-wing Congressman John Hunt was searching for ways to assure his constituents that he was on the ramparts protecting civilization against people who were threatening the foundations of the country. The immediate threat he perceived was that the poor were being taught how to write to their congressmen and senators. OEO had funded a non-profit organization called the New Jersey Community Action Training Institute, whose mission was to train poor people in the nuts and bolts of democratic participation on public boards – such as community action agencies like ours.

The Community Action Institute held seminars and classes in which representatives of the poor were taught such basics of parliamentary procedure as how to make or second a motion, how to call for a vote, and how to chair a meeting — skills the middle class pick up along the way from grade school right through to the Lions Club, but which the poor never before needed. Now that poor people were demanding and getting seats on various public agencies like the Governor's Migrant Labor Task Force, it was time to teach them how to get things done in the power structure. Part of getting things done in a democracy involves writing letters to your congressman and senators — an exercise in good citizenship, right up there with class trips to Washington, D.C. The Training Institute published a pamphlet, complete with correct forms of address, showing the poor how to write letters to people like "The Honorable John Hunt, MC."

That pamphlet, Congressman Hunt charged, was designed to create a lobby of poor people to support government programs that benefitted them. It was, Hunt declared, an insult to the entire New Jersey congressional delegation. He did not explain why letters from poor people asking for better housing were insulting while letters from members of the American Legion demanding better medical care in Veterans Administration Hospitals were not.

Having seen for myself the outpouring of letters from the poor that came in on cheap copybook paper after the CBS broadcast of "It's What's Happening, Baby!" in 1965, I thought Hunt's reactionary posturing should be challenged.

Hunt's problem, I pointed out, was that his political neighbor Charlie Sandman, the newly elected right-wing congressman for Salem and Cumberland Counties, had endorsed the Training Institute's pamphlet as a good idea. Urging people to write their congressmen sounded good and did no harm. Using form responses and a good "Auto-Pen" signature-making machine, congressmen didn't even have to personally sign the replies.

What irritated me about Hunt's criticism of a pamphlet urging the poor to write was that, like many congressman, he used phony "surveys" – political propaganda thinly disguised as questions which he mailed to his constituents at the taxpayers' expense asking their views on what he called the major issues. His first mailing went to 25,000 addresses, which seemed excessive considering he was now raising hell about the poor actually writing back. The questions were along the lines of "Do you believe anti-American, Communist-inspired protestors should be funded by your tax dollars?" I've exercised poetic license with that wording, but you get the idea. Nowhere in his survey did Hunt ask about what could be done to help the poor.

Nor did Hunt, a darling of the farm lobby, probe his constituents' thoughts on how farmworkers should be treated – whether, for instance, they should be penned off in remote farm camps and forbidden visitors, as the New Jersey Farm Bureau was urging farmers to do. The New Jersey Farm Bureau was not a government agency, however much they tried to create that impression. It was a private organization with counterparts in every state, all of which answered to the parent organization, the American Farm Bureau Federation, created by the Rockefellers and the Vanderbilts sixty years earlier to counter any populist organizations that might truly represent the family farmer. It found lucrative niches selling insurance to farmers, setting up labor contracts that brought them a percentage of whatever the farmers paid their workers, and hustling advertising to the farmers from whom they were collecting dues. They were a powerful lobby for "Agribusiness" — the huge corporate farms that were driving the small farmer off his land. They opposed every attempt to improve the working and living conditions of migrant farmworkers back to the days of John Steinbeck and FDR. Through their efforts the National Labor Relations Act, which ended the bloody labor wars of the 20's and 30's, specifically exempted farmworkers from its protection.

Their tactics were predictable; isolate the farmworkers deep inside the farmer's property; treat any visitors as trespassers; lobby to weaken state inspection of safety conditions on the farm; and make sure organizations like the Migrant Labor Board had no real power.

It would avoid difficulty, the Farm Bureau claimed, if farmers barred newspapermen, church workers, and especially anti-poverty workers from talking to migrant farmworkers at their temporary homes in the fields. To help the farmers "bring better control over trespassing," the lobby offered metal signs warning "No Trespassing Without Permission. Areas Patrolled. Violators Will Be Prosecuted." Arthur H. West, the lobby's president, was determined to head off a renewal of stories giving farmers bad publicity concerning the treatment of migrants. "No trespassing" signs weren't enough for West; he also urged farmers to contact his outfit "before making any statements, agreements, policies, or taking any action affecting farm labor."

SCOPE staffers, and especially our farmworker director Al Federici, had spent the winter months patiently visiting the farmers one by one, explaining that we were going to set up day care centers for the farmworker's kids, and evening adult education classes on basic hygiene, health, and so on. We had hired nearly 100 summer staffers and set up special training for them at Glassboro State College to prepare them to deal with farmworkers' needs. Once the farmers understood what Federici was planning, most were in favor of it. They had problems getting good pickers and knew that crop-picking families were more likely to head for farms where their kids would not have be locked in their cars while they worked. Federici, a low-key guy in jeans and flannel shirt, knew how to talk to the farmers in their own kitchens and calm their fears about unionization. The Farm Bureau's actions were now jeopardizing his efforts to win cooperation.

I was in favor of the farmworkers being unionized, but made it clear to our staff that union organization was the work of unions, and not something SCOPE should involve itself in. Our job was to help the farmworkers with the programs we had, not to organize strikes, however much they might be needed. If the farmers were willing to let us on their property to provide needed social services, it would be a breach of good faith to turn their cooperation against them on the issue of unionization.

In Salem County where Quaker farmers predominated Federici was particularly successful. In Cumberland County most farmers were practical enough to see the benefit to them of a happier work force. These were men who understood farming as a business and kept their farmworkers' housing reasonably clean and safe just as they kept their tractors and irrigation systems in good repair.

But there were tougher cases – farms that had reputations as little better than slave camps, where kids played in open sewage near live electric wires, and church and social workers were warned off with shotguns and migrant crew chiefs kept their own workers subjugated in exchange for the farmers handing the meager pay over to them for distribution to the pickers after a suitable skimming off the top.

The migrants might stay for a few weeks or a few months, but while they lived in those shacks it was their home, and they had the same rights to have people come and go as any other American. To effectively isolate their workers deep within their farms was, I charged, a latter-day version of the Nazi controls imposed in occupied Europe during the war. "The actions of the New Jersey Farm Bureau are not only unethical and immoral in terms of denying immediate aid to poor people, but may well be illegal," I wrote. "When a farmer deducts the cost of housing from a worker's wage, the worker is in fact renting his house and has the right by law to be visited by agencies or people of his choice."

SCOPE, and particularly our board chairman Bob Shaffer, had raised enough hell about the lack of legal protection for farmworkers that the Governor created a Migrant Labor Task Force to look into the matter and hold public hearings. The hearings revealed that some of the major abuses of the farmworkers came from the crew leaders — themselves ex-migrants who by force of personality and cunning recruited workers in the South and brought them along the migrant trail, exploiting them along the way. The *Philadelphia Inquirer* followed the story, reporting that

> "Scores of workers – mostly from Southern states – stepped forward to testify against the system embraced by growers in Gloucester, Cumberland and Salem Counties. The laborers accused the crew leaders of taking rake-offs on grocery purchases and medical services. .... Under the crew leader arrangement, a grower will employ a man to travel south to recruit workers for harvesting. The recruiter is paid $6 for each worker he brings north, usually in a bus. During the picking season, the crew leader will then receive a percentage of the individual harvest

> reaped by his “heads”. Witnesses said crew leaders also are cut in on trips to grocery stores. They charged the workers a “fare” for the trips in buses. The same “fare” is levied when a worker needs medical service in town.”

The hearings also brought a moment of laughter at the Board’s expense. As the *Philadelphia Inquirer* related, a Puerto Rican laborer “who has lived in New Jersey for nine years with his family of eight, said his 18-year-old son drove a farm truck for wages of ‘a piece of salami and a piece of bread.’ He said he worked every day of the year, morning and night, caring for 14,000 chickens. Asked why he had not learned to speak English, the laborer replied through the interpreter: ‘I don’t speak English because the chickens speak Spanish.’ ”

***

With the strong support of our board chairman Bob Shaffer, I participated in the New Jersey Association of Community Action Agency Directors; a collection of my counterparts around the state who faced much the same problems as did I – especially the problem of keeping the state government from diverting OEO funding away from our local agencies and into the State’s own coffers. For the most part, we were successful in keeping anti-poverty funds under local control, where the poor could have a say in how things were run.

When the brief tenure of John Bullitt, New Jersey’s first and only “poverty czar” came to an end, Governor Hughes replaced him with a man of unquestionable competence and stature. Paul Ylvisaker was a former top man at the Ford Foundation, where he had been a strong advocate of the involvement of the poor in programs funded by them. Ylvisaker was to become the first head of New Jersey’s new Department of Community Affairs, created to coordinate the efforts of local communities to come to grips with the problems of the day, from racial tensions to crime to housing to urban programs. In a gesture of conciliation with those of us who were critical of his administration's prior efforts, the Governor showed up at one of our meetings to introduce Ylvisaker. I was glad he did. Ylvisaker gave us his home phone number and invited us to call him if we had problems he could help with. Not long after, I called on him to help avoid a race riot in Bridgeton.

As the summer of 1967 wore on, LBJ's commitment of U.S. troops to Vietnam, and the ranks of anti-war protestors, grew in eerie parallel. When Johnson sent another 45,000 troops to Vietnam, 45,000 protestors marched on the Pentagon.

Vietnam and the draft provoked enormous challenges to established authority. Protestors broke into local draft board offices and poured chicken blood on draft records. Others publicly burned their draft cards. Black kids from the cities who had neither the money nor the education to get into college were drafted and died in disproportionate numbers. Most shocking of all were reports of atrocities committed by American troops – reports that horrified those of us conditioned to expect US soldiers to hand out candy bars to happily liberated little children. Now we were seeing pictures of children screaming in pain from our napalm bombs. Televised reports of US soldiers burning villages earned returning soldiers scorn and shouts of "baby-killers!"

Organized protest marches drew television cameras and police reaction, whether the protest was against the war or against racial injustice. They were not the only forces eroding established authority. In the counter-culture movement that swept the music world, drugs found a level of social acceptability that spread. Among the young, casual drug use and freely available sex became statements of rebellion against authority. To conservatives, it often proved convenient to conflate the wrongs of drug use and loose morals with the fundamental righteousness of protests against racism, and so damn all protest as evil.

Pent-up demands for racial justice and a preference of jobless young blacks for H. Rapp Brown and Stokely Carmichael's aggressiveness over the fading appeal of Martin Luther King Jr.'s policy of non-violence combined with the heat of summer to ignite race riots in the great urban slums. There were riots in Buffalo, New York; in Cairo, Illinois; Durham, North Carolina; Memphis, Tennessee; Cambridge, Maryland; Detroit, Michigan and many other places.

South Jersey had no immunity from the times. In Bridgeton, tensions rose all summer between young black men and white cops. The police department was headed by older white men who saw any angry young black man as a threat. With no regular jobs and police chivvying them off the basketball courts in mid-evening, the young blacks took to street corner meetings that led to angry curses hurled at passing patrol cars. I was asked on a hot Friday evening to attend a Bridgeton meeting to explore ways to keep the peace.

That same evening a young black man, ordered by a cop in a squad car to get off the street, told the cop to go fuck himself. The cop and his partner jumped out of the car and arrested the kid. He fought back; they applied force, and the kid ended up needing medical treatment. As he disappeared, bleeding, into the police station, rumors spread on the streets that he'd been killed. It wasn't true nor nearly true, but the crowd of angry young black men grew to nearly a hundred. The police called in reinforcements. The station house filled with overweight cops sweating in helmets and bulletproof vests, carrying S.W.A.T.-style shields, clubs, and prominently displayed guns. Everybody inside the station house was white; everybody outside was black. Police with bullhorns stood on the front steps ordering the crowd to disperse. The order produced a larger, and angrier, crowd.

I got into the police station to see the Chief, who realized the situation could spin out of control. Unfortunately, he had no idea what to do about it other than to order the crowd to disperse, which obviously wasn't working. Shuttling back and forth between the Chief and the angry crowd,

I passed on the chief's personal assurances that the alleged victim's wounds were already bandaged, and in fact he was sitting in the cell waiting for his mother to come bail him out. Few were satisfied with that response. Several questioned why it was necessary for two cops to beat one kid with clubs to get him under control, when everybody knew that particular kid was a skinny guy who couldn't fight his way out of a paper bag. Demands were made that the arresting cops come out on the steps and explain why they'd done it – demands neither the Chief nor any cop on the force was about to accept. The tensions rose. It was highly probable there were guns in the crowd outside, and there was no shortage of guns in the station house — and nervous cops carrying them. Such training as they had was to meet threats with force. None were trained in pacifying angry crowds by peaceful means.

Paul Ylvisaker, Governor Hughes' new Commissioner in charge of New Jersey's Department of Community Affairs, had given me his home phone number and urged me and my counterparts throughout the state to call him anytime he could help. Ylvisaker was then much in the news for his efforts to quell major ongoing riots in North Jersey. On July 12th a black cabdriver in Newark had swerved around a double-parked police car. He was arrested, violence followed, and an angry crowd of 200 black people surrounded the police station, enraged at rumors the cops had beaten the man to death. The rumors were untrue, but they set off a riot that lasted a week, killed 24 people, caused over $10 million in property damage, and painted Newark as a place of rage and despair. While Newark was still burning, Plainfield, 18 miles southwest, erupted when a white cop named John Gleason pursued a black kid into the ghetto, allegedly firing his pistol and hitting him. An angry black mob surrounded the cop, beat him, and shot him to death where he lay. The disorder grew as blacks broke into a nearby National Guard Armory and stole military rifles and other weapons. One firehouse was under gunfire for long hours before relief arrived. Paul Ylvisaker, the only man in the state cabinet with the credentials and credibility to do it, took to the streets of Plainfield, ordering the armored police vehicles to retreat while he and black ministers walked the streets for hours, urging calm.

From Bridgeton's police station I called Ylvisaker at his home around midnight Friday night and explained how close things were to getting out of control. He asked me to call back in five minutes. When I did, he ordered me to stay at the station house and keep things calm until the State Police arrived.

It took nearly an hour. I shuttled back and forth between inside and out as the tension grew. Nobody was shooting yet, but the first shot could come from anywhere; from the white yahoos and Klansmen who were cruising nearby waiting for a chance to start something, or from the angry blacks close enough to throw bricks and use the pistols some carried, or from the nervous and untrained, heavily armed cops inside the station. Inside, I circulated among the cops, who sweltered under their gear and helmets but couldn't shuck them so long as there was the possibility of being ordered into action. They were a mixture of hard-nosed guys willing to wade out into the crowd with clubs and guns, and others hoping the bad dream would go away. I felt the apprehension of an imminent disaster until one middle-aged cop who borrowed a quarter to buy a soda from the vending machine looked at me with frustration as he tipped up his face shield and took a swig of cold soda. "Christ, you'd think we could all find something better to do on a hot night than go through this shit!" he exclaimed. Hearing that sincere human reaction helped me keep myself calm. It was a sentiment I devoutly shared.

The State Police showed up in the person of a single uniformed trooper, who came in, spoke to the Chief and asked me for more background. I told him the major gripe at the moment was the conviction among the crowd that excessive force and police brutality were inflicted upon a guy who wasn't on drugs, weighed too little to be a threat to anybody, and who seemed to the crowd a victim of police racism.

The trooper went outside, stood at the top of the steps, waived away the cop with the bullhorn, and said he was there to answer questions.

"Why'd they have to whomp a guy who can't fight?" demanded one protestor. "How many cops does it take to arrest one guy don't weigh more than 120 pounds?"

"I don't know all the facts," the trooper replied. "Normally it shouldn't take more than one officer. We're trained to get a man under control without hurting him except in extreme circumstances."

The sudden silence among his listeners showed it was the perfect answer; a flat statement of fact that made sense and met their concern that the local police were covering up brutality. He stayed for another half-hour, calmly answering questions, occasionally getting on his radio to check the condition of the arrested man and letting the crowd near him hear the response. It was daylight before I got home. Next evening I was back at the Bridgeton police station, where a vigil had started among black residents demanding an end to police brutality. It was tense, but the actions of the trooper the previous night had effectively quieted the worst fears of the crowd about the immediate problem. On Monday I sent a letter to the Governor commending the trooper and asked that my letter be forwarded to his commanding officer, which the Governor's secretary assured me was done.

Race riots broke out all over the country in those hot July days. The Republicans, infatuated with their "Law and Order" theme, rode the wave of fear by pushing for a federal law making it a crime to cross a state line "for purposes of inciting a riot." The Bill was dubbed "the Stokely Carmichael Act," and openly recognized as a backlash against the firebrand civil rights leader who was advocating the rise of "Black Power." Their political hypocrisy of voting against jobs and housing and education and then pretending that riots were entirely the fault of guys like Stokely Carmichael angered me. My next column blasted the hypocrisy, leading off with Mark Twain's quote that "The only native American criminal class is Congress," and ending with the statement that the way to stop riots was to lock up the Congressmen who bleated about law and order while sending untrained police to deal with the horrendous conditions created by their own political posturing and irresponsibility. By the accident of circumstance, the column gained me a brief notoriety on the floor of the United States House of Representatives.

In the bucolic Gloucester County town of Pitman, where Congressman John Hunt lived, the *Pitman Gazette* dutifully ran his weekly column reporting his activities in Congress. Hunt was not only the local congressman and a Pitman hometown boy: he was also a personal friend of the owner and publisher of the *Pitman Gazette*, who thoroughly approved of John Hunt and his conservative views. Hunt's column was always given pride of place, occupying the right half of the front page.

By chance, my Mark Twain column reached the *Pitman Gazette* on the same day as Hunt's column. The publisher who would normally have ignored my column was on vacation. Filling in for him was a young relative who in the contradictions of the 60's was a long-haired liberal. He ignored Hunt's column and ran mine in Hunt's usual spot on page one. I knew nothing about it until I received a phone call from Hunt demanding to know if I wrote the column. I admitted the fact. He hung up and I forgot all about it.

A few weeks later a panicked phone call came in from one of my OEO friends in Washington, advising me that Congressman Hunt was pushing to have me charged with contempt of Congress. The Stokely Carmichael bill was coming up for a vote just prior to a vote on the appropriations bill for the anti-poverty programs, and the Republicans planned to use the first to undermine the second. My Mark Twain column calling Congress criminals had turned out to be an unexpected bonanza for the right-wingers – clear evidence that poverty fighters favored and fomented riots. It did not help that the *Atlantic City Press* had run most of that column under the provocative headline: "Joseph Wilkins Firmly Against Proposed Anti-Riot Legislation."

Various friends and contacts at OEO urged me to apologize to Hunt.

I refused, pointing out that my column never mentioned Hunt by name or district. This was, I said, a case of Hunt deciding that the guy the shoe fit was himself. Calls came in from Congressmen Cornelius Gallagher and Frank Thompson, two leading Democrats from the New Jersey delegation. Gallagher and Thompson were powerful figures, revered at the time by the liberal Democratic establishment in Congress and still several years away from their eventual indictments and convictions for corruption. They agreed Hunt was an ass, but urged me to take the medicine. Each warned I was blighting my future in Democratic politics if I didn't apologize to Hunt.

More to the point, my friends at OEO made it clear their ability to steer funds to us was in peril if I didn't put out this particular fire. I had been working hard to get funding for "The Children's Caravan," a program for farmworker's kids that was dear to my heart, and I was willing to eat a certain amount of crow to get it. By now I had learned the gut cause of Hunt's anger was seeing my column replace his own in his hometown newspaper. After hours of back-and-forth telephone discussions, I drafted a telegram worded vaguely enough that I could insist it was not an apology to Hunt but which affirmed my respect for Congress in the larger sense. My friends agreed it would probably suffice.

Hunt was to make a speech about me next day on the floor of the House. I was invited to watch the debate. Several reporters might want to interview me afterward. Next morning I was on my way to watch the show from the House Gallery when my friend Bill Green, Democratic congressman from Philadelphia who had first gotten me a job at OEO, stopped me in the hallway.

"Jesus, Joe, what did you do to piss off Johnny Hunt?" he laughed. "He's been a vegetable since he got here, and now he's on a rampage!"

"Come with me," he chuckled after I explained the situation. "We can watch it from the Speaker's Lobby." A reporter from the *New York Times* joined us at the door leading from the Speaker's Lobby to the floor of the House, and asked me to hang around after the speech so he could get a quote of my reaction. The three of us stood peering into the House Chamber as Hunt took the floor to blast away at me.

Hunt led off by quoting to the House the opening sentence of my column, which was: “Mark Twain once said that the only native American criminal class is Congress.” The *Times* man let out a chuckle. Hunt plowed doggedly on, reading my column aloud: “All over the nation this month, congressmen seeking to impress the poor, dumb, ‘folks back home’ have been making 4th of July speeches about the need to jail ‘agitators’ from crossing state lines to incite riots,” he read. *“As near as I can tell,”* he continued reading my column aloud, “Thomas Jefferson, Ben Franklin, and a number of other interstate agitators would probably have ended up breaking rocks for their one-time activities under the anti-riot bill hailed by its advocates as ‘the answer to Stokely Carmichael.’ ”

More than a few members on the Democratic side were listening and chuckling – particularly when Hunt, in a voice of outrage, read my last paragraph which said: “For my part, if I were given authority to lock up the people who cause riots, I’d take Mark Twain’s advice and head straight for the sanctimonious congressmen who bleat about “forcing respect for law and order” while making political hay out of denying needed jobs, training, and other programs for the poor.”

“It appears” (Hunt now got to the meat of the thing), “that in seeking some manner in which to make an impact upon the anti-riot bill now pending in Congress and being considered on the floor by this congressional body today, that Mr. Wilkins has injected his own conception of the quotation of Mark Twain, which will be found in “Pudd’nhead Wilson, New Calendar,” chapter 8, which reads as follows: “It could *probably be shown by facts and figures* that there is no distinctively native American criminal class except Congress.”

Bill Green laughed out loud. The guy from the *Times* listened to Hunt with an expression of delighted disbelief on his face. “Could probably be shown with facts and figures,” he repeated. Hunt wrapped it up by hauling out Shriver's original letter praising me for initiating the weekly column, making it clear that Shriver and the OEO should be held equally accountable for what he called my "attack on Congress." Then, in a twist that had me thinking back to all the "extended remarks" I read in the Congressional Record during my first years in Washington, he inserted the full text of my column into the Record at the end of his remarks. I listened with mixed feelings to Bill Green's assurance that John Hunt didn't have the clout to have me formally charged with contempt of congress. I felt vaguely disappointed, like an author whose book just missed being banned in Boston.

Chapter 20: The Children's Caravan and Yellow Dog Contracts

One Thursday morning while trolling OEO's Washington hallways for funds a friend gave me a tip about a program called "The Children's Caravan." The name intrigued me. I followed up and eventually found more information, including an artist's sketch of the proposed project.

Mort Schindel, a creative man in Weston, Connecticut, had persuaded OEO to put up demonstration grant funds for the renovation of old school buses to serve as mobile theaters in which colorful films, books and educational storytelling would be made available to children who lived in urban slums. Eight buses were to be renovated. Their seats would be removed. Soft white walls would cover the windows, and a red carpet would rise gently over steps designed as seats for the small fry. Tiny track lights were to be installed in the ceiling, and at the back of the bus a movie screen would be set up behind a gold lamé curtain that drew aside at show time. The projector was to be suspended from the ceiling over the driver's head. Colorful children's prints would be hung, lit by accent lights along the walls. An air conditioner and heater above the roof would keep the little theater comfortable year round. The exterior of the buses would be painted a cheery white, with two cartoon faces painted in red, one smiling and the other frowning, in a kindergarten version of the ancient Greek stage-masks of comedy and tragedy. Above them red lettering on the artist's sketch proclaimed "Children's Caravan." Outside, the bus would have a colorful red awning to shield the kids from the sun while they lined up behind a red velvet sheathed rope that stretched between brass stanchions. A sound system mounted above the canopy would provide music to the surrounding area. The children would enter at the front and exit using portable steps at the rear of the bus.

Nothing I had seen or imagined in the poverty wars so captured my imagination as those drawings. My friends threw cold water on my hopes, telling me only eight buses would be funded, and they had already been promised to Chicago, New York, Detroit, Los Angeles and Boston — riot-torn cities that had political muscle when it came to getting such projects. But the Children's Caravan was a demonstration project of limited reach. Only if it worked and more money later became available might there be a few more buses — a prospect that was at best a year or more away.

Whatever they said, I was determined to get two of those buses for the migrant kids in our three counties. It's hard to judge the degree by which one form of poverty outweighs another, but I had seen a sufficient variety that I had no doubts. The lives of the children of the slums are grim, but no matter how dingy their surroundings, they at least have the action and busy streets of the city to stimulate their imaginations. The children of migrant farm workers were housed in places devoid of schools, devoid of movies and devoid of streetcars and buses to reach any such attractions.

It is no easy thing to go up against the political clout of large cities on behalf of rural counties whose entire population might fit into a few blocks of Harlem or Chicago's South Side. They had friendly senators and congressmen looking out for their interests. I had two right-wing congressmen who were opposed to OEO. The cities could generate mail, phone calls, even public protest marches. My migrants hardly knew how to write and had no time off from picking crops to indulge in the luxury of phone calls. All they had was a onetime budget bureaucrat whose only edge was that I knew how the young program analysts in OEO felt when they had to sit frustrated behind a government desk hoping their work was doing some good. I spent mornings buying coffee and commiserating with junior bureaucrats yearning to affect events; afternoons poring over rival grant applications searching for defects; evenings drinking with any contact who might – maybe – and if — start to lean my way. Eventually it came down to whether I could get the program's creator, Mort Schindel, to back my play. I tracked down his address at Weston Woods Studios in Connecticut and drove up with our Farmworker Director Al Federici and Rosemarie Russo, Our Community Services Director, to see him.

His studio was a room whose floor-to-ceiling windows overlooked a green glen and a clear, bubbling brook. Fortunately for our hopes, Schindel recognized our enthusiasm and realized that, unlike the urban programs that had to contend with the bureaucracies of the big cities, we could promise and deliver whatever administrative support was needed to make the program go well. Al and Rosemarie could speak from personal knowledge of the farmworker conditions. Most of all, Schindel understood the impact his idea could have on the lives of migrant children growing up in a world where there was no color television, and no bright and happy technicolor movies and cartoons. His professional life had been built around educating children through animated films and books, including creating mobile theater units for the U.S. Information Agency in Europe years earlier. He agreed to rearrange Weston's allocations and send two buses to us if— and only if— I could get OEO to give me money for the drivers, presenters, and aides necessary to insure each bus would be fully used.

By using our already existing farmworker programs and staffing, we could do it if OEO would come through with another $50,000 or so. When my Mark Twain column drew fire from Congressman Hunt, OEO's approval of that $50,000 was on a Washington desk for signature. I was glad to find language for the non-apologetic apology that would let my friends at OEO nudge that grant along. In truth, I would have shined Hunt's shoes to get The Children's Caravan for our kids.

Our two buses arrived late in July. Al and Rosemarie were superb in organizing the project. Between Al's quiet demeanor dealing with the farmers and Rosemarie's meticulous planning and implementation, we were able to set up a regular circuit of 18 rural stops for the summer, and guarantee a full schedule among pre-schoolers once the farming season ended.

The grand opening of the Children's Caravan featured a wonderful film called "The Red Balloon," a classic of lighthearted art about a child's red balloon that escapes his room and drifts over the rooftops of Paris. From the minute they entered the magic bus and sat on the red carpeted steps to the time they left clutching free coloring books and crayons, the kids were awestruck, transported into a world they'd never imagined. I had tears in my eyes, as did Al and Rosemarie. The Children's Caravan was a hit everywhere. Both buses were in demand throughout our three counties.

After the Children's Caravan was rolling for a week or two, a pair of FBI agents showed up at my office at the Millville airport. They had information about a man wanted for murder in North Carolina and a tip he might be working for SCOPE. They produced a photograph of their man. There, staring at me calmly from the FBI file, was Walter, a driver we hired because we were impressed by his rapport with small children. My heart sank. I had not thought to ask for a police check of the background of the drivers. All I could think of was that I had sent this murderer out into remote fields among defenseless little children without taking the most commonsense precautions. "My God," I cringed. "That's him!"

Fortunately, the FBI agents were cooler heads. "Take your time. Are you sure?"

I looked again. There was no mistake. That picture was, detail for detail, a photograph of my Children's Caravan driver. Then my eye fell on the printed information, which showed the fugitive as a tall man, 6'4" in height. Walter, an extraordinarily short man, couldn't reach 6'4" if he stood on a stepladder. In fact, he had joked about whether he could reach high enough to start the movie projector. The FBI drove out to the day's location just to be sure. They called me afterward to assure me he wasn't their guy. They told me the resemblance was closer than they'd ever seen, except for the great difference in height, which was confirmed and determinative.

As the Children's Caravan buses made their welcome visits to the farmworkers housing, a pamphlet from the New Jersey Farm Bureau arrived on my desk. It reminded the farmers that, under the laws of the State of New Jersey, it was perfectly legal to permit 12 year old children to work 10 hours a day, six days a week, day or night, in farm work. They also urged farmers to deny their workers the right to have visitors. I wrote my next column about:

> "... an interesting document put out by the New Jersey Farm Bureau called "A Guide to Farm Labor and the Protection of Property Rights". Contained in that booklet are two fascinating items; a "yellow dog" agreement form that asks a farmworker to waive his right to have visitors without his employer's consent; and a notice from the State government that tells one and all in big, bold letters that it is perfectly legal to employ a 12 year old child on a 10 hour a day, six day a week basis day or night in farm work.
>
> "Out of shame for my state and its laws, I'll skip repeating the child labor notice, although it's available to anyone writing the N.J. Department of Labor and Industry. Here's the "yellow dog" agreement the N.J. Farm Bureau tells its members to have their farmworkers sign:
>
>> "I, _(farmworker)_______, understand that the land owned by my employer, __(farmer)___, is private property, and I agree not to invite or receive any guests or visitors on ___(farmer)__'s property unless I obtain written permission at least one day in advance. If I should receive an unexpected visitor, I will notify my employer immediately, and will ask my visitor to leave if my employer does not grant permission for him to stay. I understand that the issuance of visitor's permits is in the sole discretion of my employer, and I agree to accept his decision."

I again challenged the New Jersey Farm Bureau to explain the difference between the control tactics the Nazis used against people in occupied Europe and the controls the Farm Bureau sought to impose on blacks and Puerto Ricans on New Jersey farms.

***

John Steinbeck's stories of the plight of farmworkers dealt with the problems of the whites; small farmers displaced by the Great Depression and the dustbowl economics that drove families from their Midwestern farms into the itinerant life of crop-pickers on the West Coast, as with the fictitious Joad family of his 1939 Pulitzer Prize winning novel "The Grapes of Wrath," portrayed in a 1940 movie starring Henry Fonda. What existed in the stream of black migrants and farmworkers that stretched from the Deep South up along the East Coast and through our counties and on up to Maine, was worse. It traced its roots not to economic reversal or the caprice of nature, but to black slavery and the white racism that nourished and perpetuated it and kept black Americans down for a hundred years after the Civil War. The conditions in which New Jersey's migrant farmworkers lived and worked were not new circumstance. They had existed for generations, out of the public eye and shielded by the remoteness of the farms and the indifference of a white society willing to ignore and forget the occasional tragedies that came to light.

Locally, our ubiquitous presence in the summer of 1967 was forcing attention to those long-ignored conditions. Much attention followed as the simple result of introducing independent eyes and hearts to what was going on. Our staff were no outside agitators. They were intensely local; school teachers who worked in Head Start and in our Migrant Adult Education programs; counselors who worked with our Neighborhood Youth Corps teenagers; volunteers who helped out with our farmworker day care centers. These were middle-class women and men who lived in the towns and small cities and came home at night to pleasant homes and television and iced tea on the porches along shady streets where they shared with their friends and neighbors the shocking scenes they saw.

The difference they made went far beyond the dry statistics of student trips and classes taught. At a Head Start program I visited in Salem County a five-year old boy named Larry was diagnosed by our nurse as suffering from malnutrition – in a farming district lush with food crops. He didn't play with the other kids; just sat on a bench, rocking himself back and forth. He was a tiny bright-eyed little black kid. His clothing was ragged and he didn't seem to have much even of that. The local Head Start director told me that in addition to his malnutrition, or perhaps because of it, he was initially shy, withdrawn and did not communicate. For the first several days he was restless, irritable and wandered around the edge of the group.

When Larry's inattentiveness continued after he began eating the lunches we provided, the director realized that he kept up the rocking motion even when he sat on the school bus – a sign which at that age, according to the training she had received from psychologists, might be a sign of emotional immaturity. She went to a discount store and spent a few dollars on a child's rocking chair and gave it to Larry the next day. He started rocking back and forth very happily and within a few minutes began entering into the class activities – drawings, storytelling, and singing.

In that same program the cook was given a budget which provided the children a cold snack in the morning and a hot lunch. On her own, she rounded up enough donated food to replace the cold snack with a hot breakfast. Because of her personal interest, the children of poverty in that program received two hot meals a day, at least for the eight weeks they were in the program. That was a small event in the overall scale of things, but great progress for youngsters to whom malnutrition and hunger were shamefully familiar.

Sometimes our workers and volunteers on the farms and in the small towns saved lives. On a Cumberland County farm where we operated a mobile day care center, its supervisor, Helen Adamson, heard of a sick little girl in a migrant family which had arrived to pick crops only the day before. Although the children were not officially under Helen Adamson's care, she visited the migrant shack and took the mother and the two year old girl to the hospital for testing. At the hospital, through an interpreter, she learned the child had swallowed a poisonous insecticide, and that other children at home had also swallowed the poison. She went back and brought them to the hospital. For the two year old, it was too late. She died shortly after arriving at the hospital. But for the others, Mrs. Adamson's personal involvement and willingness to go and check out a report of sickness meant the difference between life and death. She stayed with the family and the children until the early hours of the following morning. The next day, Al Federici and Pat D'Augustine from our farmworkers staff worked with Reverend Juan Perez, a Spanish speaking minister and member of the Vineland Community Action Committee of SCOPE, to arrange for the funeral and help for the family in their tragedy.

These things did not always make the headlines or draw great public attention, but they became known in the local communities. People took up collections to help out such families, and talked among themselves in the small towns. The death of little children was hard to keep secret. The conditions of migrant life on New Jersey's farms were coming to light whether the Farm Bureau liked it or not.

A serious impediment to improving farmworker conditions was that once the migrants moved on at the end of the picking season, the story died in the media until the cycle started over again the next year. We were successful in focusing public attention on the wretched conditions, and had forced the state government, and particularly Governor Hughes, to start paying attention. Getting Bob Shafer appointed to the Migrant Labor Task Force, and organizing our own Farmworker's conference helped. But with the coming end of the picking season the Farm Bureau could rely on the media losing interest in the subject. It was important to keep the heat on farmworker conditions until we got significant reform.

The stories becoming public had forced the state to step up their inspections of the labor camps and to issue citations for violations that might in the past have gone unremarked. The newly-energized Migrant Labor Task Force recommended in late August that the Governor order the worst violators to close their camps altogether. It was a recommendation strongly warranted by the facts, but would result in migrant families being evicted from their housing altogether, depriving them both of their shelter and their income just as the tomato crops were due to be harvested. The Governor promised action, but was confronted by the hard facts of life.

Realizing the dilemma was in fact an opportunity for swift and strong action, I sent a telegram to Governor Hughes:

> " ... it is neither fair nor humane to toss farmworker families out into the rain because their employers have violated our laws.
>
> "I urge you to use the authority and resources at your command in a joint effort with SCOPE and following a five-point plan of action to ensure such justice:
>
> (1) Immediately close all violating camps and prosecute their owners as fully and swiftly as any rioter has been prosecuted.
>
> (2) Relocate the families affected by such closings to the National Guard Armory in Vineland, which is high, dry, clean and has toilets and cooking facilities.
>
> (3) Provide emergency funds from the Department of Community Affairs to establish a food and clothing distribution center for families moved to the Armory.
>
> (4) Establish an emergency labor pool, equipped with buses or trucks, to locate farm openings and transport workers from the Armory to the jobs, barring from use of such an employment pool any farm whose violations contributed to the emergency.
>
> (5) Provide through the Department of Community Affairs,

> emergency funds to establish an intermediate range of relocation programs to assist displaced families with finding suitable housing and employment.

The telegram was unlikely to get past whatever summer intern was opening the Governor's mail. Then the *New York Times,* displaying more clout than Western Union could muster on its best day, gave the idea a strong boost by running my suggestions in full. The Farm Bureau denied a crisis existed. The Governor didn't take the bait about the National Guard armory but, prodded by a call from the *Times*, announced he had convened a meeting for that Friday "to discuss the task force demand with top state officials." The Migrant Labor Task Force scheduled hearings for the following week in Bridgeton.

Similar conditions in upstate New York caught the interest of a wealthy Democratic congressman, Joseph Y. Resnick, who also ran into opposition from the Farm Bureau. A successful businessman who made his fortune establishing the ChannelMaster corporation, Resnick did not hesitate to take on the Farm Bureau. He organized Congressional hearings into the activities of the American Farm Bureau Federation and its affiliates in relation to the conditions of farm labor. I had achieved a certain notoriety through the *New York Times* and other newspapers for my criticism of what I termed the "Nazi-like" tactics of the Farm Bureau, and was asked to testify before Resnick's subcommittee at a Washington hearing.

Joe Gagen, a photo-journalist who had covered JFK's famous visit to Ireland for the Associated Press came aboard to teach photography to our Youth Corps kids. A first-rate reporter, he did much more, writing stories that explained in vivid detail the nature and extent of poverty in our area. He went with me the day before Resnick's hearings to photograph several of the worst camps. Gagen developed his pictures in time for me to provide them to the subcommittee. Such timely information, far more interesting than long-dated studies and statistical reports, drew considerable attention. After the story of my testimony ran in the *Associated Press*, the *New York Times*, and the *Atlantic City Press* the New Jersey Farm Bureau published my car's description and license number in its newsletter and urged its members to keep an eye out for me.

***

August and September are the great harvest months in South Jersey, when the sweet corn and Jersey tomatoes, green herbs and succulent melons and most of the rich cornucopia of crops are ripe for the picking. With the harvests arrive a new and heavy wave of migrants, in increasing numbers until the harvests are in and the migrants depart. Thus, the window for reform is a matter of weeks, gone long before the first frost or the November elections. The Farm Bureau had long ago mastered the art of delaying reform legislation until the urgency for it was lost in the turn of the seasons toward Thanksgiving and Christmas. We had done much to make public the long-hidden exploitation of farmworkers, but true reform could only come through government action at the state level. It seemed best to keep the heat on the politicians as long as possible.

In that regard, the *Atlantic City Press* and the *New York Times* were superb. The Migrant Labor Task Force, feeling the pressure and driven from within by the efforts of our president Bob Shafer, held more hearings in Bridgeton on another aspect of the machinery of poverty to which the farmworkers were chained; the "crew leaders" who recruited them and served as latter-day overseers of the mobile slavery that had replaced the old plantations. The hearings were the outgrowth of similar hearings held in June. But by now the VISTA volunteers traveling with the early migrant stream had moved on, following their community of farmworkers north. Without their testimony the August hearings might have been of dubious worth. Aside from the absence of the VISTA workers, the migrant crew leaders had adapted to our tactics and had grown aggressive in protecting their rights of exploitation. They intimidated and threatened any of their workers who came forth to testify. The *New York Times* kept with us on the hearings and reported:

> "Fred Metler, an official in the State Migrant Labor Bureau in Trenton, said that his agency was investigating charges that crew leaders were illegally withholding wages from migrant laborers and crowding migrant families into condemned shacks and shanties. Reports of assaults by crew leaders on migrants in the camps were also being investigated.... They bargain with the farmers in return for a percentage of the migrant's daily wages.... for every 15 cents that a migrant worker earns by picking a basket of tomatoes, the crew leader gets 4 or 5 cents."

There were plenty of other ways the crew leaders exploited their own workers. They charged the fresh price for milk and bread too old to be sold in stores, and doubled the price of soda, wine and cigarettes sold in the camps. They charged exorbitant fares for rides from farms into nearby towns.

A particularly brutal aspect of the chain of exploitation that began at the top and worked its way down through the farmers and the workers was that the crew leaders, almost invariably black, were often the only contact the migrants had with the community in which they found themselves. They proved the most oppressive aspect of the chain — the cruelest exploiters of their own race. *NY* Times man Ron Sullivan nailed a powerful quote from one such individual:

> "Clinton Ward, a Negro crew leader at the Cedarville farm of Dominick Sorantino, remarked 'These here are happy niggers. They like it just fine right where they are.' "

The crew leaders were bad, but there were no innocent bystanders in the whole system. In the catchphrase of the Sixties, if you weren't part of the solution, you were part of the problem. It was convenient for officials at every level of government to shut their eyes to what was going on. As weak and limited as the protections of the law were, had they been enforced with insight and vigor much could have been done. But they were not enforced, and my own Democratic Party, which then controlled our state government, bore its share of the blame. Afraid of the backlash whipped up by the conservative Republicans and their right-wing's skillful use of racial animosities, even the progressive and liberal Democrats pulled their punches. As the *NY Times* reported, one knowledgeable witness at the hearings, Ron Perrin, angrily referred to crew leaders as part of a "rotten system, backed by the farmers and the state government."

He was right. The home truth was that unless and until our elected officials championed their cause, the very poorest of the poor would continue to suffer conditions little different from outright slavery.

***

In the clash and conflict of the poverty wars there stayed always in my mind that I still had to finish law school. It was now or never if I was to realize my dream of becoming a lawyer, which was the key to any career in politics — a career for which my prospects had shrunk even as my purpose grew far stronger than any personal ambition. It was too late to transfer to a more convenient law school in Philadelphia. Unless I was willing to let another full semester slide by, I would have to return to Catholic University Law School in Washington for the balance of my courses. It was doable, but just barely. The first hurdle was persuading the Law School to re-enroll me on short notice.

In the first flush of my enthusiasm for the law I had plunged into my studies so vigorously I came out very well in academic standing – well enough to be named an editor of the Law Review. When I asked to return to classes after the interruption caused by my detour to earn my tuition the Dean, perhaps embarrassed by having a Law Review Editor drop out for financial reasons, agreed to let me back in for the fall semester of evening classes on short notice.

From my home in Brigantine to the law school in Washington was a drive of 181 miles each way. If I left Brigantine early in the morning and put in a full day with SCOPE until 4:30, I would have just enough time to drive from Millville to Washington and make the 7:30 class schedule. Allowing two hours for classes, that left me with a 181 mile drive home and a bedtime of about 1:30 a.m., three nights a week. It was a heavy schedule after days full of other responsibilities, but the time had long passed since I worried about high grades. My perspective had changed considerably during my absence from my law studies. Once willing to spend long hours delving into the finer points of anti-trust law and the niceties of the chain of title in real estate disputes, I now understood, thanks to people like Warren Lummis, that the law doesn't amount to much if you're poor and up against the bank's or the landlord's lawyer without a lawyer of your own. All I wanted now was my ticket. I picked the courses with the easiest work and the most tolerant professors. After I explained my circumstances, the law professors proved to be good sports about spotty attendance and late arrivals — so long as I passed the exams and handed in the occasional paper.

My evening commute to Washington did not slow the pace of things at SCOPE. The Migrant Labor Task Force had so focused public attention on the failures of New Jersey's Farm Labor Board with its cadre of law-violating members that Governor Hughes decided to end it. The Legislature agreed; the law was signed with all due ceremony, and the enforcement duties of the Farm Labor Board were transferred to the New Jersey State Department of Labor where there was a greater willingness to actually enforce such laws as were on the books.

The new enforcement efforts disclosed how weak those laws were – particularly those regulating migrant housing. Ray Male, the state's Commissioner of Labor, took what seemed an aggressive stance: he ordered five offending farmers to bring their labor camps into compliance or face closure. But after his agents re-inspected the camps and proclaimed them acceptable, our Chairman Bob Shafer and I toured them and found little had changed. The *New York Times* reported our complaints that:

> "The conditions in the camps we visited are still extremely deplorable. In one camp, we observed trash, garbage and debris afloat in stagnant water in an area used by children for play .... A drain pipe above ground discharging water into a stagnant pool .... a privy used by men, women and children in which human waste was up to and above ground level."

We had powerful allies. Joel Jacobson, president of the New Jersey AFL – CIO, and Irene Smith, state president of the New Jersey NAACP, were so outraged at the approval they demanded the resignation of the Commissioner of Labor. Irene Smith told the *Times* " I'm physically sick over this. The conditions in those camps are beneath slavery. How anyone could approve those places is beyond me."

Governor Hughes rejected the demands for the resignation of his Commissioner of Labor, and declined to make a personal inspection of the camps. The NAACP's Irene Smith, never one to miss an opening, lambasted the Governor for participating in a fact-finding mission to Vietnam for President Johnson when "he should have been concerned about black migrants here."

Chapter 21: Drinks with George H.W. Bush, and Five Kids in One Coffin

Even as the migrant wars heated up, our 1967 summer Head Start programs were finishing. The numbers were, on the local scale, impressive. Martha Woodward, our Head Start director, had successfully overseen Head Start programs in 28 centers, using 149 paid professional workers, 231 paid nonprofessionals, and 82 volunteers.

Our medical screening of the Head Start kids revealed that, of 1,285 kids in the program, 54 had anemia, 24 had heart murmurs, 7 had skin diseases, 30 showed signs of mental retardation, 2 had tuberculosis, 599 had dental cavities, 54 were fitted for glasses, and 435 received measles vaccines. The kids took field trips to places they'd never seen before, had breakfast and lunch every day, and learned that school could be fun. Their parents, too, had seen how their children's education could be enriched by good communication between themselves and the teachers. Our policy of letting the parents have a say in running the program paid high dividends.

The ratio of black to white was a disproportionate 2 to 1 — 815 black kids compared to 470 white. Statistically, the ratio should have been almost exactly the reverse: with 815 black kids we should have had 1,600 white kids if we were doing our jobs right. While it was true that a third of black families were poor compared to only a tenth of the white, the relative numbers mattered; nationwide, of the 24 million Americans who were poor, 16.7 million were white, and 7.1 million were black. Admittedly both urban blacks and rural whites were undercounted in the census.

I was glad we reached so many black kids. It reflected the eager participation of black parents and the organizational impetus of black churches and civil rights workers. But it underscored the dilemma that dogged the War on Poverty – was it an economic opportunity program, or a civil rights program? Were we to fight poverty on behalf of 100% of the 24 million Americans who were poor, or limit our efforts to the 33% of the poor who were black? African-Americans saw it as a program meant to atone for centuries of racial injustice. Now that the civil rights movement had come alive and the black communities were organized and militant on behalf of their rights, the jobs and benefits of the anti-poverty programs were seen by black leaders as rightfully theirs. Whites who tried to insure inclusion of the far more numerous poor whites were suspect among elite liberals as closet racists. It was no easy line to walk. Whatever the ratio, however, our Head Start program helped a lot of poor kids.

***

With the return of the school year and the onset of the harvest season we kept the pressure on for higher legal standards on migrant housing. Until now our efforts were those of advocates pushing hard to bring public attention to what we viewed as horrendous conditions. As advocates our words – and even the testimony of migrants, health inspectors, and other officials, carried only so far.

The *Atlantic City Press*, in the persons of Mary Scarpa, Vineland bureau chief, and its Millville correspondent Joyce Vanaman, decided to see for themselves. Bob Shaffer and I took them on a tour of migrant housing conditions. The August rains that made the migrant shacks exceptionally dismal had let up. The journalists reported what they found with vibrant clarity:

> "In one room on the migrant labor camp of Joseph Hepner, a pregnant woman and her three youngsters, attired in clothes not much better than rags, are huddled around a used television set.....What happens if there's a fire in these rooms, which are so crowded that is hardly room to walk in? There's a yellow bucket filled with sand hanging on a nail outside a group of the units. A healthy 120 pound reporter, straining with all her might, however, couldn't begin to lift the bucket.
>
> .... "Although the camps have many children, there are many frightening, hazardous conditions...magnified because so many of the youngsters have no adult supervision. An open

> pit by a laundry room ... a knotted electric wire just a little above ground level ... glass and rusty cans ... these are just a few easily observed problems.
>
> "At Sorantino's Level Acres Farm, a youth told how he couldn't stand to eat in his room because the smell from the nearby privy was so bad."

Accompanying the story was a photograph of the 120 pound Joyce Vanaman trying to lift the fire bucket at Joseph Hepner's migrant camp ... a bucket full of sand the rains had long since compacted into a hard mass, heavy even for a strong man to lift, hanging shoulder high on a rusty nail. That bucket, as the caption reported, was provided to protect four housing units, most of them housing women and children.

The "Ma" Hepner mentioned in the story was a piece of work. On an earlier visit I made with another reporter, she drove up in a pickup truck and threatened me with a shotgun. Angry beyond the bounds of common sense, I told her to go ahead and shoot. She backed down, driving away with a vow to call the state police. I suspect the reporter felt a certain disappointment at losing what would have been a juicy story.

What the *Press* reporters did not realize at the time was what one such farmer had going for him as landlord. He rented the used black-and-white television sets and old refrigerators to the migrants. The battered appliances cost him about $25 each; he charged $10 a week rent for them. Then he charged extra for the electricity, all of which was deducted from their pay. If he had tried to get those buildings licensed as a motel, he'd have been laughed out of town. Palming them off as migrant housing, he got away with it.

***

September brought discouraging news on several fronts. Bob Shaffer, the Presbyterian minister who was our Board President, accepted an invitation from the federal government to lead a special resources team fighting poverty in the hard-scrabble hills of Appalachia. Appalachia's gain was our loss. Shaffer's personal integrity and unstinting support was invaluable in getting us underway. He was a powerful influence in our efforts to shift control of Head Start from the school bureaucrats to the parents, and led our fight for better conditions for the farmworkers.

In the same week the irreplaceable Bob Shaffer announced his pending departure a man named John Behringer declared himself the new Grand Dragon of the Ku Klux Klan in New Jersey. "The fiery cross of the Ku Klux Klan will burn in New Jersey next summer!" Behringer pledged. I thought such viciousness should not go unchallenged. "Klan's Plan is Attacked by Wilkins" ran the next day's headline in the *Atlantic City Press*. Few other papers made much of the story. Threats of cross-burnings to come had little immediacy compared to the race riots still blazing in cities across the country.

The fires and smoke from those riots drifted in a metaphorical sense into the halls of Congress, where they were fanned by a combination of Democrats fearful of losing their seats for defending the anti-poverty programs and Republicans hoping to win those seats by hammering us for every evil we uncovered or addressed. The War in Vietnam swelled to enormous proportions and divided the country. Passions ran high.

I was still making luncheon speeches to small-town civic clubs throughout the three counties, and could see that concerns about Vietnam were no longer confined to the young and the disaffected. The weekly papers in which my columns appeared had long been running stories about which high school graduate had joined the Marines or the Army, later announcing the dates of their graduation from basic training – stories that ran in the back pages along with the news of the county fair and pictures of the prom queen. Eventually the stories reported this or that local boy had been assigned to Vietnam – news that often appeared on the bottom of the front pages. Then came the deaths — stories about those same local boys being killed in Vietnam — above-the-fold front page stories accompanied by full-dress pictures of the young man in his military uniform. Country editors began running sidebar stories about the casualty count, with headlines like "7th Local Man Killed in Vietnam," "12th County Man Dies in Combat." The questions that came at me in my speeches began to be peppered with questions about the war – not so much because I was presumed to know more about it as because the small town businessmen had it on their minds when they gathered. It was their sons and nephews who were at risk, and the unease spread.

I was ambivalent about Vietnam. The Marine Corps, even in its annual two-week Reserve training, had nourished a patriotism that made it difficult to question America when our troops were fighting. For my generation World War II was the stuff of boyish adventure and family stories. Ours was not a particularly military family, but we were proud of an ancestor who was thrown out of the peaceable Quakers for fighting in the American Revolution; and of another who answered Lincoln's first call for volunteers and fought in the Civil War.

Veterans of WWII were still much in evidence in 1967. It was only 22 years after the Japanese surrender. Many of the 20-year olds then in the service were now vigorous men in their early forties and fifties. One of my uncles navigated bombers over Hitler's Europe on runs out of England and Italy; another fought in the infantry in Italy, France and Germany. I remembered the parties and happiness when they came home unscathed after V-J day. Everyone in my generation had such uncles, fathers, or cousins. Maryanne's Uncle Mario was at Pearl Harbor when the Japanese attacked; he and his buddy ran furiously to escape a bombed and burning airplane hanger. They were strafed as they ran. Mario made it, but his buddy running beside him was killed. He was cynical about politicians, but rock-solid about what patriotism demanded.

I knew the arguments against the war — I had, after all, been in the Senate Gallery when the Tonkin Resolution unleashed its fury, and was treated to Senator Wayne Morse's denunciation of it at lunch afterward. But emotionally I found it hard to sympathize with the long-haired protesters and wild-eyed liberals and what I considered as draft-dodgers. As convincingly as my personal travels and experiences had taught me the validity of the liberal view on matters of racial and social justice, those views did not automatically carry over to the war. Even Martin Luther King Jr's linking of the social ills of America with the military misadventures in Vietnam struck me as a case of a man detouring from his chosen course. I saw little connection between civil rights in America and the War in Vietnam.

Yet there was no ignoring what was happening. When you got past the flag-burners, the shouting protestors, and the theatrical draft-card burners, there was still that constant stream of somber pictures in the small town weeklies; the surreal claims of eventual victory from generals demanding tens of thousands more troops, and the skepticism of the reporters and television journalists filing stories from the fields and jungles of Vietnam.

The expense of the Vietnamese war was drying up funding for anti-poverty work just as we were making headway with programs in job training, education, and the wide range of our efforts. Yet the War in Vietnam had an ironically beneficial local effect for some. Our job developers found new jobs for workers in local factories making military uniforms, machine parts, and glass components for military navigation and weapons systems. Men were in short supply, owing to the draft, and manufacturers were willing to work with us to find ways to put welfare mothers to work. One machine-maker rebuilt part of his assembly line to bring the work up to waist level on a conveyor belt, instead of requiring women to lift heavy parts from floor to workbench. Others helped arrange financing for used cars so welfare mothers far from bus routes could get to work. We found ways to get suitable clothing to welfare mothers so they could report for training in something better than worn out house dresses. "Foster grandparents" earned money looking after kids so mothers could take advantage of the new employment opportunities.

But the controversies we had fired up were hurting us in Congress. The great Democratic Party that had held the country together since FDR was cracking at the seams, rent by the pressures of the War, of the civil rights movement, of the anti-poverty program, and of the rebellious spirit of opposition to authority that was personified by the new music, the drug culture, and the hippies.

In Congress Democrat Edith Green, Portland, Oregon's Representative, introduced a revision to the Economic Opportunity Act that would require Community Action agencies such as ours to be officially approved by the local governing bodies – the "Bosses and Boll Weevil" amendment designed to subject the anti-poverty programs around the country to the control of big-city political bosses like Chicago's Dick Daley, and Southern courthouse politicians who would kill any hope of civil rights enforcement.

Those of us active in the field were concerned about the effect the Green amendment would have. When it came up for consideration in the House and Senate, I watched the debates from the galleries of the House and Senate. By early November, the legislative battles were in full fury. I met briefly outside the Senate chamber with Bobby Kennedy, after a particularly lively Senate session, to urge him to oppose the Green Amendment.

In the midst of the legislative clashes, I watched from the Visitors Gallery as the House debated a seemingly unrelated issue; the grant of a routine pay raise to the 3 million employees of the federal government. A handful of Republicans tried to push through an amendment that would grant the pay raise to all other federal employees, but deny it to the relatively few employees of the Office of Economic Opportunity. The floor debate on that in the House was led by Al Quie of Minnesota, freshmen Republican Congressmen Bill Steiger of Wisconsin, and a freshman Republican from Houston named George Herbert Walker Bush. It was the pettiest, meanest, and most chickenshit of attacks on the poverty programs — an attempt to deny secretaries and typists and copy machine operators a pay raise everybody else got, simply to score political points.

That evening I dined with friends in a restaurant on Connecticut Avenue near Dupont Circle known as the "Old Stein." In a booth across from us I saw George H.W. Bush, his wife Barbara, and Congressman Bill Steiger. Intrigued, I summoned the waitress and bought them a round of drinks, sending Congressman Bush a message scrawled on a napkin: *"Dear Congressman: You're driving me to drink, and I thought I'd return the favor."* I signed it: "*A community action director*." He laughed and invited me to join them for a round. We had an enjoyable conversation, but neither of us convinced the other of the rightness of our cause. He and Barbara were familiar with the community action agency in Houston from their work with various civic boards there. But their mind-set about community action was that it was a form of *noblesse oblige*; the charity owed by the privileged to the deserving poor. My argument that the surest way to eliminate poverty was to let the poor use the tools of democratic participation was met with patronizing smiles. I felt like Copernicus trying to convince the cardinals the earth revolved around the sun. Next day I sent him a letter of thanks for the return drinks.

> "Don't be too hard on Sarge," I wrote, defending Shriver. "As a business executive yourself, I think you will appreciate the added burden that is thrust upon him by a preoccupied Administration, an all-too-often reluctant Congress, an indifferent public, and an almost hopelessly disadvantaged clientele."

He didn't reply.

The still-huge Democratic majorities in the House and Senate ensured the survival of the anti-poverty programs against the onslaught of the conservatives, but we had aroused so much opposition from the big-city Democratic bosses and the Southern Democrats that several troublesome amendments passed, including Democrat Edith Green's "Bosses and Boll Weevil" amendment. Republican Albert Quie managed another blow when Congress amended the law to provide that at least one-third of every community action board had to consist of elected officials or their nominees. To those of us in the field, such measures appeared to cave in to the very people whose neglect and indifference had contributed to the problems we were trying mightily to solve.

Meanwhile, we won an allocation of 12 VISTA volunteers to work in our three counties year round. This was a substantial improvement over our previous dependency on volunteers traveling with the migrant stream. I made sure none found themselves in the sort of dead-end assignments I had seen bedevil volunteers in the big cities and on the Indian reservations of South Dakota. At an average age of just over 22, they were a touch older than the volunteers I met around the country on my evaluation trips for OEO's Office of Inspections. Eight had graduated from college; all wanted to work with teenagers and were assigned according to their wishes. Four asked to work with farmworkers, which was arranged.

Meanwhile, my notoriety led to Maryanne, loyally raising the kids, receiving sinister late-night phone calls on nights when I was driving back from Washington; calls from anonymous men ominously telling her "that road at night is really dangerous; anybody could go off the side," and "you better tell him to be careful." One said "I don't think the people in Brigantine would like to see cross-burnings." She said nothing to me about those calls until years later.

***

Our farmworker programs wound down as the harvesting season closed and the migrants moved on to other states and other crops. On October 31st our budget for day care centers for migrant children reached its planned end and the centers closed for the winter. Only a small percentage of migrants remained to pick the beets, broccoli, squash, turnips and other late crops.

Aside from providing day care, adult education and health services, we had forced important changes in the state government's oversight of migrant labor conditions. But for all the sound and the fury about improving the enforcement of such migrant housing regulations as there were, the fundamental standards for migrant housing had not improved. There was, as the Farm Bureau cynically knew, little public pressure for improvements once the migrants moved on for the year.

Nor was there realistic hope for future improvement. The state elections early in November brought in a conservative tide of Republican legislators who would take control in January. They were strong allies of the Farm Bureau. The lame-duck Democrats, responding at last to such pressure as we were able to generate, introduced bills to improve migrant housing — symbolic bills that had no chance of passage in the closing days of the existing lame-duck legislature.

Then, a few days after the fruits of the rich harvest were piled high on the Thanksgiving tables, tragedy struck. On the Jill Brothers farm in Pilesgrove Township in Salem County five migrant children, the oldest 7 years and the youngest an infant of six months, died in a fire that consumed the shack in which they lived while their mother picked crops. The *Salem Sunbeam* reported:

> "The victims were the children of Isaac and Annie Marie Taylor. They are: Ivory Lee, 7; Eugene, 4; Evelyn, 2; Wanda Elizabeth, 15 months; and Edward, 6 months.
>
> "Woodstown fire department, responding to the scene, pulled the first body from the flaming structure at 11:40 am. The last body was recovered about 12:20 pm."

It was a tragedy in which neither the farmer who owned the shack nor the state migrant bureaucracy could claim innocence. Only a few weeks before that fire, the State Migrant Labor Division, exercising its new responsibility to enforce the weak farm worker housing laws then in existence, had fined Jill Brothers $100 for violations and ordered them to build a new camp for migrant workers by the following April or face a $2,000 fine.

The loss was felt throughout our entire organization. Until we closed our farmworker day care centers, four of the five Taylor kids had been safe with us while their mother worked the fields. Only 7 year-old Ivory Lee, who suffered from brain damage and could neither walk nor talk, remained at the shack. Mabel Sibley, our supervisor of the Migrant Day Care Center in Woodstown, knew the children personally. "They were wonderful kids;" she told the *Sunbeam*. "Eugene was interested in everything; Wanda was a spunky little girl as was her sister Evelyn; Eddie, the little one, was a bright and happy boy who grew and progressed all summer long."

I stood next to the smoldering ashes of that shack next morning, trying to console the grandmother of the kids, herself a migrant worker on the Jill Brother's farm. Behind the charred remains of a metal stove, part of a wall had survived the blaze. Pinned to it, curled and scorched by the fire but still legible, were two magazine covers; the one a photograph of Pope John XXIII, and the other of John F. Kennedy. On the floor near the stove were the blackened remains of a teddy bear and a doll. The choking smell of smoke and burning and fiery deaths lay over the scorched remnants of the wood-frame shack. I felt an anger hard to express; an anger at the whole constellation of events that created that tragedy; an anger at the perversion of the profit motives that measured produce prices in children's lives; an anger at the hypocrisy of Farm Bureau lobbyists who sat in comfortable offices far away and got paid to block any attempts to reform that wretched system; an anger at the callous indifference of politicians willing to abide such horrors and campaign against programs that might end them.

Both Pilesgrove Township and Salem County refused to pay for the burial. SCOPE and the NAACP took up collections. A minister hastily summoned from nearby Woodstown did not know the farmworkers nor their religious beliefs, and could only recommend to the stunned parents that they attend church more often and accept God's will. It seemed a cold consolation.

All five of the children were buried in a single coffin. No parent, and especially no one with five children of their own as I had, could escape the horror of that image.

The anger I felt from the moment I stood in the ashes with their sobbing grandmother grew hotter when state investigators sent by the Governor reported that "while other buildings in the camp had been cited for violations of State codes or condemned, the house where the children died had passed the latest inspection."

This, as I let the Governor's office know, was abominable nonsense. The shack had failed the latest inspection, and in its wretchedness it had not differed a whit from the half-dozen other miserable shacks that stood within steps of its embers — death traps waiting for the victims of the next season.

In a telegram to the Governor, and to the outgoing leaders of the state Senate and Assembly, I urged passage of the legislation previously introduced to improve migrant housing:

> "I have just returned from a visit to the site of the farmworker tragedy," I wrote. "The deaths of these five little children is an ugly scar on the conscience of our state. We are all their parents. They died because we failed to pass laws insisting on safe, decent housing. The prevention of more such tragedies is a moral emergency of the highest priority. I urge you to use your powers to enact immediate legislation correcting the atrocious conditions which now shame our farms."

In the face of widespread public outrage, Governor Hughes called on the outgoing lame-duck Democratic legislature to pass the migrant housing legislation that had seemed hopeless only days before – threatening, if need be, to call the state Senate back into special session to act upon it. The New

Jersey Farm Bureau and its Republican friends vigorously protested. "There is no dire emergency here," the Farm Bureau wrote to its membership. "It is unfortunate that some people are attempting to use this horrible happening to cause the Legislature to adopt A957."

I pushed back hard. "There is absolutely no doubt that legislation must be passed now if New Jersey is not to become the shame of the nation," I told the *Press*. "The attempt by the New Jersey Farm Bureau to shrug off the tragic deaths of these five children is callous and shocking. The facts of farmworker conditions have been studied, debated and inspected until we have gone beyond a period of reasonableness. Even the pending legislation is very, very little and very, very late."

The opposition was determined to block the reforms at all cost. "This legislation," thundered Atlantic County's powerful Republican Senator Frank S. "Hap" Farley, "will mean the utter destruction of the farmers of New Jersey!" The Farm Bureau and the Republican leadership demanded the measure be held over until the Republicans were sworn in and took control – which would have been the end of it altogether. Those who opposed the measure, it seemed clear to me, were working on the theory that sub-marginal farmers, unlike other businessmen, had a right to stay in business no matter how many innocent children must die in the process. This battle was an old one, fought over generations – against child labor in the sweatshops of the industrial revolution, against the 12 hour day in factories, against dangerous machinery without safety guards, and against exploitation of working people by business operators too inept to make a profit unless it be by imposing dangerous conditions upon those who worked for them.

Governor Hughes, at last bringing the full weight of his leadership and personal influence to bear, refused to countenance such obstructionism. The citizens of New Jersey, he declared in a weekend telegram summoning the Assemblymen to pass the measure, "would be outraged by a callous attitude which would suggest that we do nothing and leave this responsibility to other men at other times."

Within 10 days of the tragedy, the Assembly passed the measure by a vote of 38 to 3. A week later, the Farm Bureau packed the state Senate galleries with farmers who shouted "No! No!" as the Senate debated the measure. Ignoring them, Democratic Senator Matt Feldman declared on the floor that the plight of the migrants in New Jersey was worse than Negro slaves in the South before the U.S. Civil War. The Senate passed the bill by a margin of a single vote. The Governor wasted no time signing it into law before Christmas.

After midnight Mass on Christmas Eve I came home to our Christmas tree, bright and glittering and surrounded by the toys and presents waiting to be unwrapped by our own five children. It was not visions of sugar plums, but of that charred cabin and single coffin, that ran through my head. On New Year's Eve I reached my 29th birthday, sobered by the tragedy but hopeful for what 1968 might bring.

Chapter 22: A Lost Election and Two More Assassinations

It is painful, even after the passage of almost 50 years, to write about the year 1968. Better journalists and historians than I have set in perspective the events of that cataclysmic year in which the Vietnam war, riots, burning cities, massive protests, and assassinations rocked the nation.

For me the four years after the death of John F. Kennedy were years at first of anguish, later of personal discovery and growth, and finally of understanding and hope. There are pine trees whose seeds are so protected and programmed by nature they survive the fiercest fires and germinate under the impetus of the very blaze that destroys the forest, so that in a year or so new shoots have taken root and the blackened forest is fuzzed over with new greenery.

JFK's death devastated me and many thousands like me. Yet in the years since, even as new fires broke out, here and there one could see new life, new hope, as Americans quit putting complacent trust in our institutions and government and started to ask questions and think for themselves. Violent challenges to misguided authority had, like the forest blaze, opened new seeds of independent thought and action.

I originally went to Washington hoping someday to be a senator, but having no idea what I would really stand for if I got there — like a young writer dreaming of being published but not yet having something to say. I knew now what I stood for, although the learning had taken me far to the left of the political mainstream on many issues. The more passionately I felt about righting the injustices I saw, the less chance I had to win election to Congress where I might do something about them. Yet these battles could only be fought in the political arena. The right-wing knew that, and exploited the fears and tensions of the times to win office for themselves. If the fight for social and racial justice was to be carried forward, it was clear that those of us engaged in that fight would have to fight it out in the trenches with the conservatives.

To me, the strongest and fastest growing hope as 1968 began was the emerging power of Robert F. Kennedy to bring America up out of its dead ashes into the vigorous sunlight of a new age of justice and progress. Bobby Kennedy, besieged by many elements of the Democratic Party to challenge President Johnson for the White House, was concerned such a challenge would be seen as a personal vendetta and would split the party and give the White House to Richard Nixon. Late in November of 1967 Minnesota's quixotic Senator Eugene McCarthy declared his candidacy on an anti-war platform. McCarthy's campaign brought forth an avalanche of eager young people who cut their long hair and changed their hippie appearance into a scrubbed, neatly-dressed "Clean for Gene" look. McCarthy's candidacy was of critical importance. But, to my eyes, his was a morally nearsighted campaign that challenged only the war, leaving untouched the equally great issues of ending poverty and securing racial justice – issues on which Bobby Kennedy was superior in every way.

However urgent the times, taking an active role in politics was beyond my immediate reach. I had no money, nor fair prospect of it. I could not even graduate from law school until June, nor take the Bar examination until October, nor expect the results to be announced before the following spring. It would be more than a year before I could earn my living as a lawyer – the firmest stepping-stone in my political plans. Yet I avidly followed every twist and turn of the presidential drama in the newspapers, on television, and in the government hallways and political bars of Washington.

When at the end of January 1968 the Vietcong's dramatic Tet Offensive revealed the dismal truth behind the politically soothing lies of imminent American victory and claims of seeing the light at the end of the tunnel, President Johnson obviously had come to the end of his rope. A few days later the brutality of the Vietnamese government we were supporting burst upon Americans with a sensational photograph of the Saigon police chief – part of the regime our troops were sacrificing their lives to keep in power – shooting at point-blank range on a Saigon street a Vietcong prisoner whose hands were tied behind him. The photograph, taken by Eddie Adams, captured the very moment the man died, still standing, his hair flying and his face distorted by the shock of the bullet, the pistol still to his head. At home, Alabama's Governor George Wallace, racist and proud of it, announced his candidacy for the presidency as an independent almost on the day the National Guard in South Carolina shot and killed three black men who were protesting the "whites only" policy of a bowling alley. In early March, while the political shock waves of the Tet Offensive were still reverberating in Washington, General Westmoreland, the US commander in Vietnam long ballyhooed by the Johnson White House as the sure victor over the Vietcong, asked for 200,000 more troops to be added to the 500,000 already in Vietnam.

Within 72 hours of that news the bellwether New Hampshire Democratic primary on March 12th produced a stunning 42% vote for McCarthy — a deep humiliation for President Johnson and strong confirmation that he had little hope of reelection even if he could be re-nominated, which now seemed far from certain.

The headlines proclaimed McCarthy's showing next morning. Alighting from an airplane, Bobby Kennedy answered a reporter's question by admitting he was "reconsidering" a run for the presidency. In the charged atmosphere of the day the prospect of his jumping into the race was electrifying. Liberal Democratic figures who backed McCarthy only as a last resort scrambled to get behind Bobby. The "clean for Gene" youth of New Hampshire's primary campaign were outraged that Kennedy, having, as McCarthy witheringly commented, "danced by the light of the Moon" while McCarthy carried the fight to Johnson, should now expect McCarthy to quietly fade away. Unable to resist the excitement of the moment, I haunted the Capital, justifying the time away from Millville as grant-seeking trips. That was true enough, at least until after lunch. Then I abandoned all pretense and stalked the Hill in search of every scrap of political gossip and rumor. Everywhere I went I ran across friends and figures met over the past four years, all of us engaged in the same eager quest for confirmation of our hopes that Bobby would truly run.

I was in Washington on the mid-March morning when news came that Bobby would hold a press conference in the Senate Caucus Room – the same room in which his brother Jack announced his candidacy in 1960. Eager to be on the scene I caught a cab. The traffic did not cooperate, but I arrived in time for the stand-up hallway interviews by television journalists asking this or that Senator what it meant. For me there was no uncertainty about what it meant. I had so identified with Bobby Kennedy and the causes for which he stood it would have been a betrayal of my own heart to sit the election out. I was convinced he would win both the Democratic nomination and the presidency. If I ran for Congress and won, I could be at the center of the change. And even if, as was probable, I lost, I was confident that with my experience and contacts and a law degree I could find allies and useful work in the administration of President Robert F. Kennedy.

My hopes were no secret. On the day Kennedy's announcement ran as the lead story in the *Atlantic City Press*, the banner headline in the place of honor above the masthead on Page 1 proclaimed : "WILKINS MAY SEEK NOD TO OPPOSE SANDMAN." I might have a hopeless candidacy and an empty war chest, but I certainly had name recognition.

It was too much to hope for support, or even neutrality, from the Democratic establishment in New Jersey. Governor Hughes, although a good and decent man, did not believe in turning the other cheek in politics. I had pressed him relentlessly and publicly for action to win migrant reforms and to stop the cross-burnings. For all that, I was now to pay a political price. When late in March I appeared before a meeting of the assembled Democratic county chairmen from Atlantic, Cape May, Cumberland and Salem Counties to ask for their endorsement to get my name on the party line on the ballot, a special envoy from Governor Hughes was there to torpedo any slim chance I had. The only friend I had in the room was Herb Roselle, the genial and easy-going Cumberland County chairman. Worst of all, in the eyes of professional politicians, was that Arthur Ponzio, chairman of the Democratic Party in my home county of Atlantic, weighed in against me. Ponzio was corrupt and expected a brown paper bag of cash if you wanted his support. He later spent several hard years in federal prison for accepting bribes in connection with his public office. In 1968, he was pushing the nomination of an obscure professor.

There was slim chance that in our conservative district I could unseat Charlie Sandman. Without the Democratic nomination there was no chance at all. I turned my thinking to what would happen if I took my case directly to the voters of the Democratic Party in a primary election fight. If I ran both as a candidate for the congressional nomination and as a delegate for the Democratic National Committee pledged to Bobby Kennedy, I might have a prayer. It was tempting whatever the outcome. Sometimes you have to fight even when the odds are overwhelming. This seemed one of those times.

Kennedy, as I learned from friends on his campaign staff, was facing a scheduling dilemma. The California and the New Jersey primaries, 3,000 expensive and time-consuming miles apart, were scheduled for the same day: June 4, 1968. He could focus on either, but not both. California had 172 delegates, all of which went to the winner; New Jersey only 80, which could be split county by county. The choice was inescapable. If he won California, New Jersey's delegates — a roster of dependable Democratic figures — would follow Governor Hughes's lead. Hughes, everyone understood, would undoubtedly go with President Johnson on the first ballot, and if Johnson failed would probably switch to whoever won California.

I was torn between fighting a losing battle in a war my side would win, or prudently sitting things out. Yet even as I weighed my choices, the national scene came unstitched faster and faster. Major events came like hammer blows. President Johnson, angered by General Westmoreland's demand for 200,000 more troops, relieved him of command. Nine days later, in a stunning fall from power, Johnson announced he would neither seek nor accept the Democratic nomination for the presidency. Four days after that Martin Luther King Jr. was assassinated at the Lorraine Motel in Memphis while supporting a garbage workers' strike for better wages. Black rage erupted in riots in America's cities. One of the few cities spared such rioting was Indianapolis, where it fell that dark night to Bobby Kennedy, speaking on a campaign stop to an enormous crowd of African-Americans, to announce King's death.

There were few public men in America, and only one white man, who could deliver such horrible news without inciting a riot. Kennedy was that man. In a high-pitched, tremulous voice, exhausted by the pace of the campaign, he announced the news. Shock and dismay ran through the crowd. Kennedy, at one with his audience, told them they must not give in to hatred of white people. "My brother was killed, and he was killed by a white man," he said, the words painfully straight from his heart. He ended his speech with a poignant quote from Aeschylus about "pain that falls drip by drip upon the heart until, against our will and by the awful grace of God, comes wisdom."

In the unfolding of such great events on the national scene my personal political fate was of no consequence. The reverse was not true. The national events of the day felt of momentous consequence to me. Like the millions of men who felt obliged to join the army the day after Pearl Harbor, or the hundreds of thousands drawn to Washington to add our insignificant weight to the mass showing of respect at the death of John Kennedy, it did not matter how I made out: It did matter greatly to me that I stand up and be counted for the things in which I believed.

There was no hope at all of winning the primary election. The closest and most dedicated of my supporters, my colleagues at SCOPE who shared my understanding of the need for social reform, were barred by the federal "Hatch Act" from taking an active part in the campaign. The thousands of migrants whose cause I had aggressively championed were not voters and by election day were in other states picking other crops. The people who could campaign and would vote were the school principals, the farmers, the lawyers, and the rest of those against whom I had raised particular hell. Within the Democratic Party Arthur Ponzio ran the Atlantic County Democratic organization. In Cumberland County where I might hope to do better a Vineland man was also running, which would siphon off such anti-organization vote as there was. In Salem County much of my effort to get migrant legislation passed had been directed against the Democratic state senator from that county. He bore me no love. In Cape May County the radio virulence of the Rev. Carl McIntrye and his preaching of racial hatred had poisoned both parties. To add to all of that, Robert Kennedy had decided to focus on California's winner-take-all primary and its 172 delegates. Since he did not enter the New Jersey race, I could not use his name on the ballot. Senator Eugene McCarthy, on the other hand, was running a slate of delegates statewide, which in the convoluted workings of politics meant that he was effectively challenging the enormously popular Democrat Governor Richard J. Hughes, who headed the official Democratic slate of delegates in every county. This meant the regular Democratic organizations would be working hard and steadily to get out their vote. Even if a miracle happened in the primary , neither I nor any other Democratic candidate had a hope of beating Sandman in the November election in a district where Republicans outnumbered Democrats by more than 2 to 1 and in some cases 5 to 1.

Finally, if I resigned from SCOPE, as I must if I ran, my income would stop altogether. What right had I to plunge into the strife of politics with no real plan to feed my family, other than the brash confidence that had seen me through the nine years since our first daughter was born?

Such were the arguments and emotions that filled my thoughts as the deadline for filing the necessary election petitions approached. I believed strongly that the country was coming apart and we all had a duty to do what we could. If I did not at least try, I would count myself a coward for years to come. But none of that could outweigh my obligations to support my family, no matter how miserable sitting the campaign out made me feel.

Then came a boost from an unexpected quarter. Richard Field and his wife, marvelous people and strongly supportive of our programs, on which Rich served as a board member and committee chairman, invited me to dinner at their home in Bridgeton. He knew how modest my means were, and how large my family. Over coffee he presented me with their personal check for $2,500 – the equivalent of two months salary I was then earning. It was a personal gift, they said, that I might use to carry my family through the 7 weeks between filing day and the primary election. The election would be on June 4th; my graduation from law school was scheduled for June 9th. The money would just cover my mortgage, utilities, food and other family expenses to graduation day.

Almost but not yet irrevocably committed to running, I had a few days left before the filing deadline – time to nail down several grants I was trying to get from OEO for our summer programs. The federal grants required us to raise 10% of the cost from non-federal sources. In practical terms, the best hope of finding that 10% was in the state budget — a reality that made it as necessary for me to visit the government offices in Trenton as to visit the OEO in Washington. The migrant season was fast approaching. I drove from Brigantine to Trenton, hoping to find state money I could use as the 10% lever to pry yet more anti-poverty funds out of the federal budget.

Route 206 is the road from Southern New Jersey to the state capital at Trenton where the Governor's Office and New Jersey's Senate and Assembly chambers stand. The riots triggered by the assassination of Martin Luther King were still erupting even as I drove up Route 206. Trenton was the capital of my state; Washington was the capital of my country. Both had been burning for days, with looters running rampant in the streets, sporadic shooting, National Guard patrols, and mounting death tolls.

When I reached Trenton on Route 206 I was turned back by a

National Guard unit blocking the road with a machine gun nested behind a wall of sandbags. "Sorry, sir," a sergeant informed me. "They're not letting anybody in."

It was still early in the day. Hoping to use the afternoon productively nudging the grants along by touching base with my Washington contacts, I turned around and drove down the New Jersey Turnpike and on to Washington. Coming out of the Baltimore Harbor Tunnel I heard radio reports of rioting in Baltimore proper. Looking west across the water I could see smoke rising from fires in the city. In Trenton and Baltimore and Washington the fires went unchecked because rioters shot at the fire trucks and hurled bricks at firemen and rescue workers. The radio reported a major riot that was burning and spreading along 7th Street in Northwest Washington. My route into Washington took me down the Baltimore-Washington Parkway, a lovely green journey that winds through the hills and woods of Maryland until you crest the last hill and see the distant skyline of Washington just before you take the right fork that carries you down New York Avenue to North Capitol Street. At the turnoff to New York Avenue I was stopped by another National Guard unit, with trucks on which machine guns were mounted blocking the road. I pulled over to the side and asked a lieutenant how I could get into town. "You can't, sir," he replied, "It's a lockdown. They've even got machine gun nests on the Capitol building."

In that single day I had been confronted by soldiers with machine guns blocking my path into the capitals of my state and of my country – scenes bad enough to see in banana republics but painful to find in the United States of America. I drove home thinking about Edmund Burke's apt comment that "For evil to triumph it is enough that good men do nothing." Those machine guns convinced me to run for Congress even if the only vote I got was my own. I resigned from SCOPE and announced my candidacy for Congress, and for election as a delegate to the Democratic National Convention to be held in Chicago in August.

***

It was as purely symbolic a candidacy as you could design. With no advertising money, no organization, and no time to put one together, my campaign plans involved shoe leather and door knocking – when I wasn't driving back and forth to Washington finishing up the last month of law school. I campaigned by hitting the streets two nights a week and weekends. The only patch of Democratic votes concentrated enough to make a door-to-door campaign work was Atlantic City's Northside – blocks and blocks of black homes in which Robert F. Kennedy's name was magic. I pounded the streets there for an hour, knocking on doors and getting no answer, and leaving campaign pamphlets tucked into the doors. A black kid about 15 years old watched me awhile, then asked for a pamphlet.

"You for Kennedy?" he asked.

"Yeah. I'm running for congress, and to be a delegate to the convention for him."

"You ain't gonna get nobody the way you doing it."

"Why? What's wrong ?

"You're knocking like a bill collector. Here!" He tapped so lightly on the door I could hardly hear it. "This the way you knock you want people come to the door." The door opened and I made my pitch.

"Can't bang on the door like you was doing" he said. "That's a cop's knock, or the shut-off man."

His name was Fernie Gaines, and he stayed with me for that day and on other days, passing out pamphlets and telling me who was who.

Publicity was uncertain. The guy who had the political beat for the *Press* was Frank Prendergast, a wearily cynical man built like a slouching broomstick with a serious squint in one eye not entirely attributable to the curling smoke from the ever-present cigarette that dangled from his lips. Frank, a dapper dresser, had two passions; the race track and his clothing. His idea of covering politics was to write what he was told by the local leaders, never leaning too far away from the sure thing. I was the outside challenger. The regular Democrats would have a rally of about 5 people and turn in a press release of what their candidate said when addressing what Frank Prendergast would describe as "the crowd." The organization's press releases ran as straight news. Without similar rallies I couldn't get coverage. I walked into the *Press* building in Atlantic City and spoke to its editor Chuck Reynolds, a quiet-voiced Iowan transplant, and told him I thought I was being short-changed on coverage even though I saw more people on my door-to-door campaigns than the organization could produce at their so-called rallies. Reynolds was a fair guy with a dry sense of humor. He called in Prendergast and explained my complaint.

"I think Joe's got a point," he told Prendergast. "Maybe you should go door-to-door with him and cover him that way." He had a hard time keeping a straight face when he said it. Picturing Frank walking through the rough neighborhoods I was canvassing was a comedy in itself.

"Yeah, sure," Frank answered, with the enthusiasm of a man watching his horse stumble home last. "C'mon over to my desk and gimme your schedule." When we were safely out of earshot of Chuck Reynolds, he took me by the arm and steered me out the door. "Look kid, how 'bout we do this? You go door-to-door, and then call me up with whatever you want me to say and I'll put it in the paper." This seemed eminently reasonable to me.

The publicity improved somewhat, but there are lessons to learn about bucking a political organization, no matter how corrupt and ineffective it is. The sample ballots arrived in the mail. My sister Janie, eager to vote for me, went over her sample ballot to make sure she knew where my name would appear when she went into the booth on election day. "Joe," she called, "I can't believe it! They left your name off the ballot!" I swung by her house to check it out. Arthur Ponzio as Democratic County Chairman had set things up so that Governor Hughes as "favorite son" was on Row A. Ponzio's obscure congressional candidate was also on Row A, along with all the Regular Democratic Organization candidates for delegates to the Democratic National Convention and all local offices. Row B was assigned to the Socialist candidate for President; Row C to the Free America candidate for President, and so on down to Row G, on which Jesse Gray, the black leader of a rent strike in New York, appeared as a Presidential candidate. My name was right there with him. No wonder my sister couldn't find it.

Neither could anybody else. Our polls closed at 8 o'clock, and by 9 we knew the results. The only surprise was that, having expected to get only ten percent of the vote I got twenty. After the soda and pizza, my unpaid campaign collection of cousins, nephews, nieces, brothers and sisters and friends headed home. Maryanne took our 4 year old Annie in to bed and fell asleep beside her. My attention was riveted on the California primary, where the polls wouldn't close until 11 PM East Coast time. Bobby Kennedy had battered his way through the primaries, winning where there was a heavy urban vote, losing in places like Oregon which, as one of his staffers who had coffee with him on a campaign break out there told me, Kennedy lamented was "one big f'ng suburb!" By June 4th, the numbers were such that California would be the make-or-break state. If he lost there, he couldn't get the nomination. If he won, he'd be unstoppable. The supporters of rival candidates Gene McCarthy and Vice President Hubert Humphrey went all out to stop Kennedy in California, aided by the still powerful influence of President Johnson.

My oldest daughter Jeanne-Marie, then nine, stayed with me as the televised excitement built, but fell asleep with her head on my lap before the results were clear. It was almost midnight our time when it became likely that Bobby won. The happy crowd at the Ambassador Hotel in Los Angeles went wild with anticipation, waiting for him to appear. It was the most exciting moment in American politics since his brother was elected in 1960. Bobby finally came to the podium, gave a gracious and short victory speech, hugged his wife Ethel and turned his focus to the coming Democratic Convention, urging his supporters "On to Chicago!" With that, he turned and made his way through the kitchen, where Sirhan Sirhan, his assassin, felled him with several shots to the head at point blank range. He remained briefly conscious, then lapsed into a coma.

In the action and passion of the great Presidential campaign, rumors circulated that even if he survived, he would be so disabled he could not return to the campaign. Other rumors followed, of his great personal physical conditioning, of his courageous heart, of the power of his determination and the strength of his life force. He underwent 3 hours of brain surgery on Wednesday. Through the long day the world hung breathless on the outcome. No one who believed in him could surrender the hope that, somehow, he would pull through and continue the great causes he had championed. But in the small hours of Thursday morning he died. When a friend at the *Atlantic City Press* asked me to write something, I gave him a copy of an entry in my personal journal. It ran next day in the *Press*:

A LITTLE GIRL'S EYES TELL OF THE ANGUISH

> Joseph Wilkins identified himself strongly with Sen. Robert F. Kennedy during Wilkins' unsuccessful bid for the Democratic nomination for Congress in the Second District.
>
> His young daughter was keenly interested in how both her father and Sen. Kennedy were making out in their campaigns. Wilkins tells how she accepted the news of Kennedy's death:
>
> "It's the second time for Jeannie. She's going on 10 now, and was nearly five when it happened the first time, burned into memory by four days of television.
>
> I didn't know how to tell her. When a girl is bright, and loving, and nine-and-a-half years old, life should be valentines and giggles and whispered secrets to other nine-and-a-half year old girls.

She came to me early in the morning as I poured myself a cup of coffee. She was frowsy and sleepy-eyed and wanted to know whether I had won the election and how Bobby did in California. I pulled her down to sit on my lap (when she was nearly five I could lift her onto my lap — now she's nearly ten and leggy, and is taller than I am when I'm sitting down.)

It was tough in the telling. Jeannie's the kind of girl who watches your eyes as you talk, being sure to catch every word and expression. And while you're talking, her eyes are talking back to you: merry, or curious, or exasperated with the way you don't understand the situation.

This time the eyes hit me pretty hard. There wasn't anger, or protest, or disbelief. There was only a quick sadness, and then an emptiness – a deep, lonely emptiness that made my Jeannie a thousand years old.

We made it through the day with hope going up and down, mostly down. When the kids went to bed they all prayed ... I guess there were a lot of prayers being said that night.

At seven the next morning she came into our room and sat beside me on the bed. She hadn't been told, but she knew.

There wasn't any questioning, no good mornings or small talk. Her eyes asked confirmation of what she knew in her heart.

"Jeannie ... Jeannie, Bobby didn't make it."

"I know, daddy."

***

Twice in five years all that was bright and promising about America – all the brilliant hope that our country at its best sends forth to illuminate and inspire the world – was shattered by an assassin's bullets. Not twice, in truth, but three times, for no one could gainsay the world-changing crusade of Martin Luther King, Jr., whose own grave was still unsettled. But I had never met King. However much I admired his courage and crusade, I knew him only as a figure on television and in the newspapers. The loss I felt at his death was more of the intellect than of the heart. I had personally met John and Robert Kennedy. I had shaken their hands, looked into their eyes; had engaged their attention and talked with them, had felt the energy of their personalities and the magnetism of their characters. And the course of my life had changed because of them.

I roused myself on the morning of his funeral numb with grief and shock. I do not recall how I returned to Washington that Saturday. By the bitterest of ironies, the law degree I had so doggedly pursued as the gateway to a political career offering meaning and challenge because of the inspiration of Jack and Bobby Kennedy was to be awarded to me next day in Washington. Maryanne and the kids, and my youngest brother Eddie and my widowed stepmother, all came down to Washington for the graduation in the borrowed station wagon of a cousin. We were put up overnight by friends in Bethesda. I must have driven myself down earlier in our car, but I cannot recall a mile of it. All that lies vivid and clear in memory is standing in the dark of the evening in Columbus Plaza at the grand entrance to Union Station in Washington — standing with a silent throng of thousands, waiting for the slow, slow funeral train bringing Bobby's coffin down from the morning mass at St. Patrick's Cathedral in New York. When JFK was assassinated in Dallas I had wandered around Washington in dazed grief as they brought his body home. Now I walked around Capitol Hill waiting for Bobby as the day wore on – wandering from the great hall of Union Station, up the Hill past the Senate and the Capitol Dome, the Supreme Court and the Library of Congress, past the House office buildings and along Pennsylvania Avenue's restaurants and bars where the House and Senate staffers formed the clientele and watched the television as did I, and so back again to Union Station.

The funeral train that brought him from New York to Washington was scheduled to arrive at 4:20 PM. In fact, crowds of mourners along the way so thronged the tracks that several people were killed. The train was forced to travel so slowly it ran five hours late. It did not arrive until after dark on that late summer evening. I watched as television covered the slow, mournful progress of the train along tracks that threaded through the decaying factories and decrepit neighborhoods of New York, of Newark, of Trenton and Philadelphia and Baltimore – everywhere lined with thousands of people, many of them black and poor, who stood at trackside with teary cheeks and stricken countenances as the train passed, its horn mournfully wailing, almost at walking pace to keep more pedestrians from being killed. Yet even in the countryside and the affluent white suburbs crowds lined up thousands long and dozens deep as the train passed. There were few bands or organized appearances along the route of that train. But everywhere along his route the people sang the Battle Hymn of the Republic in his honor. "Mine eyes have seen the glory of the Lord" rose as a massive prayer for Robert F. Kennedy from what seemed the very soul of America along those tracks. It was impossible, hearing that song through the day, not to think of Kennedy and of Abraham Lincoln, passing along those same tracks, their lives and deaths so similarly bound up with America's hope and its tragedy.

In the adaptive style that marked so much of what Kennedy did, the lateness of his train forced rearrangements of his funeral. No one had ever been buried after dark at Arlington National Military Cemetery; no one seemed to know if such burials violated either Arlington's regulations or the rituals or the traditions of the Catholic Church to which Kennedy belonged. When at last the train arrived and the high ceremony of the moment resumed the crowd followed the funeral cortege through the darkened streets of Washington. I walked in that friendly, subdued crowd from Union Station across the foot of Capitol Hill, west along Constitution Avenue past the Justice Department he headed as his brother's Attorney General, past the

Washington Monument and the White House, to the Lincoln Memorial where somewhere out of my sight a choir sang, and from there past the heroic golden statues that guard the Memorial Bridge across the Potomac River to the hill at Arlington that slopes up to the Custis-Lee Mansion and the eternal flame at the grave of John F. Kennedy. The crowd was too great to permit me beyond the Virginia end of the Memorial Bridge. It was enough; I was content to be there, knowing the grief I felt was shared by people of good will throughout the world.

***

For the second time in five years I was scrabbling for the nearest plank after a devastating shipwreck. In the shattered debris of hope, efforts, ambitions and ideals that followed the second Kennedy assassination thousands of Bobby's supporters, some at the peak of their careers and others, like me, at an earlier stage, awoke from shock and grief treading water, trying to piece together what had happened and what it portended for ourselves and for the causes to which we had so enthusiastically committed ourselves.

In the longer range, my desire to practice law had not changed. Receiving my Juris Doctor the day after Robert F. Kennedy's funeral was a moment of intense personal satisfaction even in the shadow of the tragedy. But New Jersey's Bar exam would not be scheduled until nearly seven months away. Even after I took that three-day exam, it would be three or four more months before the results were known. Confident as I was that I would pass the damned thing, even more time would pass before I could be sworn in. It would be nearly a year before I could start earning my living as a lawyer. Meanwhile, I had a family to feed. I needed work, and right away.

Fortunately, the Democrats were still in office and would be at least through the following January. Most of the contacts I developed over the past several years were still in place. I found work as a consultant on various projects. The New Jersey Community Action Training Institute needed somebody to edit a compendium describing what the legal requirement of "maximum feasible participation" of the poor in the design and running of community action programs meant in practical terms. That work carried me through the Fall and up to the January Bar Exam.

But it remained an emotionally disorienting time. Growing up on an island, I knew the feeling of being in an outboard motorboat coming from the ocean into the inlet and having the motor conk out. The wash of your wake and the incoming waves shove you forward with little control in your hands until you can get your engine restarted. I sensed the same phenomenon in national politics that summer. The powerful surge of Robert Kennedy's campaign was such that after his death his followers and supporters were carried forward willy-nilly, with few able to regain control of their course. Many became dispirited observers of what had become, to us, the downward trudge of an America passing from challenge and hope into a political dark age.

The time-table of the presidential election still governed. The Democrats and Republicans each held nominating conventions that summer. Early in August Richard Nixon was nominated at the Republican National Convention in Miami, even as race riots broke out there and elsewhere. He chose an unknown right-wing and secretly corrupt governor, Spiro Agnew of Maryland, as his running mate.

Six days later the Democratic National Convention opened in Chicago. In the ensuing four days of televised drama the Democratic Party imploded before the eyes of the world in unforgettable scenes of riot, bloodshed, police brutality, and shouted obscenities between convention leaders, Chicago's Mayor Richard Daley, and the on-screen shoving and bullying of TV reporters in the convention hall. Hubert Humphrey was nominated with Maine's Senator Edmund Muskie as his running mate. Humphrey, who as Johnson's Vice President had no freedom to disavow Johnson's continuance of the War in Vietnam, emerged from the Convention a bloodied candidate, begrudged by Kennedy supporters who saw him as Johnson's anti-Bobby surrogate; despised by McCarthy's supporters whose anti-war campaign engaged their passions for so many months; and distrusted by Southern Democrats suspicious of his long-standing commitment to racial justice. On election day, although Humphrey defeated Nixon in the popular vote by 43.4% to 42.7% , he lost 301 to 191 in the Electoral College where it really mattered.

***

Chapter 23: A Year in the Wilderness

Having little care for the presidential campaign after Kennedy's death, I concentrated on getting myself admitted to the Bar. Late in January I sat for the 3-day examination. With months to wait until the results would be announced, I made the rounds of Atlantic City law firms in search of employment. There were only about 50 active lawyers in Atlantic County, most of them practicing in 3 to 7 man outfits including a fair share of father and son partnerships which offered little hope of employment for an outsider. Atlantic City was an economic wasteland; the convention business had died with the coming of the jet plane that could whisk conventioneers to warmer climates. The self-styled "Playground of the World" of the roaring twenties had become a down-at-the-heels place from which the young and educated fled. Still, I wanted to raise my children in Brigantine where I grew up rather than in the impersonal environs of Washington or Philadelphia.

The nature of a new lawyer's employment had changed over recent years. When I first began law school in 1961 the old system – involving a low-pay law office clerkship working for experienced lawyers for almost a year was in place — a vestigial remnant of the day when lawyers like Abraham Lincoln read law. Fortunately for me it was replaced in 1962 by a requirement that candidates for the Bar take a "Skills and Methods" course to bring them down from the high academic atmosphere of scholarly discussions to the mundane but essential skills of finding your way to the courthouse, drafting wills, interviewing clients, and preparing cases for trial. I was spared the old-fashioned and economically threadbare clerkship of earlier years. But the mindset of the earlier tradition lingered. No matter what experience I had in government, or in managing large staffs and budgets, I was a rookie in the eyes of interviewing lawyers trying to figure out what I could bring to their practice. And until the results of the Bar Exam were announced and I could be admitted as a lawyer, my economic value to any law firm was limited.

Jim Cooper, a dynamic and successful trial lawyer who specialized in personal injury cases, gave me a job. He was a liberal Democrat in his politics, had marched in Mississippi with civil rights activists, and maintained an aggressive independence from the corrupt influences of the Republican organization that had controlled Atlantic County for generations. Of great promise to me was that I could learn how to earn good money as he had; representing plaintiffs in personal injury cases. He had just won the first million-dollar jury verdict in the history of the county. Clients were flocking to his office. His firm had 8 or so lawyers, including several about to retire and several recently admitted. In the dismal legal landscape of the city Cooper's firm was an oasis of talent and opportunity. I found myself deep in the arcane details of reviewing depositions, proposing and answering interrogatories about which witnesses saw what, and listening to the partners evaluate the monetary worth of cases.

What I had not expected, and what law school had failed to prepare me for, was that the private practice of law is a business. Like any other business, there are costs of rent, secretaries, library books, investigation, medical reports, and all the rest, and nobody takes money home to feed the kids until you have made the nut. Although Cooper's law firm was big enough he could comfortably carry young lawyers a year or two until they could earn their keep, there was no question of ignoring the economic facts of life. Nevertheless, listening to professionals weigh the cash value of human injury bothered me. Law school had featured discussions about the legal concepts of liability, as in whether it was Driver A or Driver B who caused the accident and should pay the damage. Absent from the classroom was the clinical detail of just what those damages were — how much, for example, might a jury award to an elderly woman who suffered a broken leg as the result of an accident, as compared to the award they might give an attractive young woman who was facially scarred by that same kind of accident.

These calculations reached their zenith in worker's compensation cases, of which there were many. Under worker's compensation laws, the question of fault is bypassed; so long as the worker suffered the injury in the course and scope of his employment, liability is assigned to the employer, who is required by law to carry insurance against such damages. The only question remaining is to what extent the worker has been injured and what is the appropriate financial compensation. That, in turn, is based on a complex formula that factors in such elements as the worker's rate of pay, his medical expenses, the extent of his disability and its nature as either temporary or permanent. However practical the system may be, I found it repugnant to see the loss of an arm or foot weighed and measured in such terms as X percent of disability; permanent or partial disability, and the like.

It became clear to me that my discomfort with the mechanics of calibrating human suffering with financial compensation was too serious a flaw in the makeup of a personal injury lawyer. I once again cast about for work. One of my contacts was Joel Sterns, a Democrat who worked over the previous decade in Washington in the Kennedy and Johnson Administrations before becoming Paul Ylvisaker's deputy at the N.J. Department of Community Affairs and, on Ylvisaker's resignation, Acting Commissioner. Meanwhile, he took the train daily from Trenton to New York to pursue his law degree at New York University, just as I was driving daily from Millville to Washington to get my law degree. When he was admitted to the Bar in 1968 he became Chief Counsel to Governor Hughes. Sterns was familiar with the problems I'd had with Warren Lummis and his opposition to free divorces for impoverished black women. Still waiting for the results of the Bar Exam, I drove to Trenton in mid-March and met with Sterns. He told me I could have a position as a Deputy Attorney General, assuming I passed the Bar. Or he could arrange to have the Governor appoint me to one or another of the various state boards, although those would be no-pay appointments. We discussed jobs with the Atlantic County prosecutor, but he held out little hope because, as a practical matter, they were controlled by Republican Senator Frank S. "Hap" Farley.

A job as one of the dozens of Deputy Attorney Generals for the state sounded more attractive than it was. At the time few criminal matters were within the jurisdiction of the State Attorney General to prosecute, so there was little experience in that area to be gained. The Deputy AG's were usually young lawyers assigned to represent the many state agencies in their mundane work. They were good jobs in which to gain experience in public affairs. The problem was they were full time and at $8,500 didn't pay enough for me to support the family. In any event, they offered none of the trial and law-practice experience I knew would be necessary if I were ever to strike out on my own.

My only immediate hope was to find enough consulting work to tide me over, at least for the few months until the Bar Exam results came out. Tom Karter, who played a significant role within OEO in funding migrant programs around the country, now ran a small consulting firm evaluating farmworker programs for OEO and the U.S. Department of Labor. He gave me assignments evaluating programs in the South. The Volt Information Services company hired me as a consultant and kept me afloat – barely afloat – with several assignments through the spring.

But the bottom line was that, on the eve of my becoming a licensed attorney at law, I had no definite starting place for a legal career. Any sort of local political patronage was out of the question, since the Democratic Party had no jobs to hand out even if they wanted to.

Oddly enough, my personal ties with the local Republicans were friendly. I had grown up in Brigantine and returned to it to raise my kids. The island was a Republican bastion that regularly produced heavy majorities for Howard "Fritz" Haneman, who ran the county government as Director of the County Board of Freeholders. Fritz, whose father was New Jersey Supreme Court Justice Vincent S. Haneman, was the Brigantine lifeguard who taught me how to swim when I was a boy. In an unexpected way I was a problem for Fritz and the Judge. They understood more than anybody the long-term danger of having a hometown lawyer in the opposite political party. I might be scratching for a living at the moment, but once I got my ticket and hung out my shingle, there was every probability I would in a few years be causing them political headaches. I had no ambition for local office or politics — my hopes were to someday reach the U.S. Congress and eventually the Senate. But in all likelihood any progress I made would be at the expense of the entrenched Republican machine.

Fritz, a seasoned political leader aware of my ambitions and of my bruised and battered prospects in the Democratic Party, called one day and said "the Judge" wanted me to come by for a drink. Fritz lived in a lovely home on a point that overlooked the bay as it runs southwards along Brigantine toward Atlantic City. The living room was on the second floor and featured a huge picture-window that framed a view of the bay and, at night, the bright lights of the Atlantic City skyline. Over drinks next to a cheery fireplace Justice Haneman, an earthy, bluff and friendly old fox, laid out for me the bright prospects I might enjoy if I were to switch to the Republican Party. As a Justice on New Jersey's highest court he was technically barred from political activities such as recruiting guys like me, but we all understood this was a strictly off-the-record occasion.

Justice Haneman, a life-long friend of the all-powerful state Senator Farley, promised that my path to the many political plums Farley controlled would be short and well-paved. His son Fritz, who controlled all of the Brigantine jobs and as head of the County government hundreds of county jobs, including the appointment of lawyers for the county public boards and authorities, assured me I could have my pick of them. As for higher office, nothing would please them more than to see one of their own make it to the U.S. Senate someday. Fritz had no ambitions higher than the considerable power he already possessed. The rest of the Republican organization, the Judge admitted, held few others whose abilities or hopes extended beyond the county level. In the Judge's eyes, having known me since I was a kid, I was an excellent candidate for protégée.

He had taken me to a high place and, nodding his head toward the bright lights of Atlantic City, offered me as much of the world as he could deliver. I would like to claim a biblical holiness in resisting the temptation, but in truth I was saved by the foolish optimism of youth rather than by moral rectitude. The lights of Atlantic City meant nothing to me, and if I were ever to realize my Kennedy-inspired dream and make it to Washington I did not intend to arrive wearing the livery of the Republican Party which, in my eyes, dedicated its energies to stopping the progress of social justice across the board. We parted on good personal terms. I don't think either the Judge or Fritz ever quite gave up hope that I would someday come into the fold.

As the time for learning the results of the Bar Exam approached and I was scraping the bottom of the economic barrel, my luck started to change for the better. Daryl Todd, a young and civic-minded lawyer in Jim Cooper's office with whom I had worked, was on the Board of Directors of Cape Atlantic Legal Services, the OEO-funded program that provided lawyers for the poor in Atlantic and Cape May Counties. A reform-minded young Republican, Daryl had the public-minded conscience of what were then known as "Eastern Establishment" Republicans, already losing influence in their own party. Raised with a strong belief that only Republicans could be trusted with government, he accepted as a concomitant of that belief that social justice was important. CALS, the local legal services program on whose board he sat, was in trouble. Its grant from OEO provided funds for a directing attorney and four other attorneys, three secretaries, and two investigators to provide legal services to an estimated 50,000 low-income clients in Atlantic and Cape May Counties.

Unfortunately, its initial directing attorney suffered the liberal curse of seeing every problem as one that demanded radical reform, preferably by way of Supreme Court decisions. Every case was a law-reform case made for the federal courts and suitable to go all the way to the U.S. Supreme Court. In his zeal to be at the cutting edge of law reform, he proved a poor administrator. The ordinary legal troubles of the poor with landlords, bill collectors and the gas company languished while he devoted program resources to cases that might, after two or three years of litigation, get to the higher reaches of the federal court system. When eventually he left Bob Subranni, a local lawyer with a burgeoning private practice and no experience dealing with the problems of the poor was brought in on an acting basis. He was a good man, but ill-equipped to salvage a program that was about to be closed down by the regional OEO office for its ineffective performance.

Daryl Todd, knowing of my history running OEO programs, suggested to his fellow members on the CALS board that bringing me in to run the program might keep the OEO funding alive. An evening interview was scheduled for late in April. By then, the results of the Bar Exam might be announced.

***

By early April I was at the end of my very frayed economic rope, in debt to just about everyone, chasing whatever consulting assignments I could find in Washington, Boston and New York. Days passed with still no word from the Bar Exam. I landed two days of work in Washington, where I was able to stay, free, with a friend from OEO. In Washington the flowers burst into bloom. Office workers looked for empty places on the green lawns surrounding public buildings to sit and get a bit of sun while eating their lunch. Young tourists – students from hundreds of high schools and colleges on their class trips – flocked around the Capitol. I took no joy from any of it.

I worked all night to finish a report, then drove to Philadelphia to deliver it, expecting a check for $365 that did not come through, and then drove back to Washington to log in a few more days for which the pay would be a month or more away.

When the dam finally broke, I was flooded with good news. On April 17th, a Thursday – always my lucky day — the mail came early, bringing with it a letter from the Board of Bar Examiners. Maryanne brought it to me while I was shaving and watched me open it with eager fingers. I had passed the Bar and was to be sworn in on May 13th! It took her a long time to get my shaving lather out of her hair. Also in that lucky, lucky mail, the $365 check arrived at last.

I called my friends to spread the news, and called Daryl Todd, who had set me up with an interview scheduled for that very evening with the board of the local Legal Services program for the job as director. The significance of the results seeped slowly into my heart. It had been eight long years since that hot summer day when I trudged out of Philadelphia in corduroy trousers and tweed jacket, hitchhiking to Washington with 26 pennies in my pocket.

The day was misty, with a hot sun and cool sea mist – a perfect seashore day when the island was alive with the coming of Spring. That afternoon I walked up the beach to the Seahorse Fishing Pier at the north end of the Island where I could look out over miles of a wild and empty beach and the blue ocean stretching forever, feeling for all the world like a South Pacific beachcomber, enjoying a cold beer while around me the sounds of scrubbing, painting and getting ready for the season blended with the sound of a baseball game on the radio.

That night I won the unanimous vote of the Board of Trustees of Cape Atlantic Legal Services as their choice for Chief Attorney at a salary of $15,000 per year. I was to start work on May 1st.

I could not sleep that night. I was still shifting psychological gears – trying to sort out facts, feelings, and plans. The legal services program carried a lot of responsibility with it. Steady pay would be a great relief, and the challenge was growing on me – almost against my will and better judgment. But the price was high. It would take all my energy, and much time – new time, when the freshness of practice would stimulate me. For two years I would have no private clients, and would have to stay out of politics. In return I would become expert in areas of law with little or no application to private practice.

In keeping with the old saying that "it never rains but it pours," that weekend I received a call from Art Ponzio – the County Democratic Chairman who had opposed my nomination for Congress. Now he was engaged in a bitter struggle to hang on to his control of the Atlantic County Democratic party. It was time to put together the ticket of candidates to run for the state offices. Would I be interested in being the Regular Democrat candidate for the New Jersey State Assembly? I said no with unusual vigor.

So it was that on May 1, 1969 — two weeks before I was sworn in to the Bar — I became the chief attorney of a five man law firm with 50,000 clients spread over two counties, none of whom could afford a lawyer.

Chapter 24: Running Legal Services

The world in which I was admitted to the Bar in the spring of 1969 was a far cry from what I assumed it would be when first I set out to become a lawyer. Nixon won the White House by riding the wave of middle-class reaction against the riots, protests, and chaos of the Sixties. His inauguration in January of 1969 did nothing to stop them. In April black students carrying rifles and sporting huge "Afro" haircuts seized offices at Columbia College in New York. Disturbing photographs of their leaders triumphantly brandishing rifles on the steps of the University appeared in newspapers everywhere as college administrators, in the misguided belief they were protecting academic freedom, resisted calling in the police to restore order. A week or two later 80 black students at Cornell followed suit, demanding courses in Black Studies and amnesty for themselves. In Vietnam the number of American troops reached 543,000 – a figure unimaginable in the days when I watched the Gulf of Tonkin Resolution debated in the Senate. In California thousands of Berkeley student protestors tried to seize open land on which the University planned to build dormitories. It was then that, in Governor Ronald Reagan, the right wing conservatives at last found their man on horseback. He placed Berkeley under martial law. Helicopters sprayed tear-gas on the protestors. The riot police shot and killed a man.

Such was the world when I finally took my oath as an attorney in Trenton on May 13, 1969. It was a strangely anti-climactic ceremony on a beautiful Tuesday. Dozens of us shuffled into Trenton's dull War Memorial Building, signed our names, listened to speeches, and took the oath. It was a strange oath, which included gratuitously insulting language whereby we had to swear not to steal money from our clients — a prescient indicator of the state of the Bar. A recent President of the Atlantic County Bar Association was even then under indictment for stealing client's money from his trust fund.

Much of what I faced as the new Chief Attorney of Cape Atlantic Legal Services (CALS) involved the supervision of legal matters in which I had no experience. But after a year of difficult times, just having my hands on the tiller again felt wonderful. Once more I had the authority and the funds to make things happen. The legal services program I took over had a heavy backlog of cases defending against evictions, wage garnishments, repossessions and utility shut-offs. The lawyers and secretaries were unsure their jobs would be there come next month. The files were haphazard; desks were piled with notes, memos and pleadings; documents that might be needed as evidence were buried in the mess. There was no clear policy on which cases we should fight and which negotiate. Since the program was unable to pay the salaries required to hire legal secretaries trained to take dictation in shorthand, the staff lawyers spent their time handwriting pleadings, which then had to be typed and re-typed, often through three or four time-consuming drafts. Things were so bad the Office of Economic Opportunity had concluded it would be better to shut the program down rather than waste more money on it.

Nor was OEO the friendly sponsor the anti-poverty programs knew of old. President Nixon had been in office just 100 days when I took over Legal Services. He and his Administration made no secret of their determination to dismantle OEO – the agency they had demonized in Republican election campaigns for the past four years. What programs President Nixon could quietly strangle he would; the ones with too much support in the still Democratic-controlled Congress he intended to sever from OEO and parcel out to old-line agencies before administering the final *coup de grace* to OEO itself. Head Start, for example, was too popular to kill outright. Legal Services, on the other hand, might be quietly starved of funds and red-taped to death with stringent reporting regulations and controls. The Nixon Administration had its hands full with other schemes and plans, including the illegal bombing of Cambodia and various clandestine moves to suppress dissent against the War. Compared to Vietnam, the anti-poverty war had already dwindled to a minor sideshow. To carry out his plans to shut it down, Nixon announced the appointment, just 4 days before I took over Cape Atlantic Legal Services, of a conservative Republican congressman named Donald Rumsfeld to be OEO's new director. Rumsfeld brought in as his Special Assistant at OEO an obscure 29 year old conservative congressional staffer from Wyoming named Dick Cheney, who had come to Rumsfeld's attention by sending him a strategy memo outlining the steps necessary to kill the anti-poverty programs.

In their efforts to dismantle the anti-poverty programs Rumsfeld and Cheney were handicapped by the remaining substantial Democratic majorities in Congress. Rumsfeld's speeches were accordingly designed to allay political objections, but neither he nor Cheney had any hesitation in ending programs that in their view challenged the established order of wealth and power.

I knew enough about the federal government to realize it would be a year or two before the changes they desired could be implemented. With luck and hard work, I hoped to have at least my small program shipshape enough by then to survive whatever funding crises came along. What I planned was no more and no less than traditional law, practiced with vigor on behalf of the poor.

My first action after meeting the staff was to pay courtesy calls on the judges before whom we were bringing cases. When controversies broke, as they must sooner or later, they would at least know me and have my phone number. The legal profession is intensely personal, in the sense that we want to size up whoever we might encounter in court. If people know nothing about you except by reputation, you are at the mercy of gossip. If they have a chance to shake your hand and look you in the eye, they tend to forget the gossip and form their own opinions.

The next step was to pacify the OEO, which was about to close the CALS program down. Here I had useful contacts. A few calls to Washington and a quick trip to the OEO bought us another year of decent funding. Such easy success was still possible before the Rumsfeld-Cheney team could get full control at the working level, but it was unlikely to be repeated in future years.

Reflecting the choices of its original director, the CALS law library shelves were filled with law books dealing with federal cases, Supreme

Court cases, and procedural guides about how to prepare and win cases before the Supreme Court of the United States. All this despite the fact that the nearest federal court was sixty miles away and the problems our clients faced had to do with getting the landlord to fix the toilet or turn the heat on. Prestigious law reform cases were the pet fad of liberal lawyers who thought it beneath themselves to slug it out in Landlord Tenant or Small Claims court with lawyers for slumlords and fraudulent lenders. They preferred to select just the right client with just the right test case to bring before just the right activist judge to win hoped-for sweeping edicts that would reform the law at one stroke, and help them make their reputations. I was in favor of such test cases, but believed they should be brought by the special legal services research centers which OEO had funded for just that purpose. I saw no reason why a mother with six kids should do without heat in her apartment because the local legal services office which was supposed to be battling on her behalf had its eye on higher things.

I got hold of Bill Tumulty, a bantamweight lawbook salesman who as a boy in Washington saw President Woodrow Wilson drive himself around town in a tiller-steered electric car. He helped us trade in most of our federal law library for law books that could be useful in fighting ordinary bread-and-butter cases in Landlord-Tenant and Small Claims Court, and on local issues.

I ordered new IBM dictating equipment, electric typewriters, a new Xerox machine, and had the rooms painted, the lights fixed, the windows washed and the floor carpeted. Our landlord was Lou Zaris, a World War II veteran who survived a German Prisoner of War camp. He agreed to provide weekly cleaning services and pay for the painting, the lights and the carpets in exchange for my renewing our lease for another year.

Reviews of cases in progress were sporadic, and there was little practical communication between the legal services office and leaders of the local client communities. At staff meetings I instituted a regularly scheduled full review of every case; insisted that the files be organized and brought the secretaries into the process in the belief that while the lawyers might know the law, the secretaries knew the clients and the judges' secretaries. During my brief tenure working in Jim Cooper's law office I learned how important it was to keep the file on each case so methodically arranged that any lawyer in the office could pick it up and go into court ready to plead the case confident that he had all necessary notes and documentary evidence at hand. I insisted upon a similar practice at CALS.

Technically all of the cases in the legal services program were brought in my name as Chief Attorney, even though they were handled by the staff attorneys. Still, given my total inexperience as a lawyer, I arranged to personally take on a representative selection of cases. Before long my caseload included a divorce case; a bankruptcy, a housing project complaint, a community agreement, a complaint against the urban renewal agency, a complaint against police handling of a citizen, and the incorporation of a non-profit organization.

I was helped greatly by Mrs. Barbara Camper, a tall, gentle-voiced African-American woman of competence and impeccable manners whom I inherited as secretary. Barbara had a personal dignity that set a unique tone in the office. She greeted everyone coming in and out — clients, staff and visitors — with the same quiet manners and respect. The calming effect she had on emotionally troubled clients, of whom we had many, was remarkable. One day a man harassed beyond endurance by the tactics of bill collectors entered the office in a rage. He slammed the door after himself so hard the glass shattered. I popped out of my office to see what was going on. Shards of glass covered the floor; jagged edges marked the frame of the door. The client stood there still enraged at his tormentors. Barbara didn't bat an eyelash, just looked at him quietly and said "Oh, Mr. Jones, are you all right? Did you cut yourself?" His anger evaporated. I wanted to throw the man out, but saw the wisdom of Barbara's patience.

Bob Subranni, having carried the burden of Acting Director at the expense of his burgeoning private practice, wanted to return to his clientele. I was sorry to lose him. We also had part-time attorneys advising clients one evening each week in our satellite offices. Their approach was the traditional one for legal aid, inherited from the days of volunteer programs when the best that could be done for the poor was to work out milder terms for paying debts which were, by any current legal analysis, vulnerable to challenge in court. My view was that if a client owed $750 as the result of a consumer fraud for a refrigerator that retailed for $200, it wasn't enough to negotiate a longer payment schedule for the $750. The underlying transaction itself should be fought in court. I ran newspaper ads, called all the contacts I knew, and eventually recruited a series of bright young attorneys willing to take low pay in exchange for a year or so of experience and a chance to help people in trouble.

The 50,000 clients for whose legal representation I was now responsible certainly needed lawyers who were prepared to fight for them. Of the 21 counties in New Jersey, Atlantic and Cape May counties, covered by CALS, were by every statistic the poorest. Nor was the problem confined to income. The combined population in the two counties of 234,597 was spread over an area of 1,291 square miles with practically no public transportation, which meant simply getting to the legal services offices and the courthouses was an added burden for the poor.

The potential clientele was mostly white. Their poverty was almost Appalachian in its nature, albeit hidden in backwoods cottages and trailer parks among folks caught in the confused religiosity of the Rev. Carl McIntyre's racially-coded tirades, far from the urban aggregation of black folks whose economic oppression they unknowingly shared,.

From the tip of beach on my home island of Brigantine at the northernmost point of Atlantic County, the shoreline stretched south 40 miles to the Cape May Point and back northwestwardly along the shoreline of the Delaware Bay to the Cumberland County line near Shellpile and Port Norris – about 170 miles of shoreline. Inland from there, amid the miles of pine forest, weatherbeaten cottages, trailer parks and tumbledown shacks in the woods, was where my clients lived. Generally, the closer to the ocean, the richer the inhabitants. Such was not always the case, however. In Atlantic City a large black urban population had existed for years, serving the hotel industry as maids, cooks, janitors and bellmen in summer and going on unemployment in winter. So also in Wildwood down in Cape May County, where the residences of black maids and dishwashers were tolerated by a seasonal tourism industry in need of their services.

My office was in Atlantic City, which held within its borders the largest single concentration of poor people in either county, and those mostly African-American. That large population was at last, after over a century of oppression and exploitation, becoming organized in search of civil justice and equal rights. Many leaders of Atlantic City's black community saw little reason to waste time worrying about whether the white residents of distant trailer parks were getting a fair shake from their landlords. The racial injustices they faced in their daily lives far outweighed such far-afield concerns. A black leader championing the cause of poor whites seemed incongruous to them – even though in the last months of his life Martin Luther King, Jr. had seen and begun to teach that racism was only one facet of the greater evil of poverty. But nowhere had the Poverty War provided sufficient funds to address all the poverty there was. Choices had to be made, and those choices often came down to whether help should be given to the twice-as-numerous but twice-as-scattered poor whites along obscure roads out in the counties, or to the far less numerous but equally poor blacks in the more compact and reachable neighborhoods of poverty in Atlantic City, Pleasantville, and Wildwood, where the anti-poverty dollar might go further. The tensions created by that demographic were hard to escape.

There was a limit to the number of cases any lawyer could competently handle. Each case had a cost in lawyer time. Clients had to be interviewed; pleadings prepared; evidence gathered; trial preparation organized. In private law firms, such a volume of business could be handled by renting more space and hiring more lawyers and secretaries — luxuries unavailable to legal services, where we had to cope with a rigid budget and needy clientele. The math was harsh; of the tens of thousands of clients needing help, our five lawyers would be doing well if we could handle a fifth of the cases that came in the door.

The local lawyers in private practice, while generally supportive thanks to the voluntary participation on our Board of respected young lawyers, had two points on which they were touchy. The first was a fear that we would accept clients who, by scrimping and saving, might be able to pay for a private lawyer. The second was the fear that we would start handling divorce cases.

Divorces were the Great Dismal Swamp of legal services programs. If you accepted divorce cases, hundreds of women would take up every lawyer-minute of even the largest legal services programs. The demand was so great that accepting divorce matters meant, unless you established a waiting list years long, you could not deal with evictions, substandard living conditions, or anything else.

Private lawyers felt strongly that divorces were a luxury, not a necessity, and that women who insisted on divorces should save, beg or borrow the money to pay for their divorce. The lawyer who served as chair of the Atlantic County Bar Association's Minimum Fee Committee openly boasted that he kept those fees as high as possible. In 1969 the minimum fee an Atlantic County lawyer was supposed to charge for an uncontested divorce— on penalty of being deemed "unethical" — was $400 plus $110 in court costs (about $4,000 in 2014 dollars) as published in the N.J. Lawyer's Diary for that year. This in a day when the minimum wage was $1.60 an hour – if you were covered by the minimum wage laws, which was not true of many local jobs.

It was a harsh dilemma for women with children — which was to say almost all poor women – made worse by the law's failure at that time to recognize the concept of marital rape. If she was too poor to enjoy the luxury of a divorce, a wife was at risk of forcible sex from a drunk or brutal husband. She could, of course, bring a suit for the right to move out and live apart free of his attentions. If she tried that approach, the payment of her lawyer depended upon whatever the court might order her husband to cough up. This was the ultimate Catch 22, because no lawyer would risk taking cases where his court-ordered fees had to come from husbands who often were unemployed drunks. On the other hand, if she simply moved out, that would technically constitute desertion on her part, thus disqualifying her from seeking a divorce under New Jersey's archaic divorce law of the time. Nor could she get an order compelling him to move out of the house, because the courts had not yet agreed that even the most abusive husband might be ordered out of the marital home. They clung to the concept that a man's home was his castle, with the implied sub-text that he was free to beat his wife within it.

The impact of the Minimum Fee Schedule was skewed heavily against women needing divorces. An uncontested divorce for which the published minimum fee was $400 might take a few hours of preparation and office work, and a half-hour in the county courthouse. By comparison, if you had a case before the New Jersey Supreme Court in Trenton, the highest court in the state, the minimum fee set by the Atlantic County Bar was $350.

In fact, the Minimum Fee Schedule was illegal price-fixing by the Bar Association. The justification claimed for it was that if a lawyer charged less he was competing on the basis of price, which would so depress legal fees that no lawyer could earn enough money to assure the highest standard of legal care for his clients. This, by the tortured logic of the rationale, was unethical. No one ever seemed to have been formally charged with violating the Minimum Fee Schedule, but the Schedule was approved by the county Bar Associations annually and printed in the Lawyer's Dairy every lawyer kept on his desk. Lawyers who shaved their prices felt considerable peer pressure and the possibility of being hauled before the dreaded ethics committee.

Poverty law had problems within problems, floating in a swamp of problems. The greatest challenge was the sheer volume of clients who came to us for help. My experience in running programs and getting funding freed me to a considerable extent to devote my time to actual lawyering. I had seen the problems of poverty from Washington; had visited scenes of poverty throughout America; had hired and directed scores of people to run programs to feed, educate, and find employment for the poor. But in those efforts my role was to observe, to report, to direct. Now I had for the first time a personal and professional responsibility to represent the individuals who came to me for help.

My new life as a lawyer for the poor started with my first client appointment.

Chapter 25: Saving the Household Furniture – Atlantic City Justice

The McCrackens came into the office shamefaced and shuffling their feet, fearful of their legal problems and unsure how to talk to a lawyer. When you hang impressive-looking diplomas on your wall and sit behind your desk with a secretary in the outer office, it's easy to forget how scary it is for ordinary people — the men and women who ride buses and push brooms and get their hands dirty at work and never got past the eighth grade – to talk with you.

Although the McCrackens had no children he, gray haired, open faced and dressed in clean, faded slacks and shirt, called her "mother" and she called him "father." Their thirtieth wedding anniversary was already behind them. He was a shelf-stocker for the local A&P supermarket, whose best points were that he showed up for work on time every day, was pleasant and helpful to the customers, and respectfully obedient to the succession of young managers on their way up the corporate ladder. He'd been lucky with overtime for several years. His paycheck, although slim, had gotten just that dangerous bit fatter.

Mrs. McCracken – a heavyset woman a year or two older than her husband with a sad, lined face and dispirited air, was a housewife. Their home was a one-bedroom bungalow deep in the pine barrens on the mainland. It started life as a hunting camp owned by a dozen guys from Pennsylvania, was abandoned piecemeal as the hunters got divorced, aged, or moved to Florida, and finally was offered for sale to anybody willing to do without city water and paved streets and to put up with a septic tank and bottled gas for heat and cooking. They'd lived there most of their married life. Her routine consisted of doing the everyday chores of running a home and settling down afterwards on the couch to watch TV with her husband.

It was the TV that did them in. Mrs. McCracken had an almost religious belief that everything on TV was true. Every time the TV reported a new disease, she woke up next morning with the symptoms. Off she'd go to the doctors, and home she'd come with pills, prescriptions, and the conviction that she was about to die and leave Mr. McCracken with no one to care for him.

One day the TV news carried the report of another truly horrible and inevitably fatal disease. Mrs. McCracken was certain she was its victim. The symptoms were vague, but fitted hers in every detail. There was a shortness of breath, and she had shortness of breath. There were aches and pains, and she had aches and pains. There was a rash that was exactly like that red splotch on her arm she'd been suspicious of for years. The end, she was certain, was near.

Being a generous soul and grateful for the attention of the doctors, nurses and receptionists who helped her confront the deadly disease over the next few weeks, she pushed the credit cards to the max buying "thank you" gifts for everybody. She knew this would cause no problems for Mr. McCracken because her credit insurance would pay off any debts owed on the cards when she died. The bills for all the gifts arrived at the same time Mr. McCracken's overtime was cut off.

The creditors – who preferred to call themselves by the tonier-sounding "credit grantors" – were unfazed. This, after all, was a good customer. When she maxed out the cards they granted more credit. It was as easy as selling more drinks to a drunk.

Still convinced it was only a matter of time until she passed away, Mrs. McCracken ran the cards to their new maximums, playing Santa Claus to the local health care industry. When the credit card companies finally balked at doing it again, the McCrackens headed to the Finance Company, signed a few papers, and got enough money to make partial payments on the arrearages – which freed up her credit card limit to allow her to get even deeper in debt.

Nothing lasts forever, and the day came when the encouraging calls from the finance company urging the McCrackens to take on more debt turned into questions about when they'd be making payments. However, you can't get a whole lot of money out of a guy who earns his living making sure the labels on the cans of chicken noodle soup all face outwards. It's especially tough to squeeze him when his overtime's been cut off.

The fundamental problem, from an objective point of view, was that Mrs. McCracken didn't die. She was heavy and wheezed a lot, but otherwise seemed in fair health when, badgered beyond endurance by a swelling volume of vicious telephone calls at home (her) and at work (him) from bill collectors, she and Mr. McCracken came to the legal services office to find out if they should go bankrupt.

For many Americans the stigma of personal bankruptcy had long since lost its social embarrassment. But folks at the bottom of the economic food chain like the McCrackens had an old-fashioned shame about going broke. They'd been taught that bankruptcy ranked almost as low as murder on the slide into moral depravity.

"I'm so ashamed," Mrs. McCracken blubbered, reaching out for her husband's hand. "He's worked so hard, and we've come to this!" Mr. McCracken patted her arm. "It's all right, Mother. We'll be okay," he said.

I agreed to take their case, and asked Paul Wright, a staff attorney of several years experience, to prepare the necessary court pleadings. Paul was what lawyers call "a good inside man", meaning he was useful on legal research and paperwork, but uncomfortable in a courtroom. A lawyer with 9 years at the Bar, he was honest and capable, but was handicapped by a personality quirk that sent him off on lines of thought that changed and contradicted each other almost immediately, like a movie character who steps confidently out in one direction, is hit by a sudden thought after a step or two and changes direction only to be hit by another sudden thought and another and another, until he has taken dozens of steps and yet made no progress in any one direction. His personal story was fascinating. Near the end of WW II he lied about his age to get into the Marine Corps. While aboard ship heading for Okinawa the atomic bombs were dropped on Hiroshima and Nagasaki and Japan surrendered. Paul spent his Marine Corps tour of duty in military law enforcement, patrolling the rougher parts of Chinese ports, hauling sailors out of Chinese whorehouses and waterfront bars. He returned home and got his college and law degrees, but was then confounded by the unexpected pressures of the courtroom.

The immediate decision that perplexed him was whether, since Mr. McCracken had a job and owned his own home, he and Mrs. McCracken were technically ineligible for free legal services from our office. The local lawyers, struggling in an already depressed local economy, were fearful of being driven out of business. The recent creation of the Public Defender's Office took away the bread-and-butter criminal cases on which they depended. Now Legal Services threatened their civil practice – the evictions, divorces, bankruptcies and wage executions from which fees could be earned. My predecessors at Legal Services endured protests from private lawyers about taking cases where the clients could, at least theoretically, come up with money to pay their fees. Guidelines were in place designed to measure how poor you had to be to get a free lawyer. I was not satisfied that the guidelines themselves were realistic, because they measured only the funds available to the client — not the cost of the legal services the client required. If you were poor you got a free lawyer; if a dollar over the poverty line, you were considered able to pay just as big a legal bill as the corporation that was suing you. Even the simplest calculation made it clear that the McCrackens, given the cost of their defense measured against their mountain of debt, the high interest rates they were paying, and their now harshly limited net income, qualified. And if anything was clear in their case, it was that borrowing to pay their lawyer wasn't an option. I assured Paul the McCrackens were eligible for our services.

He prepared the pleadings; the McCrackens returned to sign them, and we filed them in the federal Bankruptcy Court. Under the Bankruptcy Law, the pleadings listed each and every debt the McCrackens owed, and the name and address of each creditor. The Bankruptcy Court scheduled a hearing on the Petition for Bankruptcy, and sent postcard notices to every creditor on the list so they could come to court, prove their claim, and protest if they thought the debtors were concealing assets that should be used to pay the debt.

All this was the routine prelude to a simple mathematical calculation:

if the debts so outweighed the assets and the income it was impossible for the debtor to pay them, the assets could be sold and the proceeds pro-rated among the creditors. However, the law provided various exemptions and set a threshold protecting minimal assets from the process. Even the harshest creditor was not permitted to sell the clothes off the debtors' backs and send them naked into the world – although some of the more avid bill collectors seemed to consider even that limitation a denial of the creditor's rights. The McCrackens had so few assets and their income was so limited in relation to their bills that the issuance by the Bankruptcy Court of a complete discharge of all their debts other than the house mortgage was certain to be a routine matter. The house itself was not at risk. It could not be ordered sold for the benefit of creditors other than the bank that held the mortgage unless the house was worth a good deal more than the mortgage, which was not the case with the McCrackens. In practice, creditors faced with bankruptcy petitions of that sort rarely bothered to show up in court. Those that did were represented by a handful of lawyers on the lookout for the occasional fraudulent man trying to hide serious assets.

The Judge was Bill Lipkin, who was at that time the senior Bankruptcy Judge in the nation, having been appointed in Franklin Roosevelt's second term. He had literally been the judge in Bankruptcy since I was born.

I met the clients at the Atlantic City Hall, where Judge Lipkin held hearings every two weeks, driving the sixty miles from his regular courtroom at the federal courthouse in Camden for the occasion. The docket was heavy. My cases were well down the list. Eager to learn courtroom procedures no matter how routine, I sat off to the side, watching the process and seeing how the whole thing worked. It was, as in any court where there is a heavy volume of work for the judge, mostly cut-and-dried. A case would be called; the lawyer for the debtor would take a seat at counsel table; the debtor would walk to the witness box and be sworn in; his lawyer would ask if this was his petition in bankruptcy and if everything it said was true. If no opposition showed up the judge would announce "discharge will be granted" in a crisp monotone as he reached for the next file.

The change, when it came, hit me like a hand grenade. Another case; another witness; another lawyer; the usual questions. This time a second lawyer, who represented the same finance company to which the McCrackens owed money, stood up. "My client's claim is secured by the household furniture," said the lawyer. "I request an Order of repossession and sale." "The Order will be granted," the judge intoned. "Next case."

"What the hell's that all about?" I whispered to the lawyer sitting next to me waiting for his case to be called.

I learned with a sinking heart that particular finance company had a policy, whenever they made a consumer loan, of having the borrower sign both the note – the legal IOU for the money — and in addition a separate document giving them what is called a "security interest" in the household furniture. The furniture was essentially worthless. If the finance company tried reselling it, a living room sofa that might have cost $175 new might, with worn patches and soda stains and other wear marks, fetch $10. Of course, the last thing the finance company wanted was used furniture. What they wanted was the psychological leverage it gave them. They knew that even after the Bankruptcy Court granted a full discharge of the debt, debtors could still be shamed into paying if they faced the humiliation of having the neighbors watch repossession men carrying out the kitchen table, the bed and the TV set. For people like the McCrackens, the prospect was terrifying. This was gut-level stuff. With alarming regularity the finance company lawyer was getting "repossess and sell" orders. The McCrackens came up next.

On the witness stand I stepped them through the routine questions. Mrs. McCracken held herself together, looking appropriately sorrowful but resigned to her fate. Mr. McCracken, however, got no further than giving his name and address before he broke into choking sobs so obviously sincere they silenced a courtroom full of hardened lawyers, clerks and bill collectors.

When at last his testimony was complete, Judge Lipkin nodded his head to show as much human emotion as a lifetime on the bench still let him display, announced "discharge will be granted," and was reaching for the next file when the finance company lawyer chimed in with his request for a repossess and sell order. I stood up and objected before the Judge could grant the order. He looked up with a glint of interest. "On what grounds?"

Having no forewarning, all I could do was wing it. I stammered something about the intent of the Bankruptcy Law to give people a fresh start, about the harshness of stripping a debtor bare of every stick of furniture in the house and so on. The Judge looked at me with genuine puzzlement. "Counselor, if the debtors signed the security statement and the creditor filed it on the record as required by the Uniform Commercial Code, I can't refuse to grant the relief. Can you cite any authority in support of your objection? If not, I will grant the order." A long silence followed.

"A brief!" I blurted. "I'd like time to put together a brief with the relevant cases!"

"Counsel has no cases!" The finance company lawyer was on his feet. "I've been practicing in this court for 15 years and I've never even heard of the kind of objection he's raising. The law's as clear as daylight!" Going by his expression, the Judge thought he was right. I suspect the sight of Mrs. McCracken trying to comfort her still-sobbing husband had more effect on the Judge than whatever I said. "Thirty days," he announced. "I'll give Mr. Wilkins 30 days to produce his brief, and I'll expect a reply brief 20 days after that. Next case!"

I walked back to my office wondering what sort of brief could stop this disaster. Thirty days seemed like plenty of time, but only if one had nothing else to do while researching and writing that one brief.

***

The *Atlantic City Press* had prominently reported my appointment to run Cape Atlantic Legal Services. The publicity generated requests to speak before various groups, and a heightened awareness that there were local offices at which the poor could talk to lawyers. The already heavy caseload increased in both volume and variety.

Barbara ushered in Senor Goita, a Puerto Rican man of limited

English who was arrested in a *bodega* in Atlantic City's inlet section. The police had the store under surveillance for illegal gambling. Mr. Goita was buying cigarettes when the raid hit. He was taken to the police station at City Hall. Whether the raid was legitimate or was punishment for failing to pay off the cops wasn't clear. The police department was notoriously corrupt at the time – a third of the police force was under indictment or investigation for crimes ranging from stealing the copper pipes of vacant houses to accepting bribes. No charges were filed against Mr. Goita, whose watch and wallet were returned to him on his release hours later, less the $40 the wallet held when the police took possession of it. When Goita complained, the desk sergeant insisted the wallet was empty in the first place, which he would have known if he hadn't been drunk when they brought him in.

His flushed face and uncertain speech made him appear drunk, even in my office. But he brought with him a letter from his doctor showing that his symptoms of drunkenness were the result of a medical disorder for which he took medicine, in addition to which he suffered from a rare, and often fatal, allergy to alcohol. I called the doctor to confirm the facts, then called Mario "Mud" Floriani, Atlantic City's hard-nosed Chief of Police who was warming up to run for political office on the "law-and-order-tough guy" theme. I explained the problem and he explained where in my anatomy I could stick it. Next I called a friend at the *Atlantic City Press*. Shortly thereafter I received a telephoned personal invitation from Chief Floriani to an immediate conference. Mr. Goita and I walked the few blocks to the Chief's office in City Hall.

Loud voices from the other side of his door indicated a meeting was in progress. Eventually a stream of cops, civilians and a reporter I knew emerged, the reporter with a grin on his face. I never learned all the details, but essentially the meeting had been convened because an undertaker's war had broken out. If a man was shot or stabbed in the city, the first cops arriving on the scene would call the ambulance – which in those days came free of charge to haul you to the hospital. If, however, you were indisputably dead, they called the undertaker to pick up the body and transport it to the hospital's morgue. It was an important call because if the deceased was poor the undertakers were paid by the state and could tack charges for that initial ride to the hospital morgue onto the funeral bill. Several undertakers competed for that business in the black community, which was where many of the poor died, often violently. Eventually each undertaker reached an understanding with the cops of his choice as to how much they paid per call. This led to situations where the first cop would call an ambulance, the second on the scene call undertaker "A" and the third call undertaker "B." Whether the victim was breathing at the time became irrelevant. Eventually a fight broke out over a fallen body. The reporter got wind of it, asked Floriani for comment, and was hustled into a meeting of all parties concerned. Evidently the reporter agreed to kill the story in exchange for various other exclusives. Floriani ended the war by assigning all dead or falling bodies to undertaker "A" in one voting ward, and to undertaker "B" in the other, with appropriate threats about disciplinary actions, firings, and loss of pensions if any cop violated the arrangement.

My initial call about Senor Goita reached Floriani just as that meeting began. The second call about Senor Goita, from the *Press*, reached him just as he was trying to convince its reporter to smother the undertaker story. Hence his rapidly reconsidered decision to take me seriously. He read the doctor's letter and asked us to wait outside. Then we heard the angry tone, if not the words, of his telephone conversation with the desk sergeant in question. He emerged a few minutes later to return the forty bucks. Such was summary justice in Atlantic City.

With the help of staff lawyers like Bob Subranni, Paul Wright, Dennis Coughlin and others like Bill Blane, Charles "Sandy" Middlesworth, Dennis Braithwaite, (later my partner in private practice and still later an Appellate Court Judge) and Ward Kelsey who came as time went on I slowly fit myself into new patterns that blended casework, administrative work, continuing education, community relations and legal research. The rhythm of legal and community activity quickly enveloped me. Landlord/Tenant matters were heard on certain days of the week; small claims and wage-executions on others; divorces and family matters on still others. Client interviews had to be fitted in around standing court schedules. Research and correspondence were squeezed in where court dates and interviews permitted. My appointments book filled with scheduled court appearances, speeches, and continuing legal education seminars.

The legal problems of the poor were just beginning to be understood. Until legal services was started, law schools had taught the basic courses studied by generations of lawyers – Constitutional Law, Criminal Law, Contract Law, Wills and Estates, Family Law, and one with the somewhat biased name of "Creditor's Rights." There was no course in "Debtor's Rights," nor were there standard courses in such things as consumer fraud. The advent of legal services programs was changing things. The appearance on the scene of hundreds of young legal services lawyers representing poor people created a demand for seminars and workshops with strange new topics, such as Social Security litigation, Welfare Rights, Woman's Rights, and other subjects reflecting the legal problems flooding into Legal Services offices everywhere.

All this carried advantages and disadvantages for legal services lawyers. Reforms were coming through the pipeline that helped us immeasurably to protect our clients, if only we could keep ourselves informed and abreast of those developments. Workshops and seminars became a vital part of our professional lives. As time and funds permitted I sent a lawyer to attend, then had them present the new material at weekly staff meetings so the rest of us could keep up.

***

There were regular conferences of my counterparts from around the state where we could compare notes on problems encountered with the Bar, the judges, or the administrative agencies whose work held heavy consequences for the poor. While some reforms required massive effort to achieve, others could be implemented at the stroke of the right pen. New Jersey's state constitution makes its Chief Justice a powerful figure, vested with administrative control over every court and judge in the state and —

in matters touching upon their professional conduct — of every lawyer. The Chief at that time was Joseph Weintraub, a brilliant and singularly tough-minded jurist perfectly willing to challenge entrenched abuses in the system he ran, and capable of using the whole weight of his office whenever needed. His right hand man in carrying out his duties was Ed McConnell, who carried the title of "Administrative Director of the Courts" and answered exclusively to the Chief Justice.

McConnell invited the chief attorneys of the legal services programs to a meeting in Trenton to discuss any problems we might have. Eight or nine of us were sitting around his conference table when discussion turned to the fact that in many instances poor people who were being sued had no knowledge that the legal services programs even existed. We were encountering clients who did not find their way to our offices until the original Summons and Complaint were served, the court date reached, the case decided with the individuals having no counsel whatever, and the mess landing on our desks only when the sheriff showed up to evict them or seize whatever meager assets they had.

Someone suggested the problem might be solved if the Chief Justice issued a rule requiring every Summons to include a notice that if the person sued couldn't afford a lawyer they could contact Legal Services. McConnell seized on the idea and added the suggestion that the name and telephone number of the appropriate legal services office be included. We drafted a proposed notice on the spot. McConnell left the room, spoke to the Chief Justice, and came back with the news that the rule would be adopted.

The change so effortlessly adopted had significant repercussions. Plain folk intimidated by legal language could now read, in plain language at the top of the first page they looked at, that free legal advice was available if they couldn't afford a lawyer. The change brought protest from the sort of lawyers who prefer their targets delivered to court unencumbered by their own counsel. The lawyers for slumlords and bill collectors were a particularly unhappy bunch, insisting that most cases were uncontested; that the debtors knew they owed the money and the tenants knew they were behind on their rent and the change would stir up needless litigation and clog the court system. The Chief Justice didn't budge.

Of course, the rule brought droves of new clients to the already overburdened legal services office, but at least we now caught the cases early enough to do whatever could be done. The memory of how much positive good could be done at the stroke of the right pen stayed with me and led eventually to reform of the bail system in New Jersey.

***

Chapter 26: Illegal Drugs and Legal Traditions

Paul Wright, working away on our steadily growing caseload, asked what to do about Narco. "What's Narco?" I asked.

"Drug addicts. Reformed drug addicts, I mean. In and out of prisons. Come to think of it," he hesitated, "I dunno. Is it like an alcoholic? Once you're an alcoholic you're always an alcoholic – a whaddycallit — a reforming alcoholic? Should I say these guys are reforming addicts?" As usual, Paul had to take several detours to get where he wanted, but as always his heart was in the right place. "Anyway, these guys – black guys – Negroes? – African Americans? – say they're trying to get organized to set up a counseling program to help other addicts – reform other addicts – get them off drugs. Don't know why they want to incorporate. They asked me to meet with them tonight. Some kind of Board. Maybe they can afford their own lawyer," he shrugged. "Should I go?"

"Where are they?"

"Over on Arctic Avenue. 1705 Arctic. Some kind of storefront setup belongs to the church next door — lets them use it."

"Let's go take a look." If these were street guys trying to do something about drug addiction, I wanted to give them all the help we could as soon as we could.

The storefront was just that; a one-story building attached alongside the church, with a plate-glass store window on which was hand-painted "Narco Addicts Rehabilitation Center Organization." Under it was "N.A.R.C.O."

The tiny front room in the former beauty parlor included a couch, a counter, a chair and a chessboard. The middle room, used for group counseling sessions, was furnished with old chairs of varied description — folding, rigid, wooden and metal; an old desk, and a lamp or two. Next came a bathroom and, in the rear, a small room with a cot.

Black men, among whom drug addiction had reached epidemic proportions, made up the largest single segment of the prison population almost everywhere in America, imprisoned for a variety of drug-connected crimes ranging from robberies and burglaries to possession and sale of narcotics. For most of them, the path from drug use to prison was a closed circle, with recidivism always high. Others found in the depths of their prison misery the determination and resolve to change their lives.

John Brooks was born and raised in Atlantic City and except for a stint in the Navy and time served in prison lived there all his life. He was a man of sharp intelligence, strength of character and leadership who, as he traversed the treacherous slope of drug addiction, became a major contributor to the crime statistics of Atlantic City. In prison he found the inner resources to break his addiction, and made up his mind to help his friends also break free of drug dependency. He returned to Atlantic City, gathered a few friends and set out to establish a rehabilitation program run by ex-addicts who could and would confront the scourge.

Brooks built his team well. Richard Derry used drugs for 20 years, in and out of prison and lost his most recent job working on a trash truck when somebody reported he was a junkie. He knew he wanted to get off drugs, and had not been able to do it. His friend Clyde Waithe, another ex-addict, ran across him selling stolen record albums and brought him in to Brooks. Within a short time "Li'l Richard" as Brooks tagged him, became his alter-ego, lieutenant, and wisest advisor. They were joined by other men fresh out of prison, including Albert "Sonny" Blagrove and Wilbur "Sleepy" Kirk. The Episcopalian Diocese saw they were serious and gave them $7,500 to keep going. The cops, although never willing to support them publicly, realized they had changed their lifestyles and were serious about their work. Understanding the coming need for more organizational structure and community support, Brooks put together a local Board of Directors that included blacks and whites well-placed and respected in the community. William "Tex" Moore, a fireman and solid citizen, was board President. Karlos LaSane, one of the first elected black officials in Atlantic City, served as Vice President. Margie Jacobs, a politically active young black woman and sister to Atlantic County's first black judge, Herbert S. Jacobs, joined. Stanley "Stitz" Feinstein, owner of the leading pharmacy in Atlantic City, joined. Dr. Charles Wilson, a young and much respected black doctor, gave his active support, which proved vital in many ways. He provided medical exams to new recruits in the program; prescribed medications which helped in kicking the narcotics habit, and added strong respectability to the program among both the black and the white communities. An older black doctor, Dr. Marshall, did the same. The medical establishment began to see Narco as a useful resource.

All of the ex-addicts were convincing speakers, and much in demand among local civic groups to explain drug addiction and its consequences from the experience of their own lives. John Brooks in particular was a charismatic speaker and an imposing figure. Well over six feet tall, his "Afro" hairstyle added inches to that. There was no affectation, nothing phony, in his manner. When he was challenged he responded directly and bluntly with plain truths and ready wit; when he was angry it showed and when he smiled it lit up the room. He could use either anger or humor to make his point. The ladies of the Hadassah fell in love with him, especially when he convinced them the drug problem had expanded far beyond the black community into the world of white kids, including the affluent downbeach communities of Ventnor, Margate and Longport. He taught them how to search for hypodermic needles not only in desk drawers or behind books, but taped to the back of the toilet tank, or in the closet where you have to reach up and back over your head to find the hiding-places. The lesson hit home.

The Hadassah donated $5,000 to Narco. With that and the Episcopalian grant John decided it was time to become a formal tax-exempt non-profit corporation.

Paul Wright and I walked over to the Arctic Avenue storefront at a time when the national scene was filled with riots, racism, chaos and mean-tempered ill will on the side of law and order, opposed by angry young blacks brandishing rifles on the steps of universities. To find so bright and vigorous a presence as John Brooks and the guys at Narco fighting back against the despair and hopelessness of drug addiction lifted my spirits enormously. Here, plainly, was a leader and a cadre of dedicated and energetic men who knew what worked, had credibility among the addict population from which they themselves sprang, and who, given enough funds to work with, could make a difference of great moment. They needed more space; they needed more counselors; they needed beds and clothing and food for a residential program; they needed teachers and social workers to help recovering addicts stitch their lives back together and move uphill. All of that cost more money than could be raised speaking to civic groups in a dying city. I knew little about drug addiction; still less about what worked or didn't work to help anybody break free of it. What I did know was how to get government money out of Washington and Trenton for their effort.

As with most programs of the era, a local "in-kind" matching requirement applied, meaning each program must raise 10% of its total costs locally. This requirement had the false appeal of thrift and self-initiative. There were good arguments in its favor, including that the requirement encouraged applicants to build a local base of support, and that it served to limit the number of applications that had to be considered. In fact it often proved, as one critic derided it, "like throwing a life preserver 90% of the way to a drowning man!" Instead of dealing with the problem on the streets, guys like John had to waste time trying to raise that first 10%. Not all of it had to be in cash, and sometimes you could use a grant from one program to serve as the 10% for another. Using the Hadassah and the Episcopalian money as his matching share, John won a $59,500 grant from the Atlantic City government. He bought an abandoned roller skating rink to renovate and make into a residential treatment center. To staff it we went after a larger grant from the state. When we tried to claim the value of the newly-purchased skating rink as our 10% share, the state balked, on the grounds that real estate could not be used as the matching share. This was a major and unexpected crisis.

"We're goin' to see ol' Hap," John called me.

"Senator Farley? You've gotta be kidding!" I said. "He'll shoot us down in flames."

Republican State Senator Frank S. "Hap" Farley was one of the most powerful political figures in the state. His power sprang from the electoral history of New Jersey. For years, each of New Jersey's 21 counties held one seat in the State Senate regardless of their population. Essex County, with over a million in population, had one senator. So did Cape May County, with fewer than 100,000 people. Of the 21 counties, 13 were lightly populated, safely Republican, and conservative in varying degrees. The Republicans maintained strict party discipline, which meant they did their wheeling and dealing in a secret party caucus, then buried their differences and went out on the Senate floor and voted in accordance with the caucus position. Effectively, 7 men in the Republican caucus controlled the state of New Jersey no matter who was governor. This was the power of mal-apportionment; a system common in all state legislatures whereby thinly-populated areas controlled state governments at the expense of far more populous cities and counties. Farley, in unshakeable control of his own Atlantic County, united the least populated counties by adroitly handing out "pork" in the way of jobs, bridges, roads and public works. He seized control of his party caucus early in his career, and never let go thereafter. In 1962 the U.S. Supreme Court had finally got around to ruling such unbalanced representation unconstitutional in the famous Tennessee case of *Baker v. Carr*, which forced New Jersey and other states to reapportion the representation on the basis of "one man, one vote." But Farley had held power so long his grip on it had still not loosened.

"He said he'll see us this afternoon."

"John," I said, "don't get your hopes up. He's not likely to give us any help."

"Won't know that 'til we try. You gotta come along and run all that legal crap by him so he gets the picture."

We met in Farley's law office. John explained the problem and I added the legal details.

"So you want the state to let you use your real estate as the matching share?" Farley was a quick study.

"Yeah!" John smiled.

Farley, President of the State Senate through whom all of the Governor's budget and proposals had to pass now that the Republicans controlled the legislature, had Governor Hughes on the phone in minutes.

"Dick! How you doing, Governor? Good to talk with you. How's Betty and the kids? Fine? Glad to hear it! Listen, Dick, I've got two fellas here that need help; John Brooks and Joe Wilkins." The Governor said something to Farley I couldn't hear. I held my breath, hoping he didn't remember my giving him a hard time over migrant reform. "Anyway, Dick, they're from Narco, one of those drug rehabilitation programs. Doing a great job. Here's what they need — What? You'll see to it? Thanks Dick. Swell talking to you. And give my regards to Betty."

The conversation took about two minutes. Before we could thank Farley and get out of the office, the state budget director was on the phone. Governor Hughes wanted him to follow up on our problem. Farley put him on the speaker, told him he was looking forward to next week's budget hearing, and introduced us. "Can you help these fellows? They're doin' a swell job! You can? Thanks! Good talkin' to ya."

Within a week we were in Trenton signing the grant papers.

***

Getting and running grants came easy enough – a sort of chess game once you learned the moves. Dealing with the many facets of the human spirit that lawyers for the poor see was not as conveniently impersonal. The cases my secretary Barbara Camper ushered into my office included the farcical, the tragic, and the routine in almost equal proportions. Herod McLeod, an ancient black man who loved standing up at public meetings to berate officials for their neglect of poor people, was being slowly driven around the bend by age. Years earlier he had filed petitions to run as a candidate against Senator Hap Farley. Scraping together $50 for a tiny advertisement to run in the *Atlantic City Press* denouncing Farley as a liar and a crook, he was outraged when the *Press* refused to run the ad. Seeing their refusal as proof that the *Press* was Farley's tool — an overstated although not entirely incredible proposition — he came to legal services before my arrival as Chief Attorney and demanded a lawsuit against both the *Press* and Farley. This was denied on the diplomatic grounds it was not poverty-related. McLeod wrote in protest to OEO's Regional Office. They passed the buck back to me by writing McLeod with the suggestion he go see the brand-new Chief Attorney at Legal Services, who might reconsider the case.

"Mr. Wilkins," Barbara said in her quiet voice, "you might want me to sit in on this interview." I saw a subtle gleam of humor in her eyes and nodded. On the theory that even the misguided should be treated with courtesy, I looked over the proposed legal pleadings Herod McLeod had hand-written and noticed he had added two new defendants since his earlier effort. Now he wanted to sue the *Press* and Senator Farley and my predecessor at Legal Services, and God Almighty. God, he informed me, was an essential defendant because the United States dollar bill carries "In God We Trust" on its design, making Him an indispensable party to every lawsuit for money. Barbara, who knew the daffy old character all her life, gave him just enough time to finish the cup of coffee she poured for him, then rescued me by promising we'd get back to him when we figured out how to serve process on the Almighty. He thanked us gravely and left.

"I'm sorry to waste your time like that," Barbara said. "But if somebody doesn't talk to him he comes back every day."

"How long before he comes back now that we've talked to him?" I asked.

"Oh, he's good for six months or so now," she said, with a smile.

Not many days later Barbara came in with a worried look. "I don't know what to tell this lady. She's terribly upset. I think you should talk with her." This time Barbara did not ask to sit in on the interview.

A few minutes later a rail-thin, elderly Italian woman sat nervously in front of my desk, twisting her handkerchief as she asked how she could go about confessing to a murder.

"I killed her, and I deserve to be punished," she said. "I just don't know who to see."

Her victim, she told me, was the wife of a man with whom she carried on an affair.

"I knew he was married. I knew he'd never leave her. Then I learned she had a bad heart. So I made sure she knew her husband and I were having an affair. She had a heart attack and died that week. That's how I murdered her."

I was silent for a long time, looking at the downcast face of this tearful old woman.

"How long ago was this?" I asked at last.

"I was seventeen," she answered. "He was 35 and she was two years older than him."

Sixty years had come and gone, but her sense of guilt burdened her still. Nothing in law school offered a guide to dealing with such sadness. I knew no prosecutor would prosecute such a case. Even if it happened that morning instead of so many years earlier there was, I told her, no sure way of knowing her actions had caused the wife's death. She would not be comforted. I was the first she had ever told. After another long silence, I asked if she was religious. "I'm Catholic," she said, "but I haven't ever confessed. I haven't taken the sacraments since then." I called Vince DePasquale, a Catholic priest I knew from his work among the poor and with Narco's addicts, and arranged for her to go see him. Sixty years, and still her conscience gave her no rest.

Katherine Green came in; a voluble, stocky, usually cheerful black woman who worked at a low level job in City Hall to support herself and her kids. She walked home for lunch one day and found bulldozers and laborers from the Housing Authority program getting ready to demolish the apartment building in which she lived. Planting herself in front of the bulldozer, she raised hell with the driver until the supervisor of the program showed up. He insisted the building had been condemned to make way for a public garage; that she was served plenty of notices of the condemnation proceedings; that she never responded; and that she had to move her things out that night because they would be back next morning to tear the building down.

I called the first available judge I could reach, and was given a 3 PM hearing to apply for a temporary restraining order. I drafted an affidavit for my client to sign, swearing she never received notice. At 3 o'clock I showed up at the judge's chambers with my client. The lawyer for the Housing Authority was Isaac "Icky" Ginsburg, a seasoned veteran and energetic litigator who in his 37 years at the Bar represented, among other clients, Frank Sinatra. Icky was a tough fighter and knew the value of preparation. Between my telephone call at 1 PM asking for a restraining order, and the hearing at 3 PM he rounded up six witnesses and prepared as many affidavits to prove that my client received numerous mailed notices, signed for them, and ignored them. It was an aggressive "best defense is a strong offense" attack that rattled me considerably.

The hearing took place in the judge's chambers, with the witnesses crowded in to watch the show. I asked for time to investigate the situation and prepare my case. Ginsburg, waving his affidavits and pointing to his witnesses, claimed that thousands of taxpayer dollars were being lost due to the delay; a delay caused by a woman who in fact received plenty of notice her apartment was to be torn down. In his argument he leaned over the judge's desk, pushing his affidavits under the judge's nose. Judge Ben Rimm, who was admitted to the Bar in '28 and served the Republican organization long and faithfully until rewarded with his appointment to the Bench, hesitated. He could not see where a few more days would hurt. Ginsburg, growing more emphatic, leaned further over the desk, resting his left knee on its surface as if he were going to climb over it to browbeat the judge.

Rimm fell back abashed, and started to cave. "Well," he looked at me, "If this lady's had all that notice, why didn't she do something before now?" he asked.

I was wholly unprepared for the sight of a lawyer climbing up on a judge's desk. But that was clearly how it was done in Atlantic City, and it appeared to be working. My client was about to be bulldozed out of her home if I didn't do something. I grabbed my client's affidavit, put my knee up on the desk and leaned into the judge's face as close as Ginsburg had done. Poor Ben Rimm leaned back as far as he could without overturning his chair. The witnesses, from bulldozer driver to the Housing Authority director, were enjoying the action like spectators at a wrestling match.

"Judge," I exclaimed. "You just can't do this! This lady's got three kids living in that apartment! Think," I went on with almost divine inspiration, "what the newspaper's going to do with a story like this!" It was a telling blow. Rimm was up for his lifetime re-appointment. A story of him as a heartless judge evicting a mother and three kids was not a happy prospect. I got my temporary restraining order, which gave us enough breathing room to find out what was going on.

What was going on was that my client's apartment was in a building owned by an extremely hard-nosed Greek lady, an immigrant with a versatile ability to either understand English or not depending on the needs of the moment. She fought the City's condemnation of her building for months. She considered the appraised price so low as to be highway robbery, and defiantly intercepted every notice sent to her tenants, signed their names to the receipts for Certified Mail, and tore up that mail with righteous anger. When at last that was clear, we won an extra 60 days for my client to relocate.

***

I scheduled myself for as many cases as possible in the Chancery Division. Even though most of the cases were uncontested divorces, they at least gave me courtroom practice in such basics as putting witnesses on the stand and getting facts into the record. I was keenly aware that I was in the unique position of being chief attorney in a five lawyer program having no legal experience at all. It was also important to get to know Chancery Judge Herbert Horn, a successful trial lawyer appointed to the Bench to sweeten the odor of what was perceived as a succession of political hacks given judgeships over the years. Horn was due to become the Assignment Judge for the vicinage — a position of extensive authority over all courts and judges in Atlantic and Cape May Counties. His good will could make a difference in how our legal services efforts went.

The other judge of great significance to Legal Services was Herb Jacobs, the only African-American judge in the area. He presided over the Landlord-Tenant Court and the Small Claims Court – the lowest level county courts, where most of our legal services cases were heard. Like Judge Horn, Jacobs was honest, competent and compassionate. There is an ancient Chinese proverb that "An honest judge means the happiness of a thousand families." The more I appeared before Judge Jacobs at the bottom or Judge Horn at the top, the more I appreciated the wisdom of that proverb.

In freshman year my high school had been so close to the Boardwalk we kids spent our lunchtime money on root beers and pork roll sandwiches near the Steel Pier. Now my legal services office, only a few yards from my old school, offered the same lure of the Boardwalk and the beach and the blue haze of the Atlantic Ocean. As spring opened into early summer I found it irresistible to go out for lunchtime strolls on the Boardwalk – as did many of Atlantic City's lawyers and judges. It eased relations with adversaries to stop and chat during such strolls.

For all the press of our caseload, however, it was impossible to ignore the effect the war in Vietnam was having on the country. Late one sunny afternoon after a meeting I was having a sandwich with a fellow lawyer in a bar half a block down from the beach. Across the bar a remark was tossed from the bartender to two young women. There was laughter — and a young head tilted back to receive cold beer from a frosted mug. Outside, a passing radio that was too loud pierced the bar's silence with a metallic voice intoning *"IN SAIGON TODAY OFFICIALS SAID — "*. The door swung mercifully shut on the official word. My imagination peopled the bar with all the young men killed in that faraway land of helicopters, narrator's voices and steamy jungle backdrops for plasma bottles and bandaged eyes, always relieved by toothpaste and mouthwash jingles and instructions to stay tuned for the late show.

Combat deaths had climbed to thirty thousand – a city of the young, the strong, the bronzed young men who thought of cold beer and girls in mini-skirts. They were dead. Pete Seeger's haunting song "Where have all the flowers gone?" ran through my mind. "Picked", the song said, "by young girls every one." What of those girls? "Gone to soldiers," said the song, and the soldiers gone to their graves.

I walked back to work with disquieting thoughts.

***

There were congenial traditions in Atlantic City — traditions that increased the likelihood of chance meetings with other lawyers and the judges, and so set the context for the local practice of law. Walking the Boardwalk after lunch was one; getting your hair cut at Angelo's barbershop and bookie joint on North Carolina avenue was another; having lunch at the Stanley Restaurant still another. The Stanley was on Atlantic Avenue, a short walk from the Guarantee Trust Building which housed the county courts. Four easily identifiable groups congregated there for lunch: doctors, businessmen, lawyers, and reporters. The doctors and businessmen sat in the larger room in the back, usually at tables of four. In the front bar-room were two banquettes — long, padded benches along the wall fronted by tables joined together and chairs opposite the benches. As you entered the bar-room the tables on your left were where the lawyers and the judges sat; those on your right the reporters. The seating was open; you came in and took your seat next to whoever you found. At first, not realizing I was defining myself as an outsider in the eyes of the lawyers, I sat with the reporters, most of whom I knew, rather than with the lawyers I did not as yet know. There was a side benefit; the reporters, many as gray-haired as the judges, were free with their comments on the lawyers and judges sitting just out of earshot, telling tales of old feuds between lawyers, political maneuvering by judges anxious for reappointment, the breakup and re-formation of law firms fighting for clients, and the occasional scandals of drink, sex or embezzlement. To a young lawyer, such information helped demystify the local legal scene. Eventually, however, I learned to sit with my lawyer colleagues, where cases could be settled over coffee with the judges nodding approvingly while pretending not to hear.

***

Chapter 27: A Debtor's Brief and a White House Letter

Writing my first brief, in the McCracken bankruptcy, proved harder than I anticipated. It was what lawyers call a case of first impression. As far as I could find, no court had ever considered or decided the exact issue that I was raising – whether a debtor who signed a security agreement for his used household furniture could go bankrupt and still keep his old bed, table and chairs. Fortunately Judge Lipkin was willing to give me an additional thirty days to hand in my brief. I cleared my calender and spent several days in Washington, researching at the incomparable Law Library of the Library of Congress. There I could find the exemption-from-seizure-and-sale laws of all fifty states; any cases decided by any state or any federal court on the issue; and scholarly treatises, if any existed, on the subject. In addition, I could read the reports of the extensive and expensive commercial law services such as my old employer the Bureau of National Affairs, or the Commerce Clearing House.

Because Congress chose to allow each state to set its own level of exemption, there were fifty different levels. Western states, where the voters were farmers often in debt to Northeastern bankers, had dramatically high exemptions. In Texas, for example, the "homestead", no matter how valuable it was, stayed with the bankrupt. In a leading Texas case, a man went bankrupt owing his creditors something like \$200,000 even though he owned a home without a mortgage that was worth well over \$1 million. He kept the house and was discharged of all his other debts. Northeastern states, where debtors were often non-voting factory workers and it was the bankers who had the political clout, favored the creditors and set the lowest exemptions, which was why in New Jersey it was a tough fight to save the McCracken's worthless furniture.

Although the federal law left the question of what was and wasn't exempt up to each state, that did not solve my problem. One New Jersey law said their household furniture couldn't be taken because it was under the threshold of value exempted from judgment. Another New Jersey law said if the creditor had a security interest nailed down by a recorded financial instrument the exemption didn't save the furniture. The saving circumstance, however, was that state laws, whatever they were, could not conflict with the intent of the federal bankruptcy act to give the debtor a clean slate – a priority established by the United States Constitution, which granted Congress express jurisdiction over bankruptcy laws.

When at last I turned in my brief and served copies on the other side, it stirred up a hornet's nest of lawyers from the credit industry. If, as I argued, the core commandment of the bankruptcy law rendered useless the practice of having small loan debtors pledge their household furniture, loan companies everywhere would lose one of the most effective weapons in their armory. A trade association of credit companies asked permission to file a "friend of the court" brief opposing my arguments.

Months went by while I dealt with other matters at legal services. Eventually, the nervous McCrackens called to ask how things stood. I called the Judge's secretary.

"Are you Mr. Wilkins?" she asked.

"Yes, ma'am."

"Well, Mr. Wilkins, the Judge has not made his decision yet. Those cases you cited in your brief were hard to find. We had to send to the Law Library of Congress in Washington for most of them! He's had our conference table piled up with those books for weeks now!"

When at last the decision arrived in the mail, Judge Lipkin had ruled for the McCrackens across the board. His written opinion followed my brief almost to the paragraph. This, to a lawyer, is close to the ultimate high; to have your research so convince the judge he plagiarizes your brief.

I expected an appeal. The money and the issue involved were serious enough to the credit industry they would undoubtedly take it all the way to the U.S. Supreme Court. One ironic result was that after criticizing the so-called law reform guys for chasing sensational cases, I was getting their calls asking if they could associate themselves with me on any appellate briefs. However, within the credit industry cooler heads prevailed. If they did not appeal the case, the McCracken decision would bind only bankruptcy cases in South Jersey, although it might help persuade judges elsewhere to follow its reasoning. But if the finance company and its friends appealed, they risked establishing an unfavorable precedent that would have nationwide effect and cost them considerably more than what they must now lose in South Jersey. The higher they appealed the more risk they ran. They decided to cut their loss and forego an appeal.

In later years the fight over exemptions took place more in Congress than in the courts, although on several occasions the U.S. Supreme Court made it clear it viewed the loan company tactic tried against the McCrackens as a grab for unfair leverage having nothing to do with the value of the furniture or the size of the debt.

Late in December Mr. and Mrs. McCracken returned to the office. With glowing pride she presented me with a present. It was a letter, on White House stationary, from the President's Special Assistant James Keogh, thanking Mrs. McCracken on behalf of President Nixon for her letter praising me and "Legal Services." I kept a suitably appreciative smile on my face at her thoughtful gesture, chuckling to myself at the irony of Nixon's White House, so intent on destroying Legal Services, having to reply to her letter.

***

By late summer of 1969 most of us with responsibilities in anti-poverty programs around the country were concerned about the Nixon Administration's determination to shut down programs that had been specifically established and funded by Congress.

In California Governor Ronald Reagan had tried to turn off the tap of federal funds flowing to programs he didn't like. He was sued by Legal Services lawyers representing the poor. He lost the case and was ordered by the court to permit funds to flow through for their lawful purpose. Although his effort failed, it served to convince conservatives he meant what he said. The Nixon Administration, watching the right wing moving to take control of the Republican Party, understood the political usefulness of Reagan's gambit.

At the time, such arbitrary impoundment of appropriated funds was an essentially lawless policy. While Presidents had long had implied executive discretion to impound funds for good cause, such actions had always been within generally understood tolerances. But the Nixon Administration carried that power to extremes, refusing to spend appropriated funds for programs it opposed on policy grounds, and on a scale never before attempted. The President exercised tight control through the discipline of White House Chief of Staff Bob Haldeman and Domestic Policy Advisor John Erlichman. At their insistence Nixon's Secretary of Labor George Schultz cut $100 million from the Job Corps's existing appropriations – a third of the whole program – and closed down almost 50 Job Corps Centers, evicting over 13,000 young men and woman from the program Bill Haddad had pushed with the TV show "It's What's Happening, Baby!" that had brought in thousands of letters only a few years earlier. Other "Great Society" programs from the Johnson Administration faced similar fates. Having the President unilaterally impound funds and terminate programs he didn't like provoked a long-running controversy with Congress. These were programs Senators and Congressmen had worked hard to enact.

That controversy came home to us when the Atlantic City Neighborhood Youth Corps program run by the local Community Action Agency, after putting 178 teenagers to work in summer jobs, laid them off in mid-August on the claim that funds had unexpectedly run out. The kids elected 17 year old Michael Davis to consult legal services and find out what could be done to save their jobs.

The plight of the kids intrigued me for a variety of reasons. For too long poor people had passively accepted whatever bad news came into their lives. Talking to a young black man elected by his fellow-teenagers to fight back was welcome proof that such passivity was being left behind.

Whether the firing of the Atlantic City Youth Corps enrollees was the result of local budgeting incompetence or the result of President Nixon's "turn off the tap" national policy was worth exploring. I demanded a local audit. When that produced protests from the program's director that he'd been ordered to cut off the kids, it appeared entirely possible the local kids were victims of Nixon's new policy. With the help of Bill Blane, a thoughtful new staff attorney, I filed a federal suit against the sponsoring community action agency, and against President Nixon's Secretary of Labor George Schultz, seeking reinstatement for the kids, or at least back pay.

***

As preparation of the Neighborhood Youth Corps suit proceeded, John Brooks called from Narco. A United States Senate subcommittee was looking into the spread of drug addiction across America. The committee was chaired by Democratic Senator Harold Hughes of Iowa, a recovering alcoholic who was sympathetic to our efforts. John Brooks was invited to give testimony in Washington. He knew I had experience testifying before Congressional committees and asked me to come along.

At the hearings New Jersey Democratic Senator Harrison A. "Pete" Williams stopped by to show his support. Williams chaired the Senate committee that controlled funds for the National Institute of Mental Health. From the committee podium he complemented us on our testimony.

"I'm sure," he commented, "this is the kind of program the mental health people are interested in funding — and by coincidence," he nodded a greeting to a man sitting behind us in the front row, "the director of the relevant department is sitting right behind you gentlemen. Why don't you get together with him and see if they can get you financial help?"

This was in effect an order from their banker for the National Institutes to fund Narco. By that afternoon Brooks and I were closeted with the agency's staff at a huge office building at 5600 Fisher's Lane in nearby Bethesda, Maryland. We drove home to New Jersey with a blank grant application and instructions to fill it out as soon as possible.

Meanwhile Donald Rumsfeld, Nixon's new Director of OEO, named a new director of the national Legal Services Program even as California Governor Ronald Reagan was trying to end the program in his state. Rumsfeld's choice was 29 year old Terry Lenzner, a former civil rights lawyer in the Department of Justice. Lenzner was a friendly fellow I had met somewhere during the preceding years. When he refused to accommodate the right-wing's determination to destroy Legal Services, Rumsfeld fired him. Later he served the subpoenas on Nixon in the Watergate case.

Events tumbled upon one another. Neil Armstrong, Buzz Aldrin and Michael Collins blasted off for the first manned moon landing. Far from such stirring events, I attended the Pleasantville Tenant's Association meeting to plan strategy for getting the Pleasantville City Council to pass a rent control ordinance.

The astronauts landed on the moon. I watched the historic broadcast, mesmerized, as that first step was taken. Demonstrators parked a mule cart at the entrance to the Kennedy Space Center at Cape Canaveral to protest the persistence of poverty in a nation wealthy enough to reach the moon. The theatrically staged contrast of the space shot with the mule cart was effective. It dramatized the fact that at the moment of man's greatest adventure children died of starvation; fathers despaired of finding work; widows wept for husbands slain in war.

***

Chapter 28: Which Fight Comes First — Civil Rights or Poverty?

Mrs. Cora Boggs and Remer Quince came in. Cora Boggs was a vigorous, middle-aged black lady who lived in a row house on New York Avenue. She was one of those quiet, determined church ladies who form the backbone of their neighborhoods.

Mrs. Boggs had come to see me a few days earlier asking for legal representation on behalf of herself and her neighbors on the block. The matter had to do with the operation of the Lehigh Valley Dairy's warehouse on the street behind their homes. They lived there for years and the dairy was there for years, its warehouse serving as a distribution base for Atlantic City's boardwalk hotels and restaurants. The dairy, as far as I could gather, had either very few or absolutely no black drivers or other employees – a situation the black citizens of the neighborhood decided it was time to correct. Mrs. Boggs and her neighbors wanted me to file suit against the dairy for violating the Civil Rights Act of 1964.

They had my sympathy, but since they all owned their own homes, and had long held decent jobs at City Hall, the Post Office, and for the County, I saw no way in which their concerns fell into any category that could be called poverty-related. It was a classic civil rights case, in which a private lawyer might bring suit and a judge would have the authority to award legal fees if they won. With the volume of cases we were constantly trying to keep up with – evictions; slum housing conditions; brutal husbands and ruthless bill collectors – cases involving the truly poor — black, white and Hispanic, I needed every lawyer's hour I could direct to their care. I told Mrs. Boggs I could not accept her case, and offered to help her search for a lawyer in private practice who might take it on.

She took offense. As far as Mrs. Boggs was concerned, you could not pick and choose between fighting racism and fighting poverty; they were two sides of the same coin. My elitist friends among the liberals and the law reform lawyers would wholeheartedly agree with her, arguing that civil rights and economic justice were, in the language so beloved by theorists, "inextricably entwined." When I turned down the case, I could see in her eyes and the tightening of her lips that to her I had become just another white man finding an excuse to let racism go unchallenged. Now she had brought Remer Quince with her, convinced I would change my mind if there was a little pressure put on me.

Remer Quince was a member of my Board of Directors. He was a distinguished-looking black man with snow-white hair and mustache, a quiet manner, and an addiction to tennis. He made his living as a barber in the black community of Atlantic City, which gave him a wide circle of acquaintances. He was a long-time member of several organizations such as the NAACP, the Fair Housing Committee, Atlantic Human Resources (the local Community Action Agency), and its Midtown Community Action Council. Quince made no bones about his views. "This is *our* program," he said – meaning the anti-poverty programs in general and Cape Atlantic Legal Services in particular belonged to the black community and should serve its purposes primarily, if not exclusively.

A white person who thinks he understands how racism works against blacks is dangerously close to being a damn fool. I had seen for myself how often the currents of racism and poverty flowed together, including the viciousness of the racist farmer on a school board who insisted black kids should endure a schoolroom with a four-holer for a toilet instead of letting them use the nearby modern school because, as he put it, blacks "don't know how to use flush toilets unless you put wine in them, and then they'll use them as a drinkin' fountain!" No one could miss the unholy alliance of racism and poverty that foul statement represented.

Yet I was clear in my mind that however tightly they were so often joined, there were instances when the connection between civil rights and poverty law was not present at all. In upstate New York and Appalachia the people were overwhelmingly people of one color, and yet there was as much poverty there as anywhere. In any event, it was my job to keep the legal services office focused on poverty. I had to trust my own judgment in making such calls.

Neither Mrs. Boggs nor Remer Quince knew much about me. In an embarrassingly transparent attempt to manipulate the situation, Mrs. Boggs had reconsidered her approach since her first visit. The straightforward civil rights complaint of a week earlier morphed into a proxy complaint when she came in with Remer Quince – about the damage caused to the neighborhood by heavy dairy trucks rumbling up and down the streets, causing cracks in the walls of the homes. Evidently she thought that while I would disdain a civil rights case I might be more receptive to a traditional claim of property damages. That approach worked even less well than her first. When we reached an impasse Remer vowed to bring the matter up at the next Board meeting.

Mrs. Boggs was, like Mr. Quince, a decent person doing what she thought was right. But well-meaning or not, I resented the threat and the waste of time. A Board fight over the issue was certain to be both distracting and destructive; a breeding-ground for animosity and lingering hard-feelings, certain to hit the newspapers and bring joy to slumlords and their lawyers. This was the same fight Shriver faced in Mississippi when black activists in the Child Development Group of Mississippi received funds to run a Head Start program and used the money instead to register and organize black voters – a worthy cause, but a serious diversion from what the funds were intended for. To waste time fending off attacks from people who thought the color of their skin entitled them to hijack the poverty program disturbed me, no matter how well-intentioned they were.

Fortunately, the Board fight never came about. Jack Gilbert, a decent man and good lawyer then serving as outgoing President of the Cape Atlantic Legal Services Board, suggested a compromise. Perhaps I could send a letter to the Lehigh Valley Dairy, threatening litigation (although avoiding any commitment that Legal Services would be the one to bring it) unless they stopped damaging the neighborhood homes with their trucks. It seemed wise to try whatever compromise made for the least waste of time and resources. Mrs. Boggs and Remer Quince, knowing they had no hope of changing my mind on the greater issue and unsure the Board would back them, settled for that.

The letter produced unexpected results. The president of the dairy replied with an apology for any inconvenience his trucks had caused and informed me he was closing the warehouse entirely because the level of business in Atlantic City had declined to the point it was no longer worth keeping it open.

The affair underscored a widening gulf between my views and those of my colleagues elsewhere. I did not see poverty programs as the property of the civil rights movement, nor did I see the role of neighborhood legal services as taking law reform cases at the expense of representing individual clients in their legal travails. Still, it troubled me that the Nixon Administration was using the same positions to justify cutting funding for legal services. They were eager to tie our hands on the kinds of cases we took, but determined to slash our budgets whichever way we went. I was opposed to the conservatives for their hypocrisy, and to the liberals for their misguided foolishness. A prime example of that foolishness was the liberal proposition that legal services lawyers should represent young men who were resisting the draft if, as was easy to arrange, they did not have enough income to afford lawyers. I turned down such cases, and received criticism from various friends in OEO for not taking them. I responded to one such conversation urging me to accept draft-resister cases along the following lines:

"What in hell," I asked, "does ducking the draft have to do with poverty?"

"See, that's your problem right there, Joe," my friend said. "Once you agree they can't afford a lawyer, what gives you the right to decide what's important enough to them to file suit? Don't the poor have rights of free speech? Don't they have civil liberties? Don't they have the right to have a lawyer challenge the draft on their behalf just as much as fight a slumlord?"

"In the first place," I replied, "if you think healthy young men between 18 and 26 with no dependents are the kind of poor we're obliged to represent, you sure as hell don't know what poverty looks like. As for their worries about the draft, when I run out of slumlords and bill collectors and the rest of the slimeballs that screw the poor, I'll start worrying about draft resisters. Meantime they can sit out the war in Canada!"

Some of my friends and colleagues wondered if I was a closet conservative. Insistence on orthodoxy, whether of the liberal or the conservative variety, is as much evident in policy disputes as in any religion. I also disagreed with a third tenet of the prevailing liberal philosophy; that "Judicare," – the use of paid part-time private attorneys to represent poor people, was harmful to our mission. Liberals were convinced that the only good poverty lawyer was one who was entirely dependent on his paycheck from legal services. Judicare and variations on the theme were based on the concept of paying lawyers for the poor by the case, much as the new Medicare program was paying doctors. Governor Reagan in California and the Nixon Administration in Washington were pushing the idea, which automatically made it suspect to liberals. Rumsfeld's OEO made a few experimental "Judicare" grants, allegedly to give the idea a try. Defending full-time legal services lawyers became part of the liberal catechism, along with taking civil rights cases and chasing law reform cases. But it was clear to me that legal services never had and never would be given enough money to provide full-time attorneys on anything like the scale needed to handle the caseloads we were seeing. It might take a few years to recruit young private lawyers worth hiring by the case, but Judicare was an idea worth trying.

Eventually OEO sent an evaluation team to see how Cape Atlantic Legal Services was shaping up. The report's recommendations underscored how my views drifted from those prevailing among my counterparts:

> The evaluators found that ... Mr. Wilkins, had done an excellent job of rebuilding morale in a program which had badly needed confidence .... had created model intake procedures in terms of giving the clients dignity .... rapport with the community is extremely good.
>
> The evaluators believe, however, that Mr. Wilkins should broaden the scope of the program's activities somewhat so as

> to include student rights cases such as suspension of students from local schools. It was the evaluators' feeling that civil rights law and poverty law are inextricably linked for the poor client and should be regarded as such by the director.

It was all well and good to get a pat on the back, but I couldn't help wondering why these guys were worrying about kids being suspended from school for misbehaving when the more immediate problem was that they, and their mothers, brothers and sisters were being evicted from their homes. I was coming up against what happens when practical concerns get trumped by politics, yielding only a narrowing of available solutions.

***

Chapter 29: Retaliatory Evictions and The Pregnant Shoplifter

When the coming of the jet airplane lured winter conventions away from the chill of Atlantic City to the warmer climes of San Juan, Las Vegas and Miami, the once-profitable side-street hotels in the block that runs from Pacific Avenue to the Boardwalk slipped down market. Many converted into year-round apartments, attracting an aging population of folks who lived from month to month on their Social Security check. State laws and city ordinances required landlords to provide heat from October through April, and keep their properties in reasonably safe and sound condition. Not all did. Tenants who complained had little protection. Even if the health department sent inspectors around, and even if the inspectors weren't on the take, and even if they ordered the landlord to fix the problem, there was nothing to stop the irritated landlord from kicking the tenant out at the next opportunity. If you had a written lease and paid the rent you were safe only until the lease ended. Most leases ran for one year, after which if the tenant stayed without getting a new lease in writing, the tenancy changed to a month-to-month affair, leaving the complaining tenant at the mercy of the landlord eager to rid himself of troublemakers.

Mrs. K. .. an elderly woman of Dutch descent who filed a series of complaints with the local health officer, was told to move out after the month's notice required by law was served on her. With nothing but her Social Security check to sustain her, she came to the office demanding her rights, which on paper didn't amount to much. In Mrs. K's case, her future was predictable. If she didn't move out, the landlady would go to the Landlord Tenant court, get an Order granting Summary Dispossession (eviction, in layman's terms), and shortly thereafter the constable would put Mrs. K and her belongings out on the pavement. Under the law governing the Landlord-Tenant Court, she would not be permitted to raise as her defense that the apartment was in disrepair.

Determined to challenge the practice of such retaliatory evictions, I brought a suit in Chancery, seeking an injunction against the eviction on the grounds that both the U.S. Constitution and the New Jersey Constitution guaranteed the right of a citizen to petition the government for redress of grievances, and that filing a complaint with the health department to enforce the building code was a classic way to petition the government for relief. Going into the Chancery Court raised the stakes considerably for the landlady because it meant she was going to have to pay her lawyer for a full-blown lawsuit. I was convinced that as soon as she realized that, she'd let my client stay put; and that word would then spread around other landlords that Cape Atlantic Legal Services lawyers were ready, willing and able to fight other retaliatory evictions with the same vigor.

The strategy yielded mixed results. The landlady's lawyer was Sam Epstein, an old pro with 20 years of practicing law in Atlantic City under his belt. Sam was a short, stocky man with a boxer's misaligned nose, a perpetual Florida tan, and a taste for the latest fashions in men's clothes. Since he walked with a rolling gait like a sailor, and the latest fashions for men featured bell-bottom trousers, Sam coming down the street looked like a silver-haired old sea-dog on his way to meet his girl. He loved to tell stories around the lunch table, and told them with flair, waggling his chubby fingers to add emphasis to the tale. Like me, he had worked his way through night law school, which started us off on the right foot.

The judge we drew was George Francis — a country judge from Cape May County only recently moved up to the Chancery Court sitting in Atlantic City. Francis was a distinguished looking man; ruddy complexion, silver hair, blue eyes and easy-going in his manner. He was a combat veteran — an Army Captain in Patton's drive across France. One of his favorite stories, which he told when I paid a courtesy call as part of my get-acquainted rounds of the judges, was of a fine spring day in the war. Having liberated a bottle of French wine, he and his jeep driver were cruising leisurely along a country lane when the sound of an angry horn came from a jeep behind them. He ordered his driver to pull over to the side and was turning around to tell the passing jeep what he thought of their impatience when he realized he was looking at General Eisenhower. Unable to salute with the wine in one hand and a baguette in the other, he stood there with, as he put it, "a pretty silly-looking grin, hoping Ike wouldn't have me shot on the spot." It was hard not to like guys like Judge Francis and Sam Epstein.

The Chancery Court was on the top floor of the Schwemm Building at New York and Atlantic Avenues. The judge's chambers looked south over buildings of lower height to the Boardwalk and the sea beyond. On a sunny morning, with the sun turning the ocean blue and half-a-dozen lawyers in chambers jockeying to get their cases heard first so they could get out on the golf course, practicing law while watching distant boats cross the horizon had its charm.

It would have had even more charm if I had won. On my initial application the Judge granted me a temporary restraining order that kept my client in her apartment until the case could be heard. After several months of motions and briefings we finally came to the day of trial. My client testified; the health inspector testified; I produced for the record the landlady's resultant notice to move out. Then Sam taught me a few tricks my law professors missed. He put the landlady on the stand — another immigrant, this time from somewhere in the Baltic. The landlady swore she needed the apartment for herself, because her son was coming to live with her and the apartment she kept for herself would be too small. With the sheer incompetence of the rookie lawyer, I let her get off the stand after a brief cross examination in which she insisted retaliation had nothing to do with evicting my client. We moved to closing arguments; Sam cited an obscure law left from the war years that gave Atlantic City landlords the right to bounce a tenant if they needed the apartment for their personal use.

I protested vigorously that the apartment building in question had over a hundred apartments, many of them vacant and surely enough large ones to accommodate the landlady and her son.

"Your Honor!" Sam was on his feet. "There's nothing in the record to support that statement. There is not a shred of evidence about how many apartments my client owns! Counsel didn't even ask on cross examination if she had other apartments!"

"Of course she owns a lot of apartments!" I responded. "I've been over there myself. That building's six or seven stories high and full of apartments!"

"Objection!" Sam hit back. "If counsel's going to testify he should get on the stand and be sworn in. And he knows a lawyer can't ethically testify in a case he's handling! I demand his statement be stricken!"

"It will be stricken," Judge Francis looked at me with exasperation. "Mr. Wilkins, the time to present those facts in evidence was before closing arguments. Based on the admissible evidence before me, I am going to dismiss the preliminary injunction. Mr. Epstein will prepare the necessary order for my signature."

"But Judge!" I was stunned. Here was a case in which I had read all the relevant law; constructed a strong argument, had justice on my side, and had unequivocally screwed up on basic trial procedures. "I —"

"Gentlemen, I'll see you in chambers!" Judge Francis tapped his gavel and rose, ending my protest. I told my visibly upset client I'd be right back and headed through the door behind the bench with Sam.

The law's reliance on evidence is old and taken seriously. It may have rained like hell the day of an event, but in a trial it hasn't rained until you have produced the weatherman or his official records, and maybe a few witnesses who got wet. My failure to bring out the facts through cross-examination, or to produce evidence of the availability of those other apartments, was the kind of stupid blunder a surgeon commits when he leaves the scissors inside his patient.

"We all make dumb mistakes," the Judge said, hanging his robe on a hook behind the door as Sam quietly took a chair. They had once been rookies themselves, and knew how I was feeling.

"Sit down." the Judge said. I sat, trying to figure out what, if anything, I could do to salvage things. Before I could open my mouth, the Judge held up a warning hand. Sam had an amused, but not triumphant, look on his face. He knew his Judge. George Francis would follow the law in the courtroom, but he wouldn't let a client get hurt because her lawyer was inept. Some judges treat the courtroom as a sports field and see themselves only as referees, with justice going to the side with the best lawyers. Francis saw his job as doing justice, or coming as close to it as the sometimes strange rules of the game allowed.

"Sam," he said, "You don't seriously claim your client hasn't got extra apartments she can use, do you?" Sam silently shook his head. "Okay, then. I want you to take your time getting that order to me. Two weeks?" Sam gave a resigned shrug of his shoulders.

"Joe," the Judge turned to me, "When Sam gets that order to me, you and he will come back here and you will move to stay the order and keep the injunction in force for an additional two weeks. I will grant that motion. That gives your client a month from right now to find another apartment and move out. You can appeal if you want. If you hope to keep her in the apartment while you do you're going to have to come back again and show me why I should let her stay until the case is heard by the Appellate Division. If you don't appeal, a month's the best I can do for you."

I left that courtroom with a good deal more humility than I came in with. My client was unhappy, but I assured her we would appeal the case.

It took the best part of six months to reach a hearing before the Appellate Division. Such appeals were heard in Trenton, before panels of three judges. One of the three was Leon Leonard, another silver-haired old bull, a former Atlantic County Republican Assemblyman with a gruff voice and considerably less compassion than George Francis. Shortly after I filed the appeal Sam called me to come to a settlement conference with himself and Judge Leonard in Atlantic City in Leonard's local chambers.

"What makes this case such a big deal?" Judge Leonard demanded. "Your client had a one year lease; when it ran out it became a month-to-month; she was given a month's notice to get out; and you kept her in that apartment another what? five, six months? Just by going after an injunction! Now you want us to hear an appeal that will drag on another four or five months? What the hell's that all about?"

I was taken aback by the vigor of his attack. Fortunately, I had by then seen enough of law as it was practiced in Atlantic City to learn it was no place for the timid.

"It's about the Constitution," I answered. "My client's got every right in the world to raise hell about that apartment, and if it takes a year, so be it!"

He glared, cleared his throat, started to say something, stopped, then let me have it.

"Listen, young man. I don't like tenants that quibble about small things in their apartment when they can pack up and leave whenever they like; I don't like lawyers who think every case is a Constitutional case, and I don't like Legal Services!"

Sam, who played golf with Lee Leonard every Wednesday afternoon, rolled his eyes at the outburst but said nothing.

"Judge, if you feel that strongly, I suggest you disqualify yourself. How's my client going to get a fair hearing from you?" I raised my voice in anger. "You've decided the case alrea—"

"Don't say another word! Your client will get a full hearing and a fair decision! Now get out of here before I lose my temper!"

I left, and headed across the street for lunch at the Stanley Restaurant. By this time I had learned to sit with the lawyers and judges rather than with the reporters. As I ordered, Sam came in and sat at the table. He looked at me with a small grin. "Well," he said, "you don't back down much, I give you that! I thought Lee Leonard was going to have a heart attack!"

There was no record kept of what was said in chambers, and for all of Sam's good nature I doubted he'd side with me against his golfing buddy if I made a formal motion to force Leonard to disqualify himself. When finally we argued the case, Leonard ripped into me and my arguments while the other two judges made it clear they didn't consider the appeal strong enough to overturn Judge Francis's decision.

As I came down the stairs of the State House in Trenton where the Appellate Division heard the case, I met a friend from the State Legal Services office who wanted to know how I'd made out. I told him it was a no-hoper. He shrugged and told me not to worry. His office had drafted new legislation making retaliatory evictions illegal and establishing that any eviction attempted within a month of a complaint was presumptively retaliatory. The new law was on its way to the Governor for signature.

The law came too late to help my case, but by that time, I had kept my client in her apartment almost a full year beyond her eviction date. She didn't like it when I had to tell her we'd lost the appeal, but she found another apartment with a more amenable landlord.

***

I was living by three different clocks: the slow pace of getting cases prepared and argued at Legal Services; the normal pace of family life with the kids growing and active in their lives; and the careening speed at which the country was tearing itself apart. Publicly President Nixon proclaimed OEO an essential arm of government. He promised to preserve the Neighborhood Youth Corps, the Job Corps, Head Start, the Community Action Agencies, and the Legal Services Program. Within such privacy as the Executive branch provided, however, a grim struggle was underway as Nixon, unable to win Congressional approval to do so, tried to de-fund and dismantle the anti-poverty programs in secret. Private memos circulated among Administration officials making it clear he wanted to end them. In this he was aided by a team dedicated to his re-election, on which their careers depended. At the top was Richard Nixon, who eventually was to become the first President to resign in the face of pending impeachment. His Vice President was Spiro Agnew, who was to leave the White House in the disgrace of a plea bargain concerning his acceptance of cash bribes, sometimes within the walls of the White House. Then came Nixon's Chief of Staff Robert Haldeman and Chief Domestic Policy Advisor John Erlichman, both of whom were later to serve terms in federal prison. Next below them, the anti-poverty programs were under the dubious care of Donald Rumsfeld and Dick Cheney, who did not seem to consider themselves bound by laws their President didn't agree with.

***

Frustrated by events on the national scene, but powerless to have the slightest effect on them, I put my energy into my caseload and my duties running legal services.

Barbara brought in Senor Cozone, a short, thin Puerto Rican man who worked part-time as a parking lot attendant to support his wife and 2 kids. His English was difficult to understand, but his anguish was plain. When we got him calmed down, we learned his 22 year old wife, the mother of his 2 kids and once again pregnant, had that morning pleaded guilty to shoplifting $5.38 worth of lunch meat and been sentenced to 40 days in jail because she couldn't pay the $200 fine.

She had been shopping at an A&P in Pleasantville. At the checkout, she was told her food stamps couldn't be used for a certain lunch meat, there being a prohibition against using the stamps to buy imported foods. Not understanding what she was being told, and misinterpreting the clerk's gestures to mean she didn't have enough food stamps to pay for it, she took the lunch meat back, removed half of it from its wrapping and put it in a separate bag, leaving the remaining meat in its original wrapper on the meat display case. She went through the line, paid for her items, and left the store. A store detective brought her back in and called the police. She was charged with violating a technical provision in the shoplifting law that makes it an offense to transfer items from one package to another inside the store.

When her case came up before Sam Moore, Pleasantville's aging, ill-tempered and grim-faced Municipal Judge, he demanded to know if she left the store with the lunch meat. She spoke almost no English, had no interpreter except an almost-equally handicapped friend, and was not advised she could get a lawyer. When at last she understood the question, she admitted she had left the store with the lunch meat. He took that as a guilty plea, and imposed the $200 fine which was automatic in shoplifting cases. Her friend told the judge she had no money. He sentenced her to jail to work off the fine at $5 a day — a 40 day sentence. After the officers led her away, the friend managed to reach the husband at his work, and he hurried to see me. I drove out to the Pleasantville jail to confirm her story, then called Judge Moore to ask if he would release her without bail so she could appeal. "What for?" he demanded. "She took the lunch meat and admitted it. Puerto Ricans!" he snarled. "They're all thieves!"

I had as yet no experience in municipal court work, but was impressed with Judge Horn, who had newly moved up to Assignment Judge– the chief judge in our two counties. I called and explained the situation. "Call Sol Forman," the Judge instructed me. "Ask him to set up a telephone conference call with you and I. I'll wait here." Forman was the senior assistant County Prosecutor, a tall, balding man with thick glasses and a habit of never answering a question except with another question. Sol was a fair guy, who had no illusions about the quality of justice dealt out in Sam Moore's court. He knew, although I did not, that Judge Moore was already under investigation by the state's Supreme Court. He set up the call; Judge Horn agreed to release the young mother without bail pending the appeal, and told me to get the order ready, get Sol to sign his consent to it, and bring it to him for signature, all within the hour.

By six o'clock I was back at the Pleasantville lockup, only to learn the defendant had already been transported to the county jail fifteen miles away in Mays Landing. When I arrived there the sheriff's deputy insisted she couldn't be processed for release until the next day. Judge Horn had given me his home phone number in case there were any problems. I called from the jail, handed the phone to the sheriff's deputy and watched his face turn scarlet as he stammered from "But, but, but Judge" to "Yessir, Judge. Right away. Yessir!"

I walked my client out of the jail and went home with the happy knowledge that, however much of a bystander I was in the grand scheme of things, I had stopped one injustice in my little piece of the world. It was a powerfully satisfying feeling, until I thought about how much effort and luck it took to prevent that one single injustice. The reality was that I had spent the day and half of the evening freeing a young and pregnant mother of two from jail for having stolen five dollars worth of lunch meat. Meanwhile that judge was free to go on dealing out harsh injustice and extreme penalties secure in the knowledge that few lawyers could afford the time to champion the cause of the defendants he abused. It is all well and good to think positive thoughts, but there are times when the negative aspects of life accumulate.

And yet, even as they did, none other than Justice Vince Haneman, a card-carrying member of the Atlantic County Republican Organization who had made it to the New Jersey Supreme Court, wrote an opinion for the Court that revolutionized the law protecting tenants throughout the state. A more unlikely opinion from a more unlikely source would be hard to imagine. The case was *Marini v. Ireland*. It established the then-revolutionary principle that tenants could withhold their rent to pay for repairs. Simple as it sounded, it was precedent-shattering, and provided a pathway to raising housing standards for the poor. Until that decision, New Jersey tenants couldn't tell the Landlord-Tenant judges about unsafe electrical wiring, broken plumbing, unlit hallways, absence of trash collection, and other evils, because the law had treated those judges as robots, permitting them to ask only if the rent was paid in cash and barring them from listening to the reasons why it might not have been paid.

The case arose when Mrs. Alice Ireland of Camden rented an apartment for $95 a month and complained after two months that her toilet was cracked and leaked water. The landlord refused to make repairs, so Mrs. Ireland hired a plumber and paid him $85.72 to fix the toilet. Deducting the cost of the repair from her rent, Mrs. Ireland paid only $9.28 for her July rent, whereupon the landlord demanded the balance and eventually got a district court order evicting Mrs. Ireland. Through her local legal services office she appealed and the state Supreme Court eventually heard the case. In his landmark opinion, Justice Haneman said there is an implied covenant of habitability in every lease, even though many leases contained no specific provisions for repairs.

When news of the decision reached me, I called Justice Haneman, who not too long before had tried to persuade me to switch my party from Democrat to Republican.

"Judge," I laughed, "I can't believe you wrote that opinion. Did the other judges hold a gun to your head to make you do it?"

"Nope. In fact, I asked to write that opinion. Now make the most of it!"

The *Marini* decision became the foundation of vast changes in the rights of poor tenants, and was influential in winning similar victories in other states across the country. It eventually gave me the winning argument in what was to become the first successful rent strike in New Jersey.

***

Chapter 30: Blood in the Concrete

The new Supreme Court rule that required lawyers to stamp their Summons and Complaints with the phone number of legal services brought in cases earlier in the judicial process than ever before. Patterns emerged. Certain lawyers appeared again and again on suits brought by bill collectors, finance companies and landlords. Human nature and the adversarial nature of our legal system usually combine to work against compassion in such lawyers. When your job requires you to garnish somebody's wages, evict a family or repossess furniture on a regular basis, perhaps your self-respect demands that you convince yourself that your client is always in the right and the other party always in the wrong. Add to that the circumstance that those being evicted or subject to wage attachments are often of lower education, often darker skinned, and usually working for the lowest wages, and it is understandable that some lawyers came to view themselves as impersonal technicians employed to carry out their client's wishes rather than as independent members of a profession sworn to "weigh conflicting loyalties and guide my work with an eye to what's good, acting less for myself than for justice and the people," as the "Lawyer's Pledge" proclaims. A few, like Roy Baylinson, a Harvard Law graduate who specialized in representing landlords, were reasonable men, tough adversaries when they saw themselves in the right, but willing to work something out when we called them on a hardship case.

The lawyer who appeared most frequently for finance companies was a nice enough fellow over the lunch table but cold as ice when compassion was sought for poor people trapped in various consumer exploitation schemes. Under legal shields like the "holder in due course" doctrine, his clients were a step removed from the consumer frauds that bilked the poor. If a poor man signed a debt, no matter how fraudulently it was procured, and his original creditor sold that debt to somebody who could claim no knowledge of that fraud, that second creditor was considered a "holder in due course," entitled to collect the debt. It is a doctrine necessary in an economy based on credit, but too easily abused when applied without protections against fraud and trickery. In reality, salesmen for furniture and appliances and other goods in low income areas often got people to sign one-sided contracts for overpriced and shoddy goods that resulted in more debt than their victims could carry, at high rates of interest. When such debts went unpaid, bill collectors were turned loose on the debtor, and if their most abusive tactics failed, the debts were forwarded to "collection" lawyers like the lunchtime philosopher who brought litigation based on a fee of one-third of whatever he collected. If he garnished a debtor's wages and got $30 a week out of him, that put ten bucks in his own pocket every week, and he garnished 10 or 20 wages every week all year long. He enjoyed joining the other lawyers at our lunch tables for a civilized conversation, but his lips pursed and his eyes narrowed if you suggested the whole linked system of consumer exploitation should be outlawed.

The bill collectors were getting on my nerves. Clients who came in to fight an attachment of their wages told us they didn't mind the wage attachments so much as they did the telephone calls. There were no limits as to how many calls bill collectors could make, nor at what times, or to whom. Our clients were called at work and their employers and supervisors were told of the debt. Their wives and children were called at home with ominous and humiliating messages to "call Mr. Jones at the loan company. It's very urgent he bring his payments up to date." Neighbors were called, and any known relatives – all in a campaign intended to bring so much pressure to bear on the debtor he'd make his payments no matter how sick his kids were or how far behind he was on his rent. It would have been bad enough if the underlying debts were fair and honest. They seldom were. A television set that might cost $200 cash in the suburbs cost $500 if bought in the city on the installment plan, and the installment plans charged the highest possible interest. An inter-related system of consumer scams, reckless extensions of credit, high-pressure sales, booby-trapped contracts, relentless bill collectors, and hard-nosed lawyers showed up in our caseload. Almost without exception, what drove the debtors to the point of breakdown were the phone calls — the caustic, sneering, insistent voices that flayed the nerves and respected no personal dignity.

A man and his wife came in to fight a wage garnishment that took ten percent of his pay every week, notwithstanding that the refrigerator he'd gone into debt to buy broke down and they had to buy a replacement long before the first was paid for. When she started sobbing about the phone calls, I asked how many calls they were receiving. She kept a tally by the telephone. In one evening she got 7 calls. At work that day he received another 4 or 5. Two of their kids were yelled at by the bill collector when they answered the phone. Whatever their financial irresponsibility, if any, that family was being goaded to tensions in their home that went beyond fairness.

I filed a motion to re-open the suit in order to raise consumer fraud as a defense and to add a counterclaim for emotional damages caused by the ceaseless harassment of the bill collectors. Winning money damages for conduct where there was no physical contact – a "touchless tort" as it was called, was a remedy just beginning to be sought by personal injury lawyers. To stretch that early concept to include damages to a debtor dunned for not paying his bills was a long stretch indeed. But I could think of no other way to strike back at the abuse. I spent long hours in the library, and drafted a legal complaint so detailed it read like a horror story.

The finance company was represented by none other than the lawyer who made so comfortable a living collecting from people like my client. He called me in great irritation. "This," he said, "is unbelievable. You can't mean it! Aside from the fact there's no law to support your claim, it's the most vicious set of goddam pleadings I ever read!"

I did not bring the counterclaim in hopes of major law reform. My strategy was essentially Pavlovian – designed to change the behavior of the local bill collectors rather than reform the law itself. Many unjust practices that bedeviled the poor endured because no poor folks could afford lawyers to raise hell about them. What made the exploitation and creditor harassment profitable was that it was a low-cost and high margin, high volume business. Now that our office was on the scene with lawyers, secretaries, investigators and a law library, the poor were able to bite back. Once confronted by suits like our counterclaim, those profits would disappear as their legal fees soared. No one single case would do it, but I was sure that when word spread around our two counties that Cape Atlantic Legal Services would litigate every case of consumer exploitation and creditor harassment, the local bill collectors would get the message.

To make doubly sure, I accepted an invitation to speak to a dinner meeting of the South Jersey Association of Credit Grantors. "Credit Grantor" is what loan companies and their bill collectors called themselves when explaining to their kids how they made their living. Word had spread among their membership of the McCracken Bankruptcy case and of my counterclaim in the creditor harassment case. After reciting a few examples of abusive collection tactics culled from our legal services files, I informed them of our new policy to fight every such case. Their applause was restrained.

The finance company lawyer must have thought he'd died and gone to heaven. Here was an adversary whose main strategy was to drive up the finance company's legal fees. He happily ground out his formal answer, denying any wrongdoing while vigorously defending the rights of bill collectors to use any means short of thumbscrews.

I responded by sending interrogatories. These are the bane of every lawyer's existence when you're on the receiving end – long lists of written questions your client has to answer under oath. I demanded to know who made those phone calls, and at what times, and how often. I demanded copies of the phone bills, copies of the bill collector's files, copies of his employment application, of any complaints the finance company received, reports of what training the company gave their employees, and on and on. When the answers – as evasive as possible, came back, I scheduled depositions of the guy who made the bulk of those calls, and his supervisor. Depositions are legal proceedings in which, out of the presence of the judge but with the witness under oath and his every word taken down by an official court reporter, lawyers can ask almost any question they want and the witness must answer.

The finance company fought hard to avoid producing their man. When at last I was able to question him, under oath and before a court reporter who took it all down, I understood their reluctance. He was a deeply troubled man – a high school dropout who joined the Navy, which for unspecified reasons sent him for psychiatric evaluation two months after he joined and gave him a medical discharge as soon as the results were available. He had a severe drinking problem that resulted in a messy divorce in which his wife claimed he beat her repeatedly.

Much as I wanted to pry into that psychiatric evaluation, I had to concede that even bill collectors have rights. The key fact to emerge from the interrogatories and depositions was that the finance company for whom the man worked knew he had problems; his application for employment listed his medical discharge; his supervisor who interviewed him for the job noted on his job application something about the medical discharge being related to a psychiatric exam. Nonetheless they hired him, gave him no training, set no limits to his contacts with debtors, and paid him according to how successful he was, as their manager put it, "putting the heat on the deadbeats." Then they turned him loose on their debtors and their debtors' families.

***

Early in March I traveled again to the Library of Congress law library in search of useful precedents to support my arguments that the action of the creditor was so abusive it should be punished. The bill collector harassment case dragged on for a long time as we tussled about how much I could fish around in the records of the finance company and its bill-collecting practices. Eventually they concluded the game was not worth the candle and offered to forgive the man's debt if we dropped the case. They did not want to chance how a jury would react to the evidence we had gathered. The client was happy enough to get off the hook. The word around town afterward was that the individual local bill collectors, now aware they might face a hostile cross examination some day, eased off on their abuses. At both the state and the federal level, legislation was coming along to limit the hours and the tactics that such "torture by telephone" collectors could use.

***

A group of tenants in a housing project on Maryland Avenue far north of Baltic Avenue asked for a meeting. The streets of Atlantic City, as Monopoly players know, are named after the states of the union, which run from the ocean to the bay, while the long avenues running parallel to the beach are named after the oceans of the world. The Boardwalk is the prime property, then Pacific Avenue, then the main thoroughfare of Atlantic Avenue. North of Atlantic Avenue from Maine to Arkansas was the Northside, home to most of the City's African-American population. If you owned property at Boardwalk and Park Place you were rich and white; if you were a tenant on Maryland Avenue north of Baltic you were poor and black.

The project, Townhouse Terrace West, was built by Jack Soble and his partner. Once completed, the tenants who moved in were subsidized by the federal government. Soble and his partner retained control of the property. The rent, which included the heat, was subsidized, set at whatever Soble could get the federal bureaucrats to approve. The tenants paid a percentage based on a formula involving their income and needs. Soble collected the balance from the U.S. Department of Housing and Urban Development, with an override for managing the project.

The two-story attached townhouses looked attractive from the outside, but after a few years of occupancy the shabby construction showed. Sheetrock walls buckled, pipes leaked, and the valves on the radiators rusted shut. Mothers had to keep the windows open in biting cold weather or the kids would roast. This had a good effect on Soble's profitability, because if the utility bills went up, they recovered it from the feds, plus their override. All these complaints were aggravating, but what finally moved the tenants to organize was when human sewage backed up in their kitchen sinks.

Rent strikes to force repairs in such circumstances had been tried in Newark with indifferent success. Poor tenants had enough trouble paying the rent. Withholding it for a month or two in the expectation they would pay up when the conditions were fixed was impractical. Other bills came along and what began in good faith as a rent strike ended badly when tenants spent their rent money on other bills.

I agreed to represent the Townhouse Terrace West tenants in a rent strike on two conditions. The first was that all the tenants in the strike had to pay their rent in full and on time. The second was that they had to pay it to me, for deposit into my Attorney's Trust Fund. Under the New Jersey Rules of Court, every practicing lawyer keeps a separate trust fund for handling his client's money. That fund is subject to audit by the Administrative Office of the Courts.

It was a gamble, because the landlord was bound to seek an injunction ordering me to turn the money over to him. I reasoned that by holding the rent money in my trust account, I could assure the trial judge the tenants were acting in good faith, and that if he ordered repairs to be made out of that fund, I would have the money to do it and pay whatever the balance was to the landlord.

As expected, Soble's lawyer applied to the Chancery Division for a turnover order. Fortunately for the tenants, the judge accepted my representations that I had all of the rent money safely in my trust account, where it would stay until he ordered otherwise. I also promised to let the court know when any single tenant failed to pay the rent in any following month so the landlord could take action against that tenant while I could keep withholding the rents of all the others. That problem never arose. The tenants were united in their determination to win.

It was a large scale application of the "fix it and take it off the rent" remedy recently handed down in Justice Haneman's opinion, and it worked. Having learned the hard way from Sam Epstein about getting every scrap of available evidence on the record to support my case, I produced affidavits from the tenants about the conditions, and from private plumbers and electricians about the faulty construction, and from contractors about the cost of repairs. Manny Gottlieb, a local general contractor of great experience who had built many of Atlantic City's major buildings and voluntarily ran the renovations project at the skating rink bought by Narco, introduced me to his circle of subcontractors. Their expertise made a huge difference in my case.

Justice Haneman was helpful in more ways than his famous decision. Although the Supreme Court hears its arguments and conducts its conferences in the state capital in Trenton, his personal chambers were in the Guarantee Trust Building in Atlantic City. After the story of the rent strike hit the papers, he stopped me in the hallway one afternoon.

"Listen, Joe," he said. "and remember you didn't hear this from me. I understand the problem with filth backing up in the kitchen sinks is because he uses drainage pipes narrower than the building code requires. Have your plumbing experts rip out a wall or two and check that out."

I did, and he was right. It wasn't exactly cricket, but having survived that long in Atlantic City legal circles I was learning to take whatever breaks came my way. I have to say I seldom had an opposing party so uniformly disliked by all the judges and the other builders as Jack Soble. Atlantic City's a small town, and his reputation was against him.

He refused to settle, fearing an epidemic of rent strikes in other projects. I took Soble's deposition. After my third question his hands shook so much he couldn't light his own cigarette. I don't know what he feared, but I never confronted a more nervous litigant.

At the trial one tenant after another testified about human filth backing up from the toilets into the kitchen sink; about kids perpetually sick from extreme temperatures in their bedrooms; and about the landlord's refusal to fix sagging doors, warped storm windows, and dangerous electrical wiring. I put Manny Gottlieb's plumbing and electrical contractors on the stand to testify about the substandard construction and the probable cost of repairs. The judge handed down his decision a few weeks before Christmas. He authorized payment for all repairs out of the funds I held, ordered a 12.5% rent reduction retroactive to the beginning of the strike, and instructed me to disburse that directly to the tenants out of the money I was holding. What was left after the repairs and the rent rebate was to go to the landlord. I issued the rebate checks to the happy tenants a few days before Christmas.

***

Leon Matthews insisted I see for myself the blood in the concrete and cinder block walls of his basement — "bluud" as he pronounced it in an accent a long generation removed from the South. The blood was from a deep cut on his hand (the scar displayed with defiant pride) received years earlier while he was building the small, plain house on Washington Avenue in Pleasantville. Blood that would, together with the cinder block and the walls and roof and his memories of raising his family in that house, all go on the block at the sheriff's foreclosure sale because of the unread fine print of the sales agreement. "That's my blood," he pointed. "Right there. My own blood I put in that cement. Now the Sheriff's gonna sell my house!"

At 75 he was a short, stocky, proud black man. He had never used a lawyer before. To come to our legal services office he put on a necktie – a patterned yellow tie to accompany his plaid flannel shirt and old sports jacket. Barbara Camper knew him as a deacon in her church. She ushered him into my office with obvious high regard. He had a clutch of papers in his weathered hands — the contract he had signed to purchase a freezer on the installment plan, with fresh meat to be delivered every month. Freezer plans were popular, the idea being that you saved money by cutting out the supermarket. The salesman made it sound pretty good – swore Leon would save more than enough to pay for the meat and the freezer both.

The freezer-plan involved the debtor signing a contract to buy the freezer and the meat, but by signing a mortgage on his house Leon opened the door for the freezer company to force the sale of his home. This went far beyond the common sense understanding consumers have of what they're getting into when they agree to buy something — especially consumers who have little formal education or business experience, or have trouble reading fine print as they age.

In fact what he had signed to join the freezer plan was a bond and a mortgage which, in meticulous, cast-iron legalese bound him to pay the price of the freezer and of all the meat that was to be delivered for the following two years, plus any interest charges, court costs and attorneys fees sought by the freezer plan company if he failed to pay.

Leon understood if he didn't pay they'd stop delivering the meat, and was pretty sure they'd take the freezer back. That was fair. He knew if you buy something and don't pay for it they can take it back. There was no discussion with the salesman of what else would happen if Mr. Matthews fell sick and got behind on his freezer payments. No explanation of the legal terms and hard-to-understand phrases at the bottom of the long, small-print contract or the other fine-print pages he signed. Leon depended on his good health to see him through. Without the odd jobs he did now and then, he had nothing to live on except his Social Security, which provided barely enough for his food, his taxes and utilities, and a dollar for the collection plate on Sunday.

The freezer manufacturer went out of business; the freezer broke down, and Leon was still on the hook for meat he could no longer freeze. Then he got sick and lost the income from his odd jobs. The first he knew of the trouble he was in was when the sheriff's deputy came to his door with the papers, strongly urging him to go see a lawyer. His wife, who once handled the household budget, was five years dead.

Leon was right to insist I come see his blood in that concrete and cinder block. It was a powerful statement of something wrong with the system, when a man could build his own house and lose it because of fine print in an unfair contract. Although I had no idea how to save his house, I took the papers with me and promised to see what I could do.

Legal services lawyers everywhere were running up against the built-in barricades that kept justice from the poor in cases like Leon's – barricades founded on concepts like "holder in due course," and axioms like "the sanctity of contract, " which claimed a man's word was his bond and he must be held to it, even if one party was a corporation with highly competent lawyers drafting their contracts, and the other party was a confused laborer in his old age. There was little legal protection against consumer fraud. New

Jersey had enacted a Consumer Fraud Act in 1960 but it authorized only the state's Attorney General to bring suit for consumer fraud against commercial establishments. A bill was moving through the New Jersey legislature to permit private persons to bring such suits, and sue for treble damages, but it was not yet on the books. There was, however, a growing willingness among New Jersey's judges to consider challenges to debts based on overreaching, unfair pricing, and high-pressure selling that resulted in unconscionable consequences for the customer.

We staved off the sheriff's sale long enough to file a motion to re-open Leon's case. When that motion was granted we filed an answer on his behalf challenging the whole range of unfair practices and lopsided contractual provisions and draconian remedies that drove the profits of the freezer-plan companies. As was happening with other cases where we showed a willingness to take the fight as far as it had to go, the creditor settled, having second thoughts about risking a long and expensive fight that might result in an adverse legal precedent. Public attention to such scams was increasing as newspapers carried stories of the injustices they worked and people began to realize that consumer protection benefitted everybody from businessmen to customers, and hurt only the bad guys. Within a year the New Jersey state legislature passed the first major amendments to the Consumer Fraud Act in the eleven years since its enactment.

***

Chapter 31: A Harvest of Change

The pressure to handle divorces never let up. Most were uncontested, but the situation was complicated. What often drove the wife to seek a divorce was less her present situation than her hopes for the future. We were seeing women who had separated from their husbands two and three years earlier. After a while she might find another man, move in with him, and bear his children. Eventually it would be time for the kids to start school, with little Harry having the last name of Jones and his brother Tommy the last name of Smith and their mother the last name of Brown. Many women wanted a divorce in order to clear the way for remarriage and adoption of their children by the new father — a re-organization of their lives under one family name. In other cases women simply wanted to be free of sexual demands by unpredictably re-appearing husbands about whom they felt only fear and anger.

Whatever the reasons for the divorces, the law in New Jersey permitted divorce only on grounds of one-sided marital fault. You had to prove adultery, or extreme cruelty, or willful desertion of at least one year's duration, and that proof had to be corroborated by a witness. Worse, under the peculiar rules of the game, the party seeking the divorce had to be blameless and the other party wholly at fault. Such clarity seldom happens in real life. A woman beaten by a drunken husband might leave and eventually find a better man. Yet by the very act of moving in with him she became an adulteress and so was disqualified from getting a divorce. Everyone agreed that kids did better growing up in a two-parent home, but the combination of legal expense and archaic laws imposed a terrific impediment to that benefit for poor kids.

I explored innovations in technology in hopes new developments would let us handle the volume of cases we'd be hit with if we accepted divorces. At the annual State Bar Association meeting held each May in Atlantic City, IBM, Dictaphone and other makers of typewriters and dictating equipment had their latest models on display. IBM in particular was pushing an $8,000 Magnetic Card Typewriter which recorded an entire page of typing on a card the size of an envelope, allowing for easy correction and use of standard paragraphs. Dictating machines were becoming pocket-sized as they switched from recording on magnetic belts to recording on cassette tapes. By 1970 computers were beginning to make an appearance in the legal profession. In one room at the Bar Association gathering a company set up special telephone lines to tap a database that carried all of the recent court opinions in the State of Ohio. Having spent days researching and writing a brief trying to change the New Jersey law on retaliatory evictions, I was curious to see how long it would take using the Lexis system for Ohio. It took about a half-hour. But it would be years, I was told, before the system expanded to include New Jersey cases. And it was expensive.

Several floors below, in a less expensive exhibit area, a computer show was underway where young guys including Apple founders Steve Jobs and Steve Wozniak, wearing blue-jeans without a necktie in sight were showing a variety of gadgets pointing the way to the future. Most of the computers were cobbled together from the spare parts bin; odd-looking contrivances with wires and cables and circuit boards open to view. There were keyboards but no printers; black and white monitors that looked like old television sets or early radar screens, and no customers. The proud inventors were more interested in each other's gadgets than in lining up buyers, which was probably wise, because only a handful of lawyers wandered down to see their products.

Giving up on a technological answer to the divorce problem, I turned to a different approach. The "Judicare" concept interested me – the idea of using legal services money to hire private lawyers to represent the poor. Even if OEO survived Nixon's oppositon, it would never have enough money to fund divorces. But what if I could set up a wholesale operation and get discounts on legal fees? Was there not some way I could force the price of divorce low enough to open the courts to those needy women? Then it hit me: I had used my attorney's trust fund as a repository for funds in the rent strike case. Why not use that same device to set up a "divorce savings plan," into which women could deposit small sums every week until they had saved enough to pay for a low-cost divorce? Banks had used that approach in their "Christmas Club" plan for years. A big savings was possible because legal services was exempt from court fees for such cases. The filing and hearing fees for a divorce was $110 at the time – a considerable sum.

I sent a letter proposing the plan to Ed McConnell, the Administrative Director of the Courts:

> "I propose ... that low income persons pay into [my attorney] trust fund the sum of $225, in such installments ... as they can manage. Upon the accumulation of the sum of $225 I would, after certifying the person as eligible for legal services under our guidelines, retain a private counsel, who would represent the client in the securing of a desertion divorce in payment of a flat fee of $225. The divorce complaint ... would be filed on legal services stationery, with the attorney handling the case being listed as of counsel to myself, who would be the attorney of record. In the event the case turned out to be contested or if substantial complications resulted, the private counsel could then remit the case to me, and I would assign it to a staff attorney here in the legal services program, paying the private counsel a fair fee for services performed up to the date of his leaving the case.
>
> By filing the action on the legal services stationery, we would be able to take advantage of the filing fee waiver provided by Rule 1:13-2".

My proposal brought me into conflict with such liberals as remained at OEO, with the State Office of Legal Services, and with the Atlantic County Bar Association. OEO and the State Legal Services thought it the first downward step on the road to the hell of Judicare. The County Bar, in the person of my old boss Jim Cooper, convened an emergency committee to deal with what it considered, in Cooper's words, "socialized law."

The Chief Justice thought I should give it a try.

I put out word that I was looking for private lawyers willing to take uncontested divorces for $225 with the fee guaranteed and the court costs waived. Such was the potential of buying legal services on an aggregated basis that several lawyers even offered to go below $200 if I would channel all the cases to them. A lawyer with an arrangement like that could make good money if he could get 10 or so cases a month — certainly enough to pay his office rent and his secretary.

The theory was sound, but it proved limited in practice. Saving money for any reason is barely possible for the working poor getting by on minimum wages. For the unemployed poor on welfare, it was impossible.

***

There were other systemic barriers keeping the poor from getting good legal representation. Under the archaic Ethics Rules of the profession, lawyers were not allowed to solicit cases in any way, shape or form. Paid advertising by lawyers was strictly forbidden. Official interpretations of this ethical rule went to extremes. One opinion published by the Ethics Committee concluded that it was unethical for a lawyer whose hobby was flying to have the scales of justice painted on the door of his small private plane. I don't know who the Ethics Committee thought he would lure into his office while flying his Cessna at 7,500 feet, but there it was. It was intensely hypocritical, of course. Shady personal injury lawyers paid off cops and ambulance drivers to steer cases to them; even more distinguished ones quietly paid technically unethical "referral fees" to other lawyers for sending them cases.

The results of such nonsensical ethics were harmful to the public, who were left with no way to choose lawyers except by word of mouth. For the poor, the Ethics Rule against solicitation had wider implications. The N.A.A.C.P. lawyers in Virginia, searching for cases on civil rights, were charged with unethical solicitation of clients, and fought the Virginia Bar Association to the U.S. Supreme Court. The high court backed the non-profit civil rights lawyers, forcing at least a narrow breach in the ethics barrier. The breach was narrow because the Court was not willing to decide whether "commercial" free speech was also protected, which would have opened the door to advertising by pharmacists, doctors, lawyers and other professionals. This was a serious limitation. Without such advertising consumers had no easy way to know which lawyers specialized in divorces, or traffic court, or wills or personal injury. Nor could they learn which lawyers were willing to take consumer fraud cases as new laws came into play protecting the public against the kind of scams and one-sided contracts we at legal services were encountering. Worker's Compensation cases were another area where getting the poor into the hands of a competent specialist could make a great difference. The working poor get the most hazardous jobs; in busy kitchens where steaming ovens and slippery floors are commonplace; in collecting trash and garbage where the jagged edges of opened food cans or broken bottles lead to injuries and infections; in warehouses where lifting heavy weights brings on back problems, hernias and crushed toes. Yet there was no effective way an injured worker could tell which lawyer could get the best recovery for him.

At a national Legal Services convention in San Antonio I met Judge Alvin Ruben, a well-regarded federal judge from New Orleans. He was urging legal services lawyers to set up lawyer referral services in our home areas if none existed, which could steer clients to appropriate lawyers for the kind of case they had. A study done for the American Bar Association revealed that between a quarter and a third of contacts with lawyer referral services came from legal services. Because we at legal services were the *de facto* point of first contact between a large portion of the public and lawyers, I thought his idea made sense. I brought it up at the next meeting of the Atlantic County Bar Association, and was asked to co-chair a committee to draft a plan for such a system.

Judge Ruben's activities in promoting the establishment of Lawyer Referral Services were attempts to address the failure of Ethics Committees to adapt their Rules to the needs of modern society. The overall approach was to have a screening office or person, to whom the public could turn when they needed a lawyer. The screener would get a sense of the problem, and then refer the client to lawyers who had indicated their interest in taking such cases. It was a necessarily limited approach. If a known incompetent insisted he be put on the list for complicated litigation, there was no effective way to avoid sending him cases as his turn in the rotation came up. But it was at least a start; the Bar Association's committee would be made of lawyers, and peer pressure offered hope of informally discouraging blatant inappropriateness, by, for example, urging inexperienced lawyers to hold off asking for complex medical malpractice cases. At any rate, it offered the public something better than the bare listing of lawyer's names and numbers to be found in the telephone book.

An immediate question was how to pay the expenses. Obviously, a lawyer's referral service was useless unless the public knew it existed, which meant it would have to advertise its existence. The ABA got its ethics committee to approve advertising for such referral services, so long as it mentioned no individual lawyers in the ads. Advertising expenses would include a display ad in the yellow pages, and newspaper and radio ads to reach the wider public. A telephone had to be paid for, and somebody employed to answer calls and do the paperwork. Most lawyer referral services lived on a combination of a subsidy from the local Bar Association, a small fee charged to lawyers who wanted their names included on the panels, and in some cases a referral fee from the lawyers who received the cases. Eventually we established a plan to provide for a part-time employee hired by the Bar Association and paid for out of annual dues. A desk was found in the courthouse and the program was launched. It was slow in growing, but proved successful and durable.

A minor side effect of the prohibition against lawyer advertising was that lawyers were driven to join service clubs and civic organizations to get their names known. Several young lawyers on my Board invited me to the luncheon meetings of the Jaycees, which took place in a room at Atlantic City's famous "500 Club", in better days the venue for performers like Frank Sinatra, Sammy Davis, Jr., Dean Martin and Jerry Lewis. I attended a few meetings before concluding it was a mismatch for both myself and the

Jaycees. There was a lively moment when, in support of a protest against the national Jaycees refusal to admit women to membership, I moved to admit them to the Atlantic City chapter. This, for the Jaycees, was the equivalent of throwing a live hand grenade on the table. Sides formed, hilariously grave speeches were given, and in our chapter the motion eventually passed. Politics were seldom discussed; the problems of the poor were unknown and, I thought, uninteresting to anyone at the table other than myself. My road had by then so greatly differed from my contemporaries that I gave membership in the Jaycees up as irrelevant to anything in which I was interested, although I continued to give speeches to them and other civic groups whenever invited to explain what we were about.

***

Late in 1970 OEO Director Donald Rumsfeld and his assistant Dick Cheney attempted to rein in the Legal Services programs around the country by shifting funding authority from the national OEO Legal Services office to the directors of OEO's 10 regional offices, most of whom were not themselves lawyers. Their plan ignored a tradition of independence vital to the legal profession. Simply put, a lawyer's ability to represent his client requires that nothing except his professional judgment and the rules of his profession govern his conduct. That value is jealously guarded by the courts and the legal profession. One of the earliest, but hardest, lessons young lawyers must learn is to protect that independence – often to the irritation of paying clients who expect their lawyer to do exactly what the client wants, rather than questioning the legality, unfairness, or outright criminality of the client's wishes. To put Legal Services under the control of non-lawyers struck at the heart of that independence — especially when the Nixon Administration was trying to stop legal services lawyers from bringing suits challenging the Administration's own acts and policies. As, for example, when I sued the Secretary of Labor on behalf of the kids fired from the Neighborhood Youth Corps program in Atlantic City.

Terry Lenzner, an attorney hired by Rumsfeld to be OEO's National Director of Legal Services, opposed the Rumsfeld-Cheney plan as detrimental to the core values of the legal profession. His opposition alerted the prestigious American Bar Association and others to the plan, which was ultimately stopped. It was a courageous act. Rumsfeld fired Lenzner and within a week left OEO and moved to the Nixon White House. He was appointed Counselor to the President and took Cheney with him to become a White House staff assistant and Assistant Director of the Cost of Living Council.

Named to replace Rumsfeld as OEO Director was his former wrestling partner and roommate at Princeton, Frank Carlucci, another Nixon insider. Carlucci was a foreign service officer with a reputation for arranging the covert overthrow of left-wing governments opposed by American business interests in Congo and Brazil. All three OEO alumni – Rumsfeld, Cheney and Carlucci, would in future years serve as Secretary of Defense in Republican Administrations.

To fill Dick Cheney's spot at OEO Frank Carlucci brought in Howard Phillips as Assistant Director. "Howie" Phillips, educated at Harvard, had made a name for himself in right-wing Republican circles and did not lie about his intentions. He opposed the OEO, he remarked, because it was "based on a Marxist notion."

Observing the deliberate attempts to destroy the anti-poverty programs was an unhappy experience for me as President Nixon tightened his grip through such lieutenants as Haldeman, Erlichman, Rumsfeld, Cheney, Carlucci and Howard Phillips. After watching the differences between how Jack and Bobby Kennedy tried to improve our national life and what Richard Nixon and the Republicans were doing, life in the political arena beckoned more each day. I had committed to Cape Atlantic Legal Services for a year or so. More than two had gone by. There were still battles to fight and much to do, but thoughts of the day when I could hang out my shingle and go into private practice hovered over my desk.

***

The happy result of the testimony John Brooks gave the Senate was the eventual award to Narco of a annual grant in excess of $837,000 from the

National Institute of Mental Health. This funded a tremendous expansion of Narco's efforts. When the grant documents arrived, John asked me to review the guidelines to make sure we handled the money in accordance with government regulations. Such accountability was crucial, especially given the hostile and ever-tightening grip of the Nixon White House over programs out on the far reaches of the massive federal government. If the funds were misused, Narco would not get a second chance.

I knew so little about drug addiction and the lives of drug addicts that it seemed prudent to educate myself. Brooks suggested I start by sitting in on an intake interview with a new patient. She was 19, a lively black woman who gave her consent to my presence with a ready smile, and told us her story. At 16, she was a prostitute turning one or two tricks a week. She pitied the junkies her boy friend supplied and stole from him to supply them from time to time. In what they considered gratitude, some of them got her on to using drugs. Her boy friend drove up to New York two or three times a week, and bought between \$800 and \$1,400 worth of drugs per trip, then retailed them in Atlantic City. An \$800 buy retailed for \$2,800 and up. She said he cleared between \$6,000 and \$7,500 each week until he went to jail. When he was busted, she started tricking, working about three nights a week at about \$25 a trick, three or four tricks a night. Her beat was Pacific Avenue, which she worked during conventions. She had brothers and sisters, who were not on drugs. She had 2 children, 3 and 4 years old, both by the same man, with whom she lived. Her babies were now with her mother, who received welfare for them.

She told me that drug users used to all be black men. Now it was almost half women, and the number of white kids was going up sharply. She said the white kids had access to more goods to steal and to more money. One white kid she knew was the son of a down-beach bookie who forged \$3,800 worth of checks on his father's checking account. The amount of money that could be made selling drugs amazed me. Yet according to John Brooks, her boyfriend was small fry – a guy at the low end of the drug chain, who took all the chances getting, transporting and retailing the drugs.

"The big guys," Brooks said, "work Camden, Philly, and Newark. Atlantic City don't have enough money on the street to get 'em here, except in the summer."

I advised Brooks on ways to keep control of spending and avoid abuse and scandal, but in fact a man used to the lies, stealing and smuggling of the drug world had no problem controlling the funds for which he was responsible. There were no scandals or abuses then or ever under his leadership.

***

Meanwhile, the routine of legal services went on. I still took my share of client interviews, which kept me informed about the kinds of cases coming in and the results we were getting. They could be startling in their variety. A middle-aged woman came in about her aged father, who was growing senile and had been lured into marrying a Bulgarian immigrant. The bride, in her early sixties, returned to Bulgaria days after the wedding. A letter arrived addressed to the daughter. It was brief and to the point: "I am now in Bulgaria. When he dies, send the Social Security checks to me here at this place." The daughter conceded the scam brought no economic harm either to her father or to her, but she was angry enough to want it stopped. She was willing to pay a lawyer to handle it, so I sent her to a fellow just starting out who needed cases. On another day, two black teenagers came in; a 17 year old gum-chewing girl and her 16 year old sullen brother. Their mother was stabbed to death by her boyfriend in a drunken brawl. Now the kids were fighting over who got the stereo.

Evictions, wage garnishments, unhappiness everywhere, and in Washington nothing but power politics and foolishness. The war in Vietnam, which Nixon-the-campaigner claimed he could resolve, could not be stopped by Nixon-the-President. It was still ripping the country apart with protests, demonstrations, police beatings and all the wretched consequences of an unpopular war and Nixon-the-Commander-in-Chief's inability to win it or end it.

***

Among other progressive developments that came out of the turbulent 60's were the efforts of Ralph Nader challenging a wide range of consumer frauds through a series of consumer-advocate organizations he founded such as "Public Citizen" and the "Public Interest Research Groups." These enlisted hundreds of young volunteers. They became known as "Nader's Raiders," investigating and bringing to light unacceptable conditions and practices in almost every area where the actions of corporations and political entities adversely affected the lives of ordinary individuals.

The government agency charged with protecting consumers — The Federal Trade Commission, was spurred to new life and action by Nader's Raiders. In South Jersey there was no local counterpart to the FTC. Only the grossest frauds might draw the attention of the prosecutor, whose staff had neither expertise nor interest in combating the evils of "bait and switch" advertising, unfair collection practices, and unconscionable sales tactics. Since many scams disproportionately afflicted the poor, bringing the experience of the FTC investigators to our efforts seemed a good idea. The FTC was cooperative. We created an experimental consumer task force to probe shoddy business practices in Atlantic and Cape May Counties, working out of our Legal Services offices. The task force members included Salvatore Angiorgi, attorney in charge of the Federal Trade Commission's Consumer Protection Service in New York City, Ronald Stryshack and Earl Stackhouse, investigators for the FTC, and Frank Domenic, a special investigator for the State Office of Consumer Protection in Newark.

There was a price to pay for their cooperation: The FTC's mandate did not place priority on the problems of the poor. They were as eager to go after Boardwalk auction houses running $7,000 scams as they were to go after sleazy operators who sold $100 bunk-beds on the installment plan to desperate mothers for $350, only $20 down – at interest rates that turned a $100 bunk-bed into an $800 debt burden. Busting the infamous Boardwalk auction houses helped the FTC generate favorable publicity when it wanted to show it was doing something useful, but since the only place the FTC met consumers and took complaints was in our legal services office where only the poor came, it was the less sensational but more vital complaints of our clients that got the attention.

***

Narco's funding from the National Institute of Mental Health included mention of an "Indirect Cost Rate," whereby grants like ours might be eligible for extra funds to pay our overhead costs. Intrigued by the possibility of increasing our grant, I sent for the government publication that explained what an Indirect Cost Rate was, and how it worked. When it arrived – full of dry accounting principles, examples, forms and applicable regulations, I read through it dutifully.

Studying the documents I thought that if I could pick up another 3 or 4% for Narco, it would bring in an extra $25,000 or so to meet expenses of the rapidly growing program. Rather than fly blindly into this new territory, I drove down to the National Institute of Mental Health and tracked down the guy responsible for deciding how much of an indirect cost rate to award to applicant organizations. The negotiator was new to the National Institute of Mental Health, having spent the previous five years negotiating indirect cost rates for the Department of Defense. He knew less than I did about drug addiction treatment, but understood how much clout a friendly Senator on the Appropriations Committee had. After I gave him a brief history of Narco and of Senator Williams' help getting our grant, he suggested an early lunch in the cafeteria.

As he described his work at the Pentagon, it grew on me that big defense contractors do not think small. Their idea of a reasonable indirect cost rate was in the 40 to 50% range. As far as I could see, the man had never awarded a rate lower than 40% and Narco was his first drug-rehabilitation applicant. Over more coffee I learned that in major grants made by the parent National Institutes of Health, rates in the 40 to 50% range were routinely awarded to places like Columbia University, UCLA, Johns Hopkins, and other major medical and educational entities.

Back in Atlantic City John Brooks and I went over every Narco cost that could be considered overhead under the most expansive definitions. Since in fact we had no history of overhead costs, we applied for an "interim" rate – the budget version of a self-fulfilling prophecy, since any funds we received during the interim would by definition be spent as overhead and thus the final rate would be the same as the interim rate.

We were awarded a rate of 45.7% — effectively bringing home to Narco another $382,509 each year of the initial three-year grant period. By following up the fine print of the grant documents I had won my client an extra $1 million.

***

At long last, in mid-June of 1971 the New Jersey legislature reformed the state's antiquated divorce law. The most important aspect of the reform was that a new "no-fault" grounds for divorce was created. For years the only grounds for divorce in New Jersey had been adultery, extreme cruelty, or desertion followed by a year of separation. One party had to be entirely innocent, and the other entirely guilty, all of which had to be proved in court. Now all that was swept away. It was enough under the new law to prove two simple things: (1) that the couple had separated and lived apart for at least the previous 18 months; and (2) that there was no reasonable prospect of reconciliation. It didn't matter whose fault triggered the separation. The new law accepted what judges had long understood; that no court can trace every emotion and reaction, every life event and disappointed hope and personal failure to its source and pin the blame on one but not the other party. Gone were the lying private investigators; the hyped-up claims of extreme cruelty; the nervous uncertainty whether the judge on the hearing day would swallow the nonsense before him or show a rebellious conscience and deny a finding of one-sided fault. Now people could plan their lives — lives that often included remarriage and hopes for a happier future with a new partner – knowing they could actually make such changes. Gone too were the sending of desperate spouses to Nevada for divorces based on short-term "legal residence" qualifications – a flawed practice in itself, and useless to women who could not afford six weeks in Las Vegas. What was most helpful was that no-fault offered a way to break the back of the high minimum fees for divorce insisted upon by the Bar Association Committee on Minimum Fees.

***

Chapter 32: Final Days

By June of 1971 it was time to set the date. For nearly 15 years I had dreamt, planned and worked toward the day I would hang out my shingle as a practicing lawyer. What normally took 7 years of college and law school had taken me more than twice as long. At 32, with a wife and five kids to support and the accumulated debts of college and law school still on my books, it was now or never. Government offices in Washington were filled with guys who came to work so they could study law at night, then found by the time they graduated and took the bar exam they were trapped by a steady paycheck and growing family, too afraid to quit and go hang out their shingle. They ended up staring out the windows on gray winter mornings wondering if the snow would be heavy enough for the government to let them go home early. That prospect had scared the hell out of me when I was in Washington, and it haunted me now.

I had a month of vacation time due from legal services. In all those years Maryanne and I had taken no vacations, no trips, no time off other than weekends — and few enough of those. Jeanne Marie, our oldest, was 12. Mark was 11; Suzi 10; Tim 8. Annie, at 2 ½, was walking and talking up a storm. The prudent thing would be to use the vacation pay to carry me through my first month of private practice — but there was no telling, once I opened my law office, how many years it would be before I could again afford the time or money for a vacation. And kids grow up fast. This was as good a chance to spend time with my family as might come my way for a long time. The successor I recommended for my post at Legal Services, Bill Blane, was a hiker and camper. He urged me to take the family camping in the vast Baxter State Park that surrounds Mt. Katahdin in the great northern woods of Maine. It was an irresistible temptation. I set my resignation for October 1st, and took the month of July off, leaving August and September to wrap up unfinished business when I returned.

We rented a tow-along, pop-up camper that, with its canvas walls up and bunks slid out into position, could sleep all seven of us – so long as we tucked little Annie in the right corner. It was a delightful month of campfires, of swimming in wild rivers and ponds; of the fragrance of great pine trees everywhere; of night skies filled with brilliant stars; of watching moose wander nearby and bears open our camp cooler to get at the food. We were so far from civilization we could not find a broadcast on the car radio. The noise and bustle of the outside world faded away. My most important decision became whether to take a nap or take the kids for a swim.

After two weeks in the wilderness we headed down east to Bar Harbor, camping at Lamoine State Park on the slopes of Frenchman's Bay, where hot showers, lobster dinners, and drive-in movies were to be found—featuring two new war movies; "M.A.S.H." and "Patton." The radio news was back in reach, filled with excited reports that President Nixon had accepted an invitation to visit Communist China. I savored a copy of the *New York Times* as never before with my morning coffee at the campfire, catching up on events while the kids explored the campground amenities.

At OEO headquarters in Washington Frank Carlucci was gone, promoted to run the obscure power center in the White House known as the Office of Management and Budget. President Nixon named Philip Sanchez as the new director of OEO, although the zealous Howard Phillips remained in actual control of the agency, determined to eradicate it no matter what laws stood in his way or how much Congress disagreed with his agenda. His preferred tactic was to dismember OEO by transferring its various programs to old line agencies where, the Nixon Administration hoped, they would quietly atrophy. This the still-Democratic run Congress tried to stop.

I was present when Howard Phillips was called to testify before the House Education and Labor Committee. It was an angry panel and an angry crowd. Most of the members on the Committee had long fought for the social programs Phillips was now trying to strangle, and they resented the Nixon Administration's arrogance. I stood in the back as they cross-examined Phillips. Ralph Nader stood beside me. Bill Higgs, counsel for James Meredith in the case arising out of the integration of the University of Mississippi, was against the far wall. I thought I saw Fanny Lou Hamer in the crowd, the determined black woman who led the Mississippi Freedom

Democrats in their protest at the Democratic Convention in Atlantic City in '64. But political grudges linger; OEO's early battles still rankled with the leading Democrats. In the summer of 1971 the Nixon Administration managed to secure congressional approval to transfer VISTA and 13 other OEO programs to other agencies.

***

Back at Cape Atlantic for my last weeks as Chief Attorney, I learned that the New Jersey Supreme Court, fed up with the trend of ever-higher contingent fees for personal injury lawyers, was taking action. Traditionally lawyers for people injured through somebody else's negligence or active recklessness took the victim's cases on a fee basis that charged nothing if the client lost, but a percentage of the win if the lawyer was able to get a financial recovery from the responsible party or, as was usually the case, the defendant's insurance carrier. For years that percentage hovered between 20% and 33%. In more recent years that percentage climbed. One lawyer demanded 50% of any recovery – plus expenses – and bragged about getting it.

Early in August the New Jersey Supreme Court announced a new rule limiting contingent fees to a maximum of 33% in smaller cases, declining to 10% on the upper dollars in major recoveries. County Bar Associations around the state protested vigorously. I attended the September meeting of the Atlantic County Bar Association to argue in favor of the Supreme Court's proposal. My arguments provoked angry attempts to shout me down.

"It's a shameful system," I shouted over the din. "If a man loses an arm and a leg, he gets paid for the arm and the lawyer takes the leg!"

Lost in the passionate defense of their fees, it took time for my colleagues to notice a young man in the jury box taking notes. Asked to identify himself, he said he was a reporter for the *Press*. More angry statements followed about the meeting being private. The meeting cooled down when the well-intentioned Bar President assured the members that nothing they said would see print because, as he put it, "there's a gentleman's agreement with the *Press* they won't print this sort of thing." At this the reporter's eyes gleamed and his pen started moving at high speed.

Fortunately for me, the Bar Association dinners took place on the same day as the afternoon meetings. That night's dinner was particularly crowded, but since the *Press* is a morning paper, the assembled brethren had no clue they would be roasted in the next day's edition. Even more fortunately, in New Jersey when the Supreme Court decides to issue a Rule of Court, only the seven justices get to vote on it, and on such things they are usually unanimous or they don't propose it in the first place.

***

By mid-September I was up to my ears setting up my new law office; renting a suite; buying desks, law books, chairs, filing cabinets, conference table, typewriter; hiring a secretary; ordering stationary printed; having telephones installed and, most of all, borrowing the $5,000 I needed to pay for it all and carry me for a month or two looking, to all appearances, like a successful young lawyer in a sizeable office complete with waiting room, conference room, secretary, and the usual large desk and cushioned swivel chair for the lawyer and a wingback chair for the client.

For all the controversy in which I had been involved, an old-fashioned courtesy still existed among the private Bar which I was now entering. No one can become a practicing lawyer in New Jersey without meeting the same rigorous requirements of education and passing the Bar Exam I had gone through. You cannot be appointed to it. All the favoritism and political patronage in the world will not assure you of entry. In that sense, if in few others, there was a brotherhood of the Bar; one that stretches back far into our history. Friends sent flowers and good wishes for my opening day. Judges sent warm letters of congratulations on my entering private practice; other lawyers did the same. A surprise testimonial dinner was given in my honor at which Sam Epstein, who started as an adversary and became a mentor, presided as Master of Ceremonies.

And then it was over. Cakes and soda and a farewell lunch in the library with the lawyers and staff. On Friday the 1st of October, 1971 my secretary answered the phone in my new digs on the top floor of the Schwemm Building at New York and Atlantic Avenue with a cheery "Good Morning — Mr. Wilkins' Law Office."

How sweet that sounded!

***

Epilogue

It proved easier to leave my physical office at legal services than to walk away from the causes and movements that now formed so much of my life. The efforts of legal services lawyers all over the country were beginning to bear fruit as cases reforming the law in such areas as consumer fraud, landlord-tenant law and divorce law reached the higher courts even as legislative reforms in the states and at the federal level moved ahead. One of the greatest reforms affecting the elderly poor was the indexing of social security benefits – linking increases in social security automatically to increases in the cost of living. Another was a ruling by the US Supreme Court that it is unconstitutional to allow those who can afford it to pay fines while jailing those too poor to pay.

Nor was it all that easy to disentangle myself from local initiatives in which I had been involved. Notwithstanding the personal good wishes of many lawyers, my support of the limitation of contingent fees in personal injury cases brought heavy criticism from the organized Bar. More fire was aimed at a proposal I made that groups of clients such as members of a church congregation should band together to negotiate special legal fee rates with lawyers. The Bar Association attacked my proposal on the grounds it was unjust to lawyers to claim that legal fees were too high for ordinary people. They were evidently still under the impression there was a "gentleman's agreement" with the *Atlantic City Press* that protected them from public accountability. They learned otherwise when the *Press* took up the cudgels on my behalf in a lead editorial:

HIGH ATTORNEY FEES
ARE ATTORNEY'S FEES TOO HIGH?

> Attorney Joseph Wilkins of Brigantine says they are; his colleagues in the Atlantic County Bar Association retort that such remarks were "totally irresponsible" and degrading to the profession. .... But figures given by Wilkins in a speech last week show that fees in many cases are beyond the reach

> of people living on low or modest incomes. ....
>
> ".... Why is it cheaper today to take a round trip to Europe than it is to get a simple, uncontested divorce? Why does it cost as much to hire a lawyer for one night in traffic court as it does for most people to pay a month's rent?"
>
> "We feel these are legitimate questions, and we think Wilkins is right in raising them."

I was not finished raising them. At the next Bar Association I pointed out that the Minimum Fee Schedule was illegal price-fixing and possibly a criminal violation of the federal anti-trust laws. When I moved for its abolition the members hooted me down. I could find no second for the motion. Unknown to us all, however, the U.S. Department of Justice was investigating whether minimum fees were illegal price-fixing. At the Bar meeting the following month the Association's secretary cleared his throat and read a letter from the Department of Justice requesting copies of any minimum fee schedules established by the Bar Association. There was a long silence. I rose and again moved to abolish the Minimum Fee Schedule and the Minimum Fee Committee. Realizing that to defend the minimum fee in the face of a possible criminal interpretation by the Justice Department was inviting trouble, not a peep of opposition came from any lawyer. My motion passed and the Minimum Fee died a quiet death.

Within a few years the Supreme Court struck down the archaic ethics rules that prohibited advertising by lawyers and other professionals. The case arose from two young lawyers running a legal services clinic in Arizona, who took out a newspaper ad informing the public of their low prices for such matters as divorces, wills, and the like. The Arizona Bar disciplined them; they challenged it, and the Supreme Court came down heavily in favor of consumers – a ruling that opened the way not only for lawyer advertising, but for pharmacies, doctors, dentists, and other professions to advertise their services and prices.

There were other major problems in the legal system, such as the abuse of the bail system. Because the Legal Services programs did not deal with criminal matters except an occasional minor municipal matter I had, as yet, no experience in that field. The fastest way to get such experience was to take on criminal defense cases. Bob LeGore, the county's Public Defender, agreed to send me cases in which his office had conflicts.

I spent one whole beautiful day in May trying to get a mother of five kids out of jail. They locked her and her husband up on a Saturday. She was 50, her husband was 51. They were charged with welfare fraud because she made money cleaning houses for which she was paid cash she didn't report. The papers were very big with it. The detectives were reported to have gotten word the couple was going to flee – notwithstanding, as the detectives well knew, that there were five kids; one in a local college on a scholarship, three under 16. The newspaper noted police concerns that the couple would flee as soon as the kids got out of school, omitting the minor fact that school would not let out for another month, and that parents with scholarship kids aren't generally thought of as high bail risks. Her bail was set at $6,000, which she did not have. Even the prosecutor agreed the bail was high, and came down to $1,000, and signed it. But the Judge on the bench said no, because he had seen in the newspaper that they might flee the state. Not long before, that same judge had dropped bail by $50,000 on a convicted killer charged with 16 counts of armed robbery and assault with intent to kill police officers. It took a week to get her bail reduced.

Aside from the kind of harshness judges like that could display, the bail system was exacerbated by the corruption rampant in Atlantic City. If a hotel dishwasher got arrested for a barroom brawl on Saturday night, his bail might be set at $5,000. To get out of jail he had to call for a bail bondsman from an insurance company which would guarantee the bail for 10% of the amount, plus another fee for the bondsman who wrote the bond – usually another 1%. The catch was that the defendant never got the money back. Even if he showed up for court and was found innocent, he was out the $550 he paid the bondsman. Effectively, the cop who arrested you cost you

$550 without a hearing. Abuse crept in; the word on the street was that certain cops and bondsmen, and maybe the bail clerk, had a deal going in which the bail bondsman collected the premium and posted the bond, but did not inform the insurance company or forward their $500 premium. The $550 would be split three ways, between the bondsman, the bail clerk, and the cop. Local cynics suspected the judge also got a cut, but there was no proof of any of it.

After wasting an entire day (for the $15 paid by the Public Defender's Office for such motions) trying to get a dishwasher out on his own recognizance, I arranged lunch with Assignment Judge Herbert Horn, the chief judge in the area. He listened to my frustration, and suggested I look into a 10% bail system devised by the Vera Foundation under a Ford Foundation grant in Illinois. Under the Vera plan, a defendant could post 10% of his bail directly with the court. If he showed up for his hearing, he got the money back. It took a while to work up the guidelines and necessary forms with the help of Charles Middlesworth, a legal services attorney later in life a Superior Court Judge. By the summer of 1972 Judge Horn had the approval of the Chief Justice to try the program in Atlantic County as a one-year experiment. The system was installed, and after the first year it was extended throughout New Jersey. It effectively saved the poor all over the state an enormous sum of money. I was certain the amount of direct economic benefit that came from the 10% bail program amounted to more than the entire budget for New Jersey's Public Defender and Legal Services programs combined.

***

Even as my attention turned to building my private law practice, I kept abreast of the fate of the anti-poverty program. Days before his second inauguration, President Nixon appointed OEO Director Phillip Sanchez Ambassador to Panama. This left Howard Phillips as OEO's "Acting Director," in undisputed control of what was left of the Office of Economic Opportunity . His honeymoon was brief. Hardly had Nixon's hand come down from the Bible than Phillips notified all ten OEO regional offices their funds would be terminated. This abuse of his authority was challenged in court – on the grounds, among others, that the Administration had no right to refuse to spend money Congress appropriated for programs established by law. Another successful attack was more personal; that Phillips had no authority to run OEO because the Senate did not "advise and consent" to his nomination. With this challenge the Court agreed. Phillips was out.

It was an empty victory. In his State of the Union message President Nixon announced that community action agencies were no longer needed; that the functions they performed could be carried out by other departments and agencies. His plan met no applause from the Democratic congressional majorities. It did not help that more news of corruption in the White House and Nixon's cover-up of the Watergate scandal was coming to light every day. But the damage was done. In the glare of such great events as Vietnam, the Watergate impeachment proceedings, and Nixon's eventual resignation in disgrace, the War on Poverty faded into obscurity. The single term of Jimmy Carter's Presidency that followed did not bring it to life again. With the ascendancy of Ronald Reagan to the White House in the election of 1980, the very idea of fighting poverty was ridiculed in the glorification of wealth and militarism that marked the long triumph of the right wing. After September 30, 1981 when the Office of Economic Opportunity's successor, the Community Service Administration, went out of existence, there no longer existed a single-purpose anti-poverty agency at the federal level.

***

With the advantage of 40 years of hindsight, what are my own thoughts and conclusions about how we fared? What sticks with me after all those years? What did it all mean, and what good did it do?

It needs no caveat to alert the reader that I view these matters through the prism of politics — often partisan politics, for which I offer no apology. My political opinions are strong and long-standing. I have known, admired and voted for Republican candidates, and will surely do so again. But when it comes to the Republican national leadership there has been little to admire in my lifetime. I see fault enough in the Democrats, but for the Republican

Party, when I think of its betrayal of the spirit that nourished Abraham Lincoln and demanded the abolition of slavery, I confess to a harsher judgment. And that judgment is harshest when I contemplate the fate of the War on Poverty, in which the national Republican leadership abandoned all pretense of higher purpose and sold its birthright for political office. To explain that, I must talk bluntly about race.

Roosevelt had made sure the New Deal was seen as intended for whites, with any progress for blacks only an incidental benefit. He favored civil rights, but he knew how volatile the problem was, and how quickly his opponents would pounce if his programs appeared as though they came at the expense of poor whites. It took Harry Truman to integrate the armed forces after FDR's death. Roosevelt understood fully the nature of the national Republicans — those he called "the malefactors of great wealth" — and the identification of his programs with poor whites was vital to his purposes. And it worked. To this day when you see photographs of the WPA, the CCC, and other New Deal program beneficiaries, they are usually poor whites. And to this day when you go into West Virginia, Tennessee, and the poor white communities of Appalachia, you find an abiding reverence for Franklin Delano Roosevelt. Against that the Republicans made little headway for a generation.

But times changed. The War on Poverty and the Civil Rights law were both passed in 1964, called into life by the same President and set into motion by the same Administration. President Johnson thought the Economic Opportunity Act was a Rooseveltian measure; a blow struck at the ancient evil of poverty. But it was joined at birth to the Civil Rights Act, and the Republican Party had learned the dangers of Roosevelt's appeal to poor whites. It would not let programs aimed at securing racial justice and economic justice, those two noble efforts, both be nourished in the same society at the same time. President Johnson remarked, as he signed the Civil Rights law, that it would cost the Democratic Party the South for a generation or more, and so it has. Within a year Richard Nixon and his colleagues were moving to create the infamous "Southern Strategy," whereby the Republicans cast their lot with latter-day Klansmen who masked their racism under appeals for "Law and Order" and thinly-coded denunciations of anti-poverty efforts. By 1980 Ronald Reagan defiantly began his Republican campaign for the Presidency in Philadelphia, Mississippi, calling for "states rights" in an unmistakable bid for racist votes in the very county in which the three civil rights workers of 1964 were murdered under police authority.

When those trying to eliminate poverty made mistakes — and there were many, as this book discloses — the Republican policy was essentially one of "Gotcha!" There were excesses here and there, but for the most part the money was spent wisely. When that Chicago straw boss handed out cash to the kids cleaning a trash-strewn lot he was wrong, but so, perhaps, was the law.

In the main, the G.O.P. opposition had a mixed result; the Civil Rights law survived and was strengthened; much of the poverty program died. It was worth it, but I have no doubt that the War on Poverty was part of the price paid for progress on Civil Rights.

Did the War on Poverty do any good? Perhaps the best proof of our work is to be found in the fact that fifty years after the Economic Opportunity Act was signed by President Johnson, many of the individual programs to which it gave birth still exist in one way or another. Legal Services programs are still open and active, despite the efforts of Republican Presidents Nixon, Ford, Reagan and both Bushes to stifle, divert or malnourish them. The Head Start programs have become a permanent part of America's educational resources. Since its inception Head Start has served over 22 million pre-school age children and still includes the heavy involvement of the poor and of volunteers in over 1,600 programs. More than 170,000 Americans have served in VISTA, which continues today as part of President Clinton's AmeriCorps. Today's Job Corps boasts 122 centers open nationwide, training 70,000 new enrollees each year. So I do not believe our effort was wasted. Many benefitted immediately; others benefit to this day.

Nor do I regret the derailment of my own political dreams. It is enough for me to remember, on the annual anniversary of Robert Kennedy's death when commentators discuss the chaos that was the year 1968, that I stood up to be counted for the things in which I believed.

As to whether and how poverty will ever be eliminated in America, I think we shall one day succeed. Not necessarily through the political process or through government programs, although each have their role to play. The great programs of FDR's New Deal continue to thrive. Social Security to this day helps the elderly live with a measure of dignity and independence. Federal unemployment benefits temper the blow of layoffs and plant closings, and LBJ's Medicare and Medicaid ease the impact of ill health on the aged and the poor.

But if we are to eliminate poverty, a fundamental clearing of our vision — a doing away with the present distortions of our view — is essential. Age-old superstitions and taboos impede progress on many fronts, as the controversy over stem-cell research demonstrates. Xenophobia – our primitive fear of strangers — is too easily exploited by those eager to gain power. We must rid ourselves of the worship of Mammon. As long as our religious leaders strut about in wealth obscene to the memory of a man whose only display of anger was against the money changers in the temple; as long as our political leaders see money as the mother's milk of political success and the moneyed appearance of success as the key to electoral victory; as long as our media celebrate the trappings of wealth and fame and judge wisdom only by dollars, we will not eliminate poverty.

I have read too much history to deceive myself about the prospects of success in the near future, or even a good bit beyond. Capitalism has its insufferable excesses, but Communism proved even worse. Religion has powerful claims, but charlatans arise almost daily. Political demagogues sprout with depressing regularity and the election of pious hypocrites has become routine. Yet I have too powerful a faith in Democracy – and perhaps the ultimate goodness of mankind, despite the likes of Hitler and Stalin — to abandon hope. Something in me, nourished by what I have seen along my journey, tells me we will prevail.

On a personal level, I often wonder how the kids I met made out – the ones in poverty and the young VISTA volunteers who tried to help them. What became of Little Laughing Thunder and Miss Fire Cloud, those bright-eyed and merry little girls on the Sioux Reservation? And what of the huge family in Plattsburgh that lived in a cold house at Christmas time? And the red-sequined whirlwind clearing that trashy lot in Chicago? And of the young people who wrote seeking help after seeing "It's What's Happening, Baby!" And what of the teenagers I met amidst the coal mines of Appalachia and among America's migrant farmworkers?

There is no way to know, but I hope they remember that there was a time when America gave a damn about them.

Acknowledgments

I acknowledge, with love and deep appreciation, the help of Maryanne Wilkins, the sort of wife who stood by me, as readers of this book will have seen, through years of raising our five children in a warm and loving home on an uncertain budget even as I pursued college and law school and followed the rushing eddies and currents of my career. It is to her constancy and loyalty that I owe the joy of having our children and grandchildren and great-grandchildren sit around our family table at Thanksgiving and Christmas sharing love and laughter with us and with each other. She proved the sort of wife who understood that someday the notes and reports and clippings my activities generated would come in handy.

Even with those notes, copies of reports and letters I wrote and received, newspaper clippings, and material stored in the National Archives, this is nonetheless a memoir, with all the limitations of memory and personal perspective the genre implies.

My thanks to the staff at the National Archives at College Park, Maryland for tracking down boxes of files from the Office of Economic Opportunity and its successors, and to my friend Alan Kligerman, who read the early draft of the manuscript with a keen eye for errors. Thanks also to my later volunteer manuscript readers Joe Gagen, Charles Pancoast, Richard Moore, Leonora Wilkins, Norma Michelle, Joe Cowley, Gary Lefkowitz, Heather Simpson and Alfred Tubach.

And my special thanks to Louis Toscano, a world-class journalist, author, and an editor's editor, who stole time from his own work in progress to give me the benefit of his professional guidance. Any errors remaining after all that are my own responsibility, or the result of advice I foolishly chose to skip over.

Joseph T. Wilkins
Smithville, N.J.
August, 2014

About the author

Joseph T. Wilkins, N.J. Press Association award-winning columnist, is a semi-retired lawyer and former municipal judge who lives in Galloway, NJ. In addition to *Kennedy's Recruit: Tales from the Poverty Wars*, he is the author of *The Speaker Who Locked up the House*, and *The Skin Game and other Atlantic City capers*, a richly comic account of the stick-up of an illegal card game in Atlantic City. His books are available as ebooks, and can be ordered in print at Politics and Prose Bookstore in Washington, DC (800) 722-0790. His columns can be read on his website at www.josephtwilkins.com and at www.shoremedia.com

A graduate of LaSalle College in Philadelphia and Catholic University Law School in Washington, D.C., Mr. Wilkins has practiced law over 45 years in a varied career in which he has represented the very poor and the very wealthy. He served as Chief Attorney for a legal services program for the poor and has served as corporate counsel for multimillion dollar corporations and as Founding Chairman of the State Bar Association's Committee on Casino Law. He has been the chief lawyer for the City of Atlantic City, and served as a municipal judge for seven years.

He lives in Galloway, New Jersey and is the father of 5, and has 11 grandchildren and 3 great-grandchildren.